THE OBSERVER BOOK

Frances Perry is an internationally known and respected gardening writer and lecturer who has made many television appearances and broadcasts. She is the gardening correspondent of the *Observer* and has written nineteen books.

She was the first woman county horticultural education organizer, being appointed to that post in Middlesex in 1951 and was sub-sequently Principal of Norwood Hall, a college of further education in horticulture. For her work in this field she was awarded the MBE in 1962.

She was the first woman to be elected to the Council of the Royal Horticultural Society (founded in 1804) and is now its first and only woman Vice President. She has received both the Veitch Memorial Medal and the Victoria Medal of Honour, the latter being the highest honour the Society can bestow.

She is also one of only two overseas 'members at large' of the Garden Club of America, a signal honour, and was awarded in the USA the Sara Frances Chapman medal for 'literary excellence' for one of her books, *Flowers of the World*.

Some of the material in this book has appeared or been suggested by articles in *The Observer*, although in the main the contents owe their inception to letters or queries received from readers of that paper and from radio listeners and lecture audiences. These reflect the problems besetting all gardeners – novices and professionals.

Inevitably there are people to thank and I should like to express my appreciation – first to Observer Newspapers for their blessing on this project, then to my husband, for his help and back-up at all times, and to L. P. Smith, the eminent agricultural meteorologist who supplied the interesting weather lore pieces for each month's work. To Dr Joe Stubbs I am indebted for help with the section on pests and diseases, to Rosemary Wise and Kenneth Midgley for their painstaking drawings.

The Observer Book Of Gardening

The Year In The Garden

Frances Perry

CORONET BOOKS
Hodder and Stoughton

Copyright © 1982 by Frances Perry

First published in Great Britain 1982
by Sidgwick and Jackson Ltd

Coronet edition 1984

British Library C.I.P.

Perry, Frances
    The Observer book of gardening.
    1. Gardening
    I. Title
    635   SB450.97

    ISBN 0-340-34598-5

Printed and bound in Great Britain for
Hodder and Stoughton Paperbacks, a
division of Hodder and Stoughton Ltd.,
Mill Road, Dunton Green, Sevenoaks,
Kent (Editorial Office: 47 Bedford
Square, London, WC1 3DP) by
Cox & Wyman Ltd., Reading

Contents

 JANUARY

The Month in the Garden

Cutting winds and icy rains are the main enemies of winter flowers. Snow does far less damage unless it freezes on buds or open blooms, though heavy falls of snow can weigh down evergreens so much that their branches break.

Masses of flowers cannot be expected outside in January, but there will always be some stray blossoms in well planted gardens, and colourful effects can be achieved by growing a few coloured-leaved conifers, or trees with ornamental bark and twigs. Plants which are useful for this purpose are listed on p. 10 and further discussed in *Winter in the Garden* (p. 13).

Some shrubs and trees produce flowers in sheltered places – or even in exposed situations in mild winters – notably certain viburnums like *Viburnum farreri* whose sweetly scented blossoms stud the naked branches from the end of October until mid-March. The hybrid *V.* x *bodnantense* is another, as well as the evergreen, shade-tolerant *V. tinus*. The winter jasmine, *Jasminum nudiflorum,* should also be displaying itself as well as various heathers, and the sky-blue *Iris unguicularis.* As the month advances *I. histrioides,* the witch hazels (*Hamamelis* species and varieties), several hellebores and the green-catkined *Garrya elliptica* put in an appearance, and there are berries to enjoy on skimmias, pyracanthas, hollies and cotoneasters.

Plants such as these are worth fostering for they shine like jewels against sombre backgrounds. Anyone can have a charming garden in June, but it takes skilful planning and good planting to induce anyone to visit gardens on a cold January day.

It is in winter, however, that an unheated alpine house comes into its own. The plants it contains may be perfectly hardy to cold but succumb to excessive wet, particularly when this is followed by severe frosts. Yet, kept dry at the crowns and planted in well-crocked containers, with a 'collar' of granite chippings or brick rubble, many small bulbs and alpines will flower freely in January and February. Arranged on a waist-high bench they are easy to see without stooping. Other plants can be brought from frames into the alpine house, to succeed those that have faded and to maintain the continuity until such time as there are plenty of flowers in the open garden.

General Tasks Garden work at this time of year consists mainly of repairing structures, building new garden features when the weather allows, ordering seeds and plants for spring sowing and planting, and general tidying up everywhere.

Trees and Shrubs Check all trees and shrubs for dead or diseased branches, cutting these back to the trunks or clean healthy wood. Paint all pruning wounds more than 1 in. (2.5 cm) across with Arbrex or a similar sealing compound.

Plant new specimens in suitable weather and fork between established trees and bushes.

Dwarf rhododendrons and azaleas keep their roots near the surface; cover the root area with dry leaves or dead bracken in severe weather. Remove the protective covering when the weather improves.

Shake snow from evergreens.

Any plants which arrive from nurseries in inclement weather should have their roots freed from the hessian wraps (mice have been known to nest in these), their roots covered with dryish soil, and be kept in a frost-free shed until conditions are suitable for planting outside.

Climbers Check on protection around doubtfully hardy climbers and renew if necessary.

Tie in stems which have broken loose in winter gales.

Roses Complete planting of new bushes, or heel them in for a time if the weather is bad. See also March, *Roses* (p. 60).

Lawns Check that all tools and equipment are clean and in working order. Book a date for machinery in need of a general overhaul and sharpening of blades.

Hardy Plants Order new plants for spring delivery.

Take root cuttings of oriental poppies, anchusas, *Anemone japonica* and catananches. Insert these in pots or boxes of sandy soil and leave in a cold frame to root.

Firm any plants put in during autumn which may have been lifted by frost.

Bulbs Bring in batches of forced bulbs from their plunge beds for flowering in the home. See September, *Bulbs for Forcing* (p. 196).

Pick *Iris unguicularis* flowers regularly.

In severe weather place sheets of glass over *Iris danfordiae*.

Rock Garden Plants Remove fallen leaves nestling between plants. Such debris may rot and kill alpines and also harbours slugs and woodlice.

Order new plants for spring delivery.

Water Plants Keep pools filled with water. If this freezes over, provide an air space so that fish can breathe. See May, *Water Gardens* (p. 112).

Vegetables Plant rhubarb and surround the crowns with strawy manure. Force an early rhubarb crop by covering first with straw, then with boxes or large inverted pots.

Lift seakale and chicory roots and plant in boxes of good soil. Store under the greenhouse staging and exclude light with a covering of black plastic in order to force the crowns.

Sow mustard and cress on a kitchen window sill, the cress three days before the mustard.

Fruit Check on fruit in store, discard or use any showing signs of decay.

Finish tar-oil spraying of apples and other fruits (see December). Prune apple and pear trees, except in frosty weather; collect and burn prunings.

Plants under Glass Take cuttings of chrysanthemums intended for late-autumn flowering. Young shoots about 3 in. (7.5 cm) long are ideal, severed just below a joint and rooted in sandy compost in pots or boxes. A soil-warmed bench or heated propagating frame accelerates rooting; thereafter the young plants should be individually potted. Sort out pots, pans and compost, and order seeds ready for sowing under glass next month and in March. Water sparingly, and when necessary apply it in the mornings.

Remove faded flowers from primulas, cyclamens and the like.

Sow sweet peas four or five to a 3 in. (7.5 cm) pot.

Sow leeks this month (for good-sized stems) in a heated greenhouse.

Sow tomatoes in a warm house with a temperature of 13°C (55°F) or more.

WEATHER

'At New Year's tide, the days lengthen a cock's stride' is one of the few solid facts in the weather calendar, but the corollary is often equally true: 'As the day lengthens, so the cold strengthens', for the coldest winter weather almost always comes after Christmas.

Seasonal cold is not unwelcome in the January garden, if only because heavy rain is less likely when temperatures are low. There is a French saying that 'a bad year comes in swimming'.

A month of snow can be helpful in the garden; beneath the white blanket the soil and small plants will remain much warmer than if they were exposed to the full severity of winter frosts which occur over bare ground. 'Snow cherisheth the ground and anything sown in it' as Francis Bacon said.

It is always wise to brush heavy snow-falls off branches and shrubs to prevent them from being broken down by the sheer weight. Plants may also suffer during a thaw from water-logging around their stems and surface roots if the melting snow cannot drain away quickly enough, but otherwise snow is more of a boon than a curse.

One type of January weather that is generally disliked and almost dreaded is unseasonal warmth. This causes premature emergence from winter dormancy which in turn leads to tender growth that will inevitably suffer when cold weather returns. The full adverse effect of such out-of-season warmth is often not obvious until later in the year, which explains the saying that 'January commits the fault, and May gets the blame'.

The old plea 'January warm – the Lord have mercy!' was the prayer of many a peasant; modern gardeners will surely agree, even if a warm January means a reduction in their heating bills.

Sow begonias and gloxinias very thinly, barely covering the seed with soil. Maintain a temperature of 18°C (65°F).

House Plants Water only when the compost is dry.

Give plants plenty of light, particularly during the day; move them away from windows at night unless these are double glazed.

Keep forced bulbs in good light and out of draughts.

Water flowering azaleas with soft water; spray the leaves frequently, particularly in hot rooms, but avoid water on opening blooms.

PLANTS IN THEIR PRIME

Trees and Shrubs in Flower
Chimonanthus praecox (winter sweet): *Daphne mezereum; Garrya elliptica;* heathers (*Erica carnea*); *Jasminum nudiflorum; Lonicera fragrantissima;* mahonias; viburnums.

Berried Shrubs Aucubas (laurels); pernettyas; pyracanthas; *Skimmia japonica*.

Hardy Plants Hellebores; *Iris unguicularis;* winter pansies.

Bulbs Crocus species; *Eranthis hyemalis* (winter aconite); *Iris danfordiae, I. histrioides*.

CROPS TO ENJOY

Vegetables Brussels sprouts; broccoli (purple- and white-sprouting); cabbage; kale; leeks.

Root crops in store: Jerusalem artichokes; beet; carrots; onions; parsnips; salsify; scorzonera; swedes.

Greenhouse: lettuce; mustard and cress.

Fruit Apples and pears in store.

PLANT ASSOCIATIONS

Mass winter heathers in front of a silver fir or silver cedar.

Red-berried pyracanthas look spectacular alongside bamboos.

Garrya elliptica growing by a wall associates with *Viburnum tinus* in front.

GARDEN PROBLEMS

Snow weighing down conifers and other trees and shrubs.

Inadequate protection round doubtfully hardy plants.

Newly established plants lifted by frost; tread these back in place.

Rotting amongst dahlia tubers in store; cut out diseased areas and dust with flowers of sulphur.

Ties and stakes loosened by gales.

Decaying fruits and root vegetables in store.

Plants of the Month

ANEMONES

Brightly coloured anemones, from Cornwall and the Isles of Scilly, are favourite cut flowers in January. *Anemone coronaria,* the poppy anemone of Palestine, is the main parent of these and apparently arrived in Western Europe at the time of the Second Crusade. Bishop Umberto of Pisa, after blessing a contingent of soldiers leaving for the Holy Land, suggested to the sailors conveying the troops that for ballast they brought back soil from Palestine instead of sand. This sacred earth was intended to provide a last resting place, at the Campo Santo at Pisa, for the illustrious dead.

Anemone coronaria

The mission was fulfilled and the following year, to everyone's amazement, the ground was spangled with unknown red flowers. This was looked upon as a miracle, and the flowers, which of course were poppy anemones, became known as 'blood drops of Christ'. In due course plants were donated to other religious houses, and eventually some reached private gardens, including that of a seventeenth-century French florist called Maître Bachelieu who had the good fortune to obtain several 'sports' or mutations, with flowers of different shades, and even with double rows of 'petals'. These he grew on and constantly hybridized but would never part with any seeds or plants. For ten long years he retained his unique collection until the Burgomaster of Antwerp, who had long coveted the fine, long-stemmed, richly hued flowers, paid him a visit. While walking round the garden he had the misfortune to drop his fur-trimmed civic robe on one of the beds and, after apologizing to his host, called his servant who took the offending garment back to his carriage. As he had anticipated, the fur had collected plenty of fluffy seeds, which the Burgomaster then sowed. Proud of his successful ruse, the Burgomaster made no attempt to hide the manner in which he had originally obtained the seed, but he was a generous donor and the plants – which later became known as the French Anemones – soon reached a wide and appreciative public.

VIOLETS

Napoleon's favourite flower is reputed to have been the violet, which he said reminded him of the Corsican woods where he played as a child.

Viola odorata

When he married Josephine she wore violets, and on every anniversary the Emperor presented her with violets – a gesture which did much to stimulate their cultivation and the development of large-flowered cultivars in France.

Years later when banished to Elba, Napoleon told his followers 'I shall return with the violets in spring', a prophecy which came true following his escape from the island. His many supporters were quick to sport bunches of violets, the ladies wore violet dresses and a mass of his favourite flowers greeted him at the Tuileries. But his triumph was short-lived, and the final defeat at Waterloo led to his exile on St Helena. Before leaving he was allowed to visit Josephine's grave, where he plucked a few violets and wore them in a locket round his neck for the rest of his life.

With the return of the Bourbons, violets went out of fashion, but were restored to popularity by the Empress Eugénie, who apparently first met Napoleon III when he was touring his new empire. Asked by Napoleon the way to her bedroom, Eugénie replied 'through the church door', but at a court ball that night she wore a violet gown and violets in her hair as a tribute to his 'great ancestor'. This apparently so pleased Napoleon III that he asked for her hand in marriage.

Violets were also the favourite flower of Queen Alexandra, wife of Edward VII; up to five thousand plants were at one time cultivated in frames at Windsor Castle.

Winter in the Garden

Only in the tropics is it possible to have a garden ablaze with colour throughout the year. In temperate climates, there are peak months in summer and poor months in winter. But the winter garden need not be dreary if careful thought is given to the placement and selection of suitable plant material.

Winter colour can be achieved in various ways. Although few in number there are certain winter flowers, as well as bright berries, coloured-leaved evergreens and trees with attractive barks. November through to February is the dullest time of the year and the period which needs to be considered most carefully. A winter walk in bad weather is scarcely inviting and indeed may not be possible for some members of the household, so plan for part of the winter garden to be visible from the house.

Such plants as heathers and golden conifers maintain their character for many weeks and naturally provide the backbone of winter displays. I would not willingly dispense with such heather varieties of *Erica carnea* as 'King George' and 'Vivellii', both rich crimson, or 'Springwood White' and 'Pink Spangles'; nor *E.* x *darleyensis* 'Arthur Johnson', pink, and 'Silberschmelze', white. All these are evergreen, tolerate most soils, even limy, put up with bad weather, do not snap their stems in storms and last for years yet keep on flowering, providing the house with useful material to blend with Algerian irises, early narcissi, anemones, and other winter blossoms.

To my mind heathers look best when grown on undulating ground – on hummocks and in valleys, an effect which can be produced by building up or removing soil in various places, then covering the whole bed with 3 in. (7.5 cm) of moist peat. If the heathers are planted out from pots, to avoid root disturbance 12–18 in. (30–45 cm.) apart, they establish themselves without trouble and in a year or two coalesce to form broad patches of colour.

Heathers also blend splendidly with small conifers, and added colour may be introduced by inserting the odd plant of *Thuja orientalis* 'Aurea nana', *T. occidentalis* 'Rheingold' or 'Sunkist', all golden-leaved, or the silver-foliaged *Picea pungens* 'Globosa' and *Chamaecyparis pisifera* 'Boulevard'.

FLOWERING SHRUBS

Taller winter-flowering shrubs include several deciduous viburnums, like *V. farreri* (*V. fragrans*) which begins blooming in October and continues producing stray blossoms until the new leaves appear in April; others are *V. grandiflorum* and *V.* x *bodnantense,* the latter a hybrid between the two species, with flower heads rather larger than those of *V. farreri* and pinker in bud. All grow to an eventual height of 12 ft (3.6 m), unless kept shorter by annual pruning, and all have fragrant flowers in compact heads, and neat privet-like leaves.

Lower-growing, but sweeter-scented and later-flowering than any of these, is the deciduous *V. carlesii* which forms its cherry-red buds in autumn but needs a warm spell for them to open into waxy white flowers. It was discovered in Korea in 1883 by a consul called Carles, but only reached Britain early in this century. Hybrids from it include the earlier, evergreen

V. x *burkwoodii,* which starts blooming in January, and the deciduous
V. x *carlcephalum* with exceptionally large flower heads.

A well-known viburnum which flowers continuously from late autumn
to early spring is the evergreen laurustinus, *V. tinus,* which needs a sunny
position to flower freely. The flowers are borne in flat heads with many
white, pink-budded but scentless florets. This viburnum also makes a good
hedging plant; and there is a form with creamy-yellow leaf variegations.

V. rhytidophyllum is also useful for winter effect. It bears large, oblong,
heavily veined evergreen leaves densely coated beneath with rusty hairs.
The small creamy flowers (or pink in the variety 'Roseum') appear in May,
but if two plants are grown in close proximity they will pollinate each
other and produce large clusters of oval fruits, red at first but ultimately
black.

Winter-flowering plants: *Jasminum nudiflorum* (left); *Erica carnea* 'Vivellii' (centre);
Viburnum farreri (right)

Other winter-flowering shrubs which invariably please include the green-catkined, evergreen *Garrya elliptica,* which is best grown as a wall plant; *Abeliophyllum distichum,* a slow grower with clusters of four-petalled, fragrant flowers of pinkish-white on the bare stems about February, and *Chimonanthus praecox* the winter sweet, aptly named since a single spray of its waxy, purple-blotched, yellow flowers will scent a fair-sized room. They are borne on the leafless branches in the midst of winter. *Jasminum nudiflorum* usually shows its first starry, yellow blossoms around Christmas, as do certain witch hazels, particularly *Hamamelis japonica* 'Arborea' – which also assumes handsome autumnal leaf tints prior to leaf-fall – and the spicily scented *H. mollis* 'Pallida'. The mezereon, *Daphne mezereum,* is another fragrant shrub; its small lilac-purple flowers are borne thickly along the tops of the naked main shoots around February. There is also a white-flowered form 'Alba'.

For lime-free soils there are several early rhododendrons like the *R. arboreum* varieties 'Blood Red' and 'Roseum', whose bell-shaped flowers are bunched in globular heads. The hybrid rhododendron 'Nobleanum' is one of the earliest, with funnel-shaped, rosy flowers with crimson spots and white interiors. These all bloom from January until March. Other subjects for lime-free, sheltered gardens are the evergreen camellias and pernettyas.

BERRIES AND FRUIT

For winter berries I can think of no better plants than the evergreen skimmias, for although not tall (they average 4 ft (1 m)) their stems are smothered with scarlet berries for most of the year. It is essential, however, to have a male plant nearby as pollinator for the females. *Skimmia japonica* has fragrant white flowers in April and May which are as arresting as the berries, and *S. reevesiana,* although shorter, has the merit of being hermaphrodité so only one plant needs to be grown. Both are shade-tolerant.

Bright berries are a feature of several cotoneasters, like *C. conspicuus,* an evergreen shrub with scarlet fruits which the plant explorer Frank Kingdon Ward, who discovered it in south-east Tibet, described as a 'bubbling red cauldron of berries'. The small, tree-like, deciduous *C. frigidus* is similarly laden with red berries. *C.* x *watereri* we grow as a wall shrub, cutting away most of its new young shoots in autumn so as to display to the full its heavy trusses of orange-scarlet fruits. Only in very severe winters are these taken by birds. The deciduous *C. horizontalis,* with herring-bone branches, makes a handsome small wall shrub or, like *C. microphyllus* (evergreen) and *C. adpressus* (deciduous), can be planted as ground cover to trail over rocks and banks.

Pernettyas have white, pink, red or wine-coloured, marble-sized fruits, but require a peaty soil. Since the sexes are borne on different plants, male and female plants are necessary in order to ensure pollination. Pyracanthas and hollies are others which bear showy berries throughout the winter.

TREES WITH WINTER BEAUTY

There are not many winter-flowering trees, but outstanding are the autumn cherry, *Prunus subhirtella* 'Autumnalis' and the evergreen strawberry tree, *Arbutus unedo*. The cherry makes a small deciduous tree up to 20-30 ft (6-9 m); its small, semi-double, white or blush-pink flowers are produced in bursts – according to the weather – from November to March. In our garden the strawberry tree always flowers around Christmas, usually among the round, scarlet, strawberry-like fruits from the previous season. Its white, urn-shaped, waxy flowers occur in pendent panicles which contrast pleasantly with the small, glossy, dark green leaves. *Arbutus unedo,* although ericaceous, tolerates limy soil and seaside plantings but the branches occasionally snap in heavy gales. *A.* x *andrachnoides* is similar with the added merit of fine cinnamon-red bark and branches.

In addition to *Arbutus* x *andrachnoides* the bark of most birches warrants a second glance. Our native *Betula pendula* has a silvery-white trunk with occasional black patches, but that of *B. papyrifera,* the paper birch, is even whiter, very smooth and often peeling in paper-like layers, a characteristic shared by *B. utilis,* except that here reddish-brown patches usually appear between the silvers. The trunk of *B. albo-sinensis* is orange-red and again peels off in layers while that of *B. maximowicziana* is orange, brown, grey and whitish.

Handsome barks are also common in some maples, particularly the snake-barks *Acer pensylvanicum*, *A. capillipes* and *A. davidii,* all of which have trunks with longitudinal white stripes; in *A. pensylvanicum* the young branches are streaked green and white and look especially arresting.

PERENNIALS AND BULBS

Few herbaceous plants brave winter's cold, but among the few exceptions are hellebores, particularly the well-known, white Christmas rose, *Helleborus niger*. The tall, green-flowered *H. corsicus (H. lividus corsicus)* flowers in our garden at the end of January, and even in December there are blooms on our *H. orientalis* where these grow in sheltered corners. The white, greenish, pink, red or crimson flowers, often spotted in other shades, are a joy to behold for several months and we even have one of primrose-yellow. They associate especially well with blue hepaticas and red camellias. The white-flowered toothwort, *Dentaria pinnata,* which grows 1½ ft (45 cm) tall and has clustered heads of four-petalled blooms above clumps of divided leaves, is a late winter perennial which also does well in shade. One invasive plant which may be useful in certain situations, but should be avoided near cherished specimens, is the winter heliotrope, *Petasites fragrans.* This has white vanilla-scented flowers on 6 in. (15 cm) spikes around February, followed by large rounded leaves. Winter pansies are useful for sun or shade and come in various colours.

Several small bulbous plants bloom in winter but need to be grouped for maximum impact. They include the buttercup-like winter aconites *(Eranthis),* early crocuses, snowdrops, *Cyclamen coum, Scilla tubergeniana, Anemone blanda* and the related hepaticas, *Narcissus cyclamineus* and *bulbocodium,* as well as precooled daffodils which are sold by some bulb firms. Precooled bulbs flower well ahead of the normal time, even in January in mild areas. The small *Tulipa pulchella* blooms in February and is followed by the water-lily tulip *T. kaufmanniana* and its varieties, and by other species. Finally there are several irises, particularly the sky-blue *I. histrioides,* which even survives light falls of snow, the yellow *I. danfordiae,* and the delightful Algerian iris *I. unguicularis* which should be planted in a sheltered south- or west-facing position against a wall so that it is reasonably dry at the roots in winter. Then it will flower from November until April, with large blue flowers on 6-12-in. (15-30-cm) stems. Slugs are inordinately fond of its flower buds so a lavish scattering of slug bait or several applications of liquid slug killer are advisable, especially in damp weather.

Greenhouse Gardening

In Victorian times conservatories attached to the side of a house, with a 'viewing' area from the living room, were all the rage, and there were also free-standing conservatories housing displays of ferns and orchids, with other foliage and flowering plants. Regardless of the weather there was always colour and variety within these houses.

Heating and labour costs have caused most of these elaborate structures to disappear, and today one would have to go to Kew Gardens or some of the stately homes to find an example. Yet greenhouses are still erected, and glass-sided garden room extensions are added to homes; the former are used to raise and house plants, the latter as extra living rooms, for people and plants. There is sound logic in attaching a sun room to a house. As it is close to essential services, such as heat and water, it will be easy to look after, and by trapping the sun it helps to keep the home warm while providing a pleasant leisure area for the family.

A free-standing greenhouse offers more scope for the growing of plants, but is more expensive to keep warm in winter. Nevertheless, if you can keep out frost it will enable you to raise many seedlings and cuttings, produce early flowers for the home and safeguard tender kinds during the worst of the weather. Even a cold (unheated) house can do some of these things, although the plants will come along later than in a warm greenhouse. Tomatoes can be grown inside in summer, or the whole house can be converted to an alpine house, with displays of rock plants and small bulbs in pots and pans. Placed on a waist-high, shingle-covered bench such alpines can be particularly enjoyed between December and March when outdoor flowers are at a premium. (See also February, *Plants under Glass*, p.35.)

CHOOSING A GREENHOUSE

For whatever purpose the greenhouse is intended, it is essential to shop around before purchase. Study the different shapes and sizes of houses, the materials from which they are made, and the quality of workmanship. Wood used to be cheap, but is now a luxury; teak, oak or Western red cedar look splendid against old, weathered brick but are very expensive to purchase and will need constant maintenance in the years to come.

Aluminium is competitive in price and needs little maintenance. There is an old prejudice against metal houses, because people believe they are colder than wooden ones. In reality there is very little difference, because most heat losses occur through the glass, not through the glazing bars.

Shape is of little importance. Aesthetically the traditional dog-kennel shape may not be exciting, and in some instances the newer hexagonal or twelve-sided greenhouses may look more attractive. However, these are more expensive and in some ways not so easy to manage as most interior equipment is geared to the traditional rectangular or square houses.

For a single greenhouse I would always opt for one with glass to the ground. With fuel costs in mind we need to make the best use of a greenhouse, and if this has glass to the ground, greater use can be made of the space beneath the benches. This area is invaluable for storing plants brought inside for the winter, such as geraniums, dahlias, chrysanthemums, gladioli and begonia tubers. Most foliage plants like ferns, ivies, aspidistras and tradescantias are quite happy growing in the light shade under greenhouse benches.

The benches themselves will be occupied by growing plants, and over these can be fitted more shelves on which to stand rooted cuttings of geraniums, fuchsias and other plants. In spring the shelves may be utilized to sprout seed potatoes and begonia tubers, and boxes of seedlings will appreciate being in full light near the glass.

There are several points to watch when comparing and evaluating greenhouses. First, how much growing space will you have? A path down the centre is essential, running to 2-3 ft (60–90 cm) from the far end. Benches should be no more than $3\frac{1}{2}$ ft (1 m) wide or they are difficult to reach across. After working out the area of the house subtract that of the path and you will be left with the space available for plants either in borders or on benches.

There is almost half as much space again in a house 10 ft long by 8 ft wide (3 m by 2.4 m) as there is in one 8 ft by 6 ft (2.4 m by 1.8m), yet the larger house will not cost half as much again as the small one.

Other things to consider include the robustness of the glazing bars, the fit of ventilators and doors, and the erection of the house. Modern trends lean towards large panes of glass that slide into grooves and need no putty or mastic. With these, overlaps – and the laborious task of cleaning algae from the overlaps – are eliminated and no heat is lost through them.

Many of the larger garden centres stock a good range of houses – indeed some are devoted solely to greenhouses and sheds – where it is possible to make detailed comparisons.

SITING THE GREENHOUSE

To make the best use of modern equipment, electricity and water should be available, so it is advisable to site a greenhouse as near as possible to sources of supply. Ideally, it would be sited close to the dwelling house, to do away with cold treks in the dark, maybe in snow, to check that all is well. The chores of watering, damping down, opening and shutting ventilators are more likely to be carried out on a regular basis if the greenhouse is near at hand.

For these reasons there is much to be said for a lean-to house built against a south- or west-facing wall of the dwelling-house. Such a greenhouse will gain some heat from the house wall, and it may be possible to run a radiator into it from the central heating system. With water and electricity near at hand the installation of a lean-to costs very little.

A free-standing greenhouse, used chiefly for raising seedlings and cuttings early in the year when light is at its lowest, should be constructed to run east-west, with the door at the west end. Thus the plants can make full use of the low-angled spring sunshine.

A greenhouse intended for growing orchids, cacti or other pot plants is best sited on a south-north axis, with the door at the south end. In such a situation sun heat during the day will be less intense and there will be fewer problems with ventilation and shading.

Greenhouse plants: *Cymbidium* orchids, flowering in February (left); *Streptocarpus*, flowering from May to October (right)

HEATING

Greenhouses can be heated by various means: a solid-fuel boiler, free-standing paraffin heaters, gas from a main supply or butane gas cylinders, or by electricity. The latter is undoubtedly the best and most adaptable; the heating is automatic and can be controlled by thermostats to within very tight limits. In addition, soil warming can be combined with space heating to effect economies which cannot be achieved by other heating methods.

Whichever type of fuel is used, the cost of keeping a greenhouse at a night minimum temperature of 7°C (45°F) will be doubled when this is raised to 10°C (50°F), and it will be almost doubled again if the night minimum is increased to 13°C (55°F).

SOIL-WARMING CABLES

Most of the plants grown by amateur gardeners are quite happy with a night minimum of 7°C (45°F) provided that they have a root temperature around 13°C (55°F) – perhaps a little more for certain plants. A higher root temperature is easily and reliably provided by the installation of electric soil-warming cables laid under the soil of a greenhouse border or bench. Such heating cables are thermostatically controlled so that both the air and soil temperatures can be provided at monitored cost. Soil warming is the key to economic electric greenhouse heating.

To install soil warming in a greenhouse bench, construct a base of corrugated asbestos sheeting well supported by cross bearers. Fit a wooden framework 8 in. (20 cm) deep all round the bench, and over the asbestos base spread 2 in. (5 cm) of sand with the soil-warming cable on top. Cover this in turn with another 1 in. (2.5 cm) of sand. The heating cable should be controlled by a rod-type thermostat inserted in the sand base.

Pots and seed trays can then be stood on the soil-warmed sand base – which should always be kept moist as heat rises through damp sand but not so easily through dry sand. Water is a good conductor of heat, air is not.

It is also important to pack moist peat around pots or boxes on the sand base in order to retain the heat; otherwise the warm air causes a mild draught as it rises. The soil in pots on a soil-warmed bench which is not packed with peat can actually be colder than if they were standing on a bench *without* soil warming.

And now an important point which is rarely mentioned in advertising copy or manufacturers' literature: a greenhouse thermometer that is accurate to within plus or minus one degree.

Assuming that it costs £20 a year to heat a small greenhouse to 7°C (45°F) night minimum, it will cost £40 a year to keep it at 10°C (50°F). This means that every degree Fahrenheit above 45°F will cost £4. The dials on a thermostat only provide a rough guide to the temperature setting, and you have to check carefully over several nights, with a reliable maximum-minimum thermometer, that the setting of the thermostat is really keeping the temperature at the desired level.

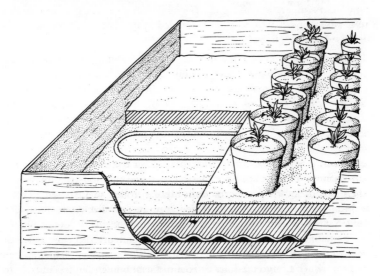

Electrical soil-warming cable laid on sharp sand and covered with another layer of sand

If the thermometer is showing a night minimum of 7°C (45°F) when in fact the heating thermostat has been keeping it at, say, 8°C (47°F) you will be paying £8 a year more than necessary.

Fan-assisted or blow heaters are the easiest electrical heaters to install because all that is required is an ordinary three-pin 13 amp socket. They contain a heating element and a fan which blows air across the element and into the greenhouse. Thermostatically controlled, some models can have the heating element switched off while the fan circulates air round the house; this can be very useful at times, for example when chrysanthemums are opening their flowers and there is a risk of moisture condensing on the blooms and causing spotting.

Fan heaters eventually wear out, and heating elements can fail. Tubular heaters are far more reliable. They come in several lengths and whatever the size of the greenhouse, enough tubes can be installed to provide the desired heat level. If the element in one tube fails, it is a simple matter to obtain and fit another, and in the meantime the other tubes should provide enough heat to keep frost out.

It is rather more expensive to install tubes than a socket for a fan-assisted heater, but for a small house I would always opt for tubes.

GREENHOUSE AIDS

Refinements such as benches, shelves, heating, lighting, automatic ventilation, electric vapourizers for pest and disease control, and automatic watering can be added to a greenhouse as and when the cost becomes feasible. A fully automatic house can look after itself for short periods, even up to a month. True, greenhouse equipment is expensive, but there is no need to buy it all at once.

Automatic ventilation With electricity in a greenhouse, an extractor fan for automatic ventilation can be installed, controlled by a rod-type thermostat, the best and most sensitive for both tubular heaters and extractor fans.

Non-electric automatic ventilators are also available, notably those which push up ventilators or open louvres (set in the side or roof of a house) as the temperature rises above a predetermined figure and close when the temperature falls. They are fine for light aluminium ventilators and for louvres which fit into the sides or roof of metal houses, but less suitable for heavy, old-fashioned ventilators.

Electric fans Electric vapourizers are available for pest and disease control, but a small electric fan mounted in the apex of the roof farthest away from the door and pointing downwards at an angle of 10 degrees helps considerably to prevent plant diseases. It performs the two functions of keeping the air moving in the house and drying the condensed moisture on plant foliage, thus reducing the risk of infection by diseases. In our own greenhouse we have hardly ever had to spray for disease control since we installed a small electric fan. It is also a splendid heat-saving investment as the fan pushes down warm air as it rises towards the roof ridge, thus preventing all the heat escaping through the glass.

I have experimented with thermometers at ground level and in the roof and have found a temperature difference on some nights of as much as 8°C (14°F). With the fan working day and night, at negligible running costs, the temperature difference has been reduced by more than two-thirds.

Propagating cases Greenhouse electricity permits the installation of heated propagating cases – efficient for raising seedlings and rooting cuttings. They can be purchased in various sizes ready for plugging into the electric circuit. A handyman can construct his own over a soil-warming cable on the bench by erecting a wooden frame of convenient size over the bench and covering it with a sheet or two of glass. This will maintain an inside temperature high enough to root cuttings or germinate seeds.

WATERING AND SHADING

With automatic heating, ventilation, and pest and disease control taken care of, there only remain watering and shading to consider for the house to be fully automatic.

Various automatic watering systems are available, some which drip feed water to individual pots and others, much simpler to install, which work on the sub-irrigation principle. To install these the bench is lined with plastic sheeting and covered with either sand or plastic matting obtained from a garden supplier. The plants in their pots are stood on the sand or matting, kept permanently moist manually or by an automatic system. The plants draw up water via their roots as and when they need it.

Plants in plastic pots, which have several drainage holes, adapt particularly well to sub-irrigation. Clay pots can also be used, with a bit of doctoring. Dispense with the piece of crock normally used to cover the drainage hole and replace this with a wick of glass wool pushed through the hole so that it is in contact with the bench at one end and the compost in the pot at the other end. Water rises in the pots by means of capillary action and the plants take up as much as they need.

My tutor at horticultural college used to say that if we learnt how to water plants properly we were halfway to becoming gardeners. The subject of watering in the open garden is discussed in April (p. 95). While outdoor watering is of the utmost importance, a certain amount of tolerance is acceptable and one can be a bit hit and miss with the watering programme without disastrous results.

Greenhouse watering, however, is a much more exact affair. As with pot plants in the home, so more greenhouse plants are killed by overwatering than by being kept too dry. Indeed in the case of many pot plants it is an advantage to allow them almost to dry out between waterings. In winter they may need watering only once or twice a week, while in a scorching summer, and especially in small greenhouses where it is sometimes difficult to keep the temperature down, watering may be necessary twice a day.

Much depends upon the size of the pot and the size and nature of the plant. A large leafy plant obviously transpires more moisture than a small one. Plants in clay'pots also dry out faster than those in plastic because moisture evaporates through the sides of clay pots. For that reason I avoid mixing clay and plastic pots; watering is that much easier if they are kept separate.

The best way of finding out if a plant needs water is to lift up the pot and feel its weight. One soon learns to tell the difference between a dry plant and a wet one. Many pot plants are grown in loamless composts based on peat, and once these composts dry out they are difficult to moisten again: soak the compost thoroughly, leave it for an hour to drain, then water it again.

Keeping the humidity in a greenhouse at a benevolent 55 to 60 per cent is not easy in hot weather. Gardeners working daily in or near greenhouses can damp down several times a day by splashing water generously over benches and floor, though on hot days the water evaporates in an hour or so. Sub-irrigation benches which constantly supply water to pot plants have the added advantage of evaporating water into the air, thus creating a moist atmosphere.

From early April the sun gains strength, and young seedlings will need some protection from its heat. Green plastic sheeting can be hung in front of a bench to intercept the sun's rays, or newspapers can be propped over the plants and removed when the sun begins to go down.

Roller blinds made of plastic materials are excellent and available in different standard lengths and widths for fitting outside or inside the house. What is important is to remember to raise and lower them as necessary during the day; in my experience many gardeners forget to lower the blinds when the sun shines and forget to raise them when the sky clouds over.

Technology has made it possible for greenhouse blinds to be raised or lowered automatically, the controlling mechanism being activated by the sun's rays. However, these systems have so far proved too expensive for the average gardener to install.

Blinds fitted to the outside of the house are preferable because they also reduce the amount of heat going into the house. Fitted inside they do a reasonable job of protecting plants from direct sun rays, but not a great deal to prevent the temperature from rising too fast or too much.

The simplest method of providing shade is to spray or paint the outside of the glass with a shading compound. It is also cheap and can be quickly applied with a long-handled broom. One proprietary compound has the remarkable property of staying on the glass during even the most torrential downpour. Yet come autumn when shading should be removed, a duster or rag tied to a broom will on a fine day rub it off in minutes.

New Gardens

Every week thousands of people change homes. Some may have attractive gardens, but many will have nothing to commend them, or they may be brand new plots tacked on to brand new houses. In the case of existing gardens it is wise to wait for a year before making major alterations. This gives you time to become aware of problems and to discover what plants turn up in borders or in rough grass.

With a brand new garden you will start from scratch, and that means thoughtful planning. A garden, like a home, reflects the personality of the owners, their tastes and interests, and since all members of the family will share it they should be consulted at the planning stage. This will help you to decide whether the garden is basically to be a place in which to relax, a play area for children and pets, a source for fruit and vegetables, or a bit of all these elements.

Start by committing your ideas to paper, preferably graph paper on which it is easier to calculate the scale of beds, paths and other features. Better still, draw up a scale map of the garden, cut various shapes from differently coloured paper to represent lawns, flower beds, trees, paths and service areas, and arrange and rearrange these on the plan until you arrive at a satisfactory effect.

LAWNS AND PAVING

A lawn or paved area provides a welcome sitting-out or play area and also makes a garden look more spacious. Planting right up to the house can overshadow the rooms, cause dampness to the walls and be depressing to look at during the dull winter months.

Most gardens are rectangular, and with a lawn of the same shape, the side borders will inevitably be rectangular, too. Avoid this static look by introducing other shapes. A simple method of softening a tailored lawn is the introduction of a few island beds of flowers. Where the lawn adjoins a flower border, make the edges wavy rather than straight.

A town garden (35 × 46 ft: 10.5 × 14 m) on two levels, with climbers and window boxes to add a third dimension, can be a real joy for many months of the year

In small gardens or with young children it is advisable to have hard paving near the house. It will take heavier wear than turf and also dry out more quickly after rain. A few tubs of flowers, a garden seat or a bird bath will soften the hard appearance of paving.

PATHS

Main paths should be strong and wide enough to take a wheelbarrow. If possible avoid a path across the lawn and instead set a few stepping stones just below the level of the turf. They will take the worst of the wear and the mower can ride over them. It will be necessary, however, to trim their edges from time to time to check encroaching grass.

Paths should always lead somewhere – never finish abruptly at a boundary fence. Avoid a straight path running through the garden, cutting it in two; any path looks more attractive if it winds round the various features. Crazy or formal paving of natural or simulated stone gives a more attractive finish than concrete. Gravel paths are dry to the feet, durable, easily patched and weed-free for months after an application of weedkiller. Grass paths look beautiful, but need a lot of upkeep: mowing, edging, weeding and feeding.

A large but easily managed garden (100 × 156 ft: 30 × 47 m), planted mainly with trees, shrubs and ground-cover plants set in an informal lawn. The island bed with bulbs, flowers and foliage plants provides interest in every season.

SECLUSION

If you want your garden to be private, fencing or hedging will be needed. Walls make the most pleasing boundaries but are expensive to have constructed. Hurdles or wattle fencing – if you can find them – give quick privacy and are easily erected; close-woven fencing is also effective and gives suitable support for climbers. Open-weave fences are less stable and give less privacy for a time until massed boundary shrubs in front are growing strongly. Hedges are probably the cheapest, but take time to mature; they also deplete borders of nutrients and must be trimmed at least once or twice during the growing season.

A tapering garden (80 × 120 ft: 24 × 36 m): blending curves with straight lines and introducing plenty of shrubs breaks the formality of this corner plot. The kitchen garden is masked by hedges, while the pool area is quiet and secluded

Ugly views beyond the garden or surrounding buildings can create problems, but quick-growing trees, or a summer house festooned with climbers, can help to block them out. Examine the garden and its surroundings from all angles and if there is anything you would rather blot out from view, mark it on the plan as in need of screening.

Trees create shade as well as provide flowers and/or fruits, but huge forest trees are not suitable for small gardens. Remember that young seedling trees will go on growing, so choose the type of tree which at maturity will be in proportion to the size of the garden. Standard apple trees, for example, give shade, beautiful spring flowers and fruit.

The secret of making a long, narrow garden (140 × 30 ft: 42 × 9 m) exciting is to divide it with hedges to provide informal lawn areas and to create surprises

VEGETABLES AND FRUIT

Kitchen garden crops should actually be kept at the far end of the garden, hidden by a pergola covered with roses, a border of shrubs or a rock garden. For temporary cover, a screen of summer leaves has plenty of eye appeal.

The compost heap and tool shed should also be out of sight from the house; dustbins can be hidden behind a low hedge or a few largish shrubs in tubs. A greenhouse is different, since most gardeners will prefer to have this near to mains water and electricity. However, it should not be sited where the house blocks out sunlight nor where it interrupts the view.

IMPORTANT DESIGN POINTS

If you have planned your new garden along these lines, after a couple of years you should not be able to view the whole garden from any given point. Surprise is the essence of good design, with each twist and corner revealing a new vista or viewing angle.

Grow herbs close to the kitchen.

Leave a small bed near the house to accommodate very late or very early flowers, such as winter heathers, hellebores and snowdrops, where they can be enjoyed from the house in bad weather.

Small fruit trees like cordons and espaliers take up less room than bush trees; they can be planted fairly close together, crop well and make a convenient screen to the vegetable plot.

Plan most flower beds where they will receive plenty of sun, although there is a good choice of plants for sunless borders (see October, *Growing in the Shade*, p.219).

There are other hedges besides the ubiquitous privet (see December, *Hedges and Screens*, p.263).

Pools should be in open situations and in full sun. While children are small use pool excavations as sandpits as a safety precaution.

Herbaceous borders should be at least 6 ft (approx. 2 m) wide for telling effect.

Study gardens in the neighbourhood as a guide to plants likely to succeed in your particular soil and area.

 # FEBRUARY

The Month in the Garden

February is a difficult and unpredictable month for gardening. The weather determines both practical outside work and the presence of blooms in beds and borders.

In many ways February spells the turn of the year, with colour appearing, although not in large quantities. Instead, look for it in small flower groupings amongst bare branches and indeterminate shades of green.

General Tasks Whenever conditions are favourable get on with outdoor tasks, particularly anything of a constructional nature.

Tidy tool sheds; replace or repair tools as necessary.

Wash out pots and seed trays in readiness for next month's sowing.

Order seeds and plants for spring delivery.

Trees and Shrubs Prune shrubs which normally carry their flowers from mid-summer onwards, on shoots made during the current year.

The winter-flowering *Jasminum nudiflorum*, for example, should be pruned after blooming, the old flowering shoots being cut back to within $\frac{1}{2}$ in. (1 cm) of the old wood. On *Buddleia davidii* (*B. variabilis*), cut last year's shoots back to within 1 in.

(2.5 cm) of the older wood in order to obtain better quality blooms and to keep bushes shapely and compact; remove weak or damaged shoots altogether. Prune *Hydrangea paniculata*, *Ceanothus* 'Gloire de Versailles', *Campsis radicans*, spiraeas and tamarisks in a similar manner.

Plant deciduous hedges when the weather is mild. Cut back and 'lay' overgrown hedges.

Firm back newly planted shrubs which have been lifted by frost.

Climbers Cut last season's growths of *Clematis* x *jackmanii* back to 12–18 in. (30–45 cm) from the ground. On other clematis remove frosted, dead or broken shoots and shorten others to prevent overcrowding.

Roses In mild spells, continue with

planting of new bushes. Firm any which have been lifted by frost.

WEATHER

The French call February 'double-faced' and 'the shortest and worst of all the months', and they are often right. Soil temperatures are at their lowest at this time of the year, and only the bravest flowers are to be seen in most gardens. The snowdrop, also known as 'Fair Maid of February', often appears early in the month, while the crocus is dedicated to St Valentine and should be in bloom about 14 February.

February can be a very cold month indeed if the winds are blowing from the north or from the east and southeast. If westerly winds are strong and Candlemas Day (2 February) 'brings clouds and rain, then winter is gone and won't come again'. This is the belief of many countrymen, but spring is still a stranger to most parts of the country, and it is only the tips of the south-west coasts which experience an upsurge of temperature.

February is also known as 'fill-dyke', but this is more a request then a firm statement. The plea 'February fill the ditch, black or white, we don't care which' expresses the need for winter rains to fill up the soil with moisture at all levels, so that plants can better withstand the drier and warmer months to follow. Once the soil is at capacity moisture, the drains will run and the ditches will be filled.

For the gardener, February is a month to be endured, not enjoyed. If it brings a few dry mild days, do not be in too great a hurry to start spring sowing, for this is the time of the garden year when patience is a sensible virtue.

Lawns Brush off wormcasts and apply wormkiller if the weather is mild. Regardless of weather conditions refrain from cutting the grass until March.

Hardy Plants During suitable weather sprinkle a general fertilizer such as Growmore between herbaceous plants and lightly fork it in. At the same time remove large weeds and cut back dead stems.

Bulbs Protect crocuses and polyanthus from bird damage with a deterrent spray.

Bring the last of the bulbs indoors from plunge beds.

Keep those which have finished flowering in a frost-free place until they can be planted outdoors.

Vegetables Prepare beds for seed sowing when weather conditions allow. Sow parsnips and, in the south of England, broad beans and early peas; but wait for another fortnight before following suit in the north.

Plant shallots.

Herbs Split and replant chives.

Prepare new herb beds, incorporating organic matter on heavy and poor soils.

Fruit Apple and pear trees which were not given a tar-oil winter wash in December can be given a bromophos in oil spray as an alternative at the end of the month. This will control red spider mites and other fruit-tree pests (see also August, *Plant Disorders*, p.176).

Cut back the side shoots of young fan-trained peaches and nectarines, and wall-grown plums and cherries, to within 12-18 in. (30-45 cm) according to space available.

Spray peaches with dithane 945 or

Bordeaux mixture when buds swell in order to control peach leaf curl.

Tip summer-fruiting raspberry canes; cut all canes of autumn-fruiting kinds down close to the ground.

Plants under Glass In February the alpine house comes into its own, repaying earlier labour with a rich harvest of miniature bulbs and flowers. Heat is not required, only the protection against wind and wet afforded by the glass panes. This is sufficient to induce many small bulbs like dwarf cyclamen, narcissi, crocuses and species tulips, as well as primulas, mossy saxifrages – their dumpy hummocks of leaves spangled with small jewel-like flowers – and even dwarf gentians to burst into early bloom.

Seed sowing should start this month. Great heat is not necessary for germination, 10-13°C (50-55°F) being sufficient for a wide range of half-hardy annuals and tender perennials for planting outside in late May or early June.

Sow seeds, also, of plants such as streptosolens, gloxinias, coleus and celosias, for greenhouse decoration later in the season. Germinate them in a warm propagating frame, temperature 16-18°C (60-64°F) and, when the seedlings are large enough, pot them separately in small pots.

Dormant herbaceous perennials, like asters, anthemis, phlox, achilleas and campanulas, can be lifted and boxed in good potting soil, stood on a greenhouse bench and sprayed over from time to time to start them into growth. When the shoots are about 3 in. (7.5 cm) high they can be severed from the crown and used as soft cuttings (see July, *New Plants from Old*, p. 154). The cuttings can be rooted in a closed propagating case.

Start dormant tubers of strepto-carpus and tuberous begonias in boxes of moist peat kept on a warm bench or in a propagating frame, temperature 13-16°C (55-60°F).

Water and start into growth fuchsias, heliotropes, hydrangeas and abutilons which have been dormant all winter. Keep in a temperature of 10°C (50°F) and spray over their tops daily with tepid water.

Dormant fuchsias can be started into growth in February

Cut back robust greenhouse climbers like passion flowers, streptosolens and plumbago to within a few inches of the old wood.

Sow carrots ('Early Nantes' and 'Early Market') in a cold frame. Keep the lights closed for a week or two before sowing in order to warm the soil, which should be light and finely raked.

Sow an early batch of parsley in a cold frame or under cloches. Water the soil with boiling water beforehand to hasten germination.

House Plants Clean smooth, large-leaved plants with damp cotton wool and soft water containing a few drops of milk.

Take smooth, small-leaved plants to the kitchen sink if possible, cover the soil in the pots with foil (to prevent excessive wet) and spray the foliage with tepid water.

Care of indoor plants: (A) a watering can with a hole under the spout is excellent for watering pot plants; (B) for sub-irrigation, fill a tray with pebbles and keep wet; (C) keep plants in saucers for easy watering; (D) a sprayer is very handy for watering

Towards the end of the month, start feeding established plants, using a proprietary soluble feed at half the recommended strength. Repeat after two weeks.

Repot pot-bound plants in fresh compost.

Throw out ungainly codiaeums, dracaenas and other woody plants which are unlikely to break lower down on the stems. Prune to shape others which have a ragged appearance.

PLANTS IN THEIR PRIME

Trees and Shrubs in Flower Alnus;
camellias, *Chimonanthus praecox,
Cornus mas; Corylus avellana* (hazel);
Daphne mezereum; D. odora; ericas
(heathers); *Garrya elliptica; Hamamelis
mollis* and others (witch hazel);
*Lonicera fragrantissima, L. standishii;
Mahonia japonica; Prunus subhirtella*
'Autumnalis'; *Rhododendron arboreum,
R. mucronatum* and varieties;
*Sarcococca humilis, Stachyurus praecox ;
Viburnum farreri; V. grandiflorum;
V. tinus.*

Climbers *Clematis cirrhosa* 'Balearica';
Jasminum nudiflorum

Hardy Plants Helleborus of various
kinds, particularly *H. corsicus; H.
lividus; H. orientalis; H. viridis; Iris
unguicularis; Petasites fragrans;* various
pulmonarias.

Rock Garden Plants *Anemone
blanda;* corydalis; *Primula juliana*
varieties, *P. vulgaris;* saxifrages;
violas (winter pansies).

GARDEN PROBLEMS

Wormcasts on lawns.
 Bud-picking by birds.
 Slug damage.
 **Mice eating crocus corms or
seedlings, especially under glass.**
 Loose shoots on climbers.
 Dead tree branches.

GARDEN HINTS

Avoid walking on frosted lawns.
 **Do not dig snow or frost into the
soil.**
 **Tread back newly planted shrubs
and perennials lifted by frost.**
 **Shake newly fallen snow from
evergreens.**
 **Check ties on wall shrubs and
climbers after gales.**

Bulbs Crocuses; *Eranthis hyemalis* (winter aconite); galanthus (snowdrops); *Iris danfordiae, I. histrioides, I. reticulata; Narcissus* 'February Gold', *N. pseudo-narcissus; Scilla bifolia; Tulipa celsiana* (*T. persica*).

CROPS TO ENJOY

Vegetables Broccoli; sprouting broccoli; Brussels sprouts; celery; kale; lettuces (under glass or cloches); leeks; savoys; turnip tops.

Root crops in store: Jerusalem artichokes; beetroot; carrots; onions; parsnips; potatoes.

Fruits Forced rhubarb; stored apples and pears.

PLANT ASSOCIATIONS

Camellias of any colour can be carpeted with *Helleborus orientalis*.

Prunus subhirtella 'Autumnalis' with a ground cover of *Helleborus corsicus*.

Red winter heathers (*Erica carnea* forms) interplanted with early mauve crocuses and *Iris histrioides* 'Major'.

In shelter, yellow primroses will come up with snowdrops and crocuses.

Jasminum nudiflorum against a wall, fronted with winter pansies and *Skimmia japonica* behind these.

Corylus avellana 'Contorta' as a lawn specimen plant with blue *Anemone blanda* and *Colchicum* 'Waterlily' which comes into leaf when the anemones have died down and will flower in autumn.

Snowdrop, *Galanthus nivalis*

Plants of the Month

SNOWDROPS

Native to European woods and damp meadows and naturalized in Britain, especially on Skye. On 2 February, Candlemas Day, which is the Feast of the Purification of the Virgin Mary, it was for many years customary to clean images of the Virgin and to fill the niches with snowdrops as a symbol of purity. Fragrant varieties, brought from south-eastern Europe, used to be especially popular; they still turn up occasionally in naturalized plantings. Snowdrops are also known as Mary's Tapers, Candlemas Bells and February Fair Maids.

ORCHIDS

The orchid family is the largest in the world, with representatives in practically every country and in diverse places – from icy arctic bogs to the jungle forests of the tropics.

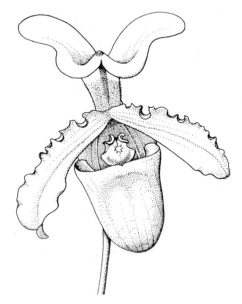

Slipper orchid, *Paphiopedilum spiceranum*

At this time of year enthusiasts with warm greenhouses are able to flower a variety of species, many of them brought to Britain in the last century when 'orchid fever' was at its height. One slipper orchid, *Cypripedium spiceranum* (now more correctly *Paphiopedilum spiceranum*), was discovered in Bhutan by a teaplanter named Spicer who sent it to his mother in Wimbledon, where it was seen and bought by Veitch, one of the great nurserymen of the nineteenth century. When exhibited by Veitch the plant attracted much attention and was greatly in demand. In those days orchids were valuable commodities, often changing hands at hundreds of pounds per plant, and it is hardly surprising that others tried to locate the source of *C. spiceranum*. In 1870 a German professional plant hunter called Forstermann went to Bhutan to find Mr Spicer and from him obtained information as to the plant's habitat. Having found the location he packed all the plants he could carry, then systematically set to work to exterminate any remaining specimens – a move which not only destroyed it for ever as a wild plant but enhanced the value of those he had purloined. With skilful propagation forty thousand plants of *C. spiceranum* were sold in auction rooms only fourteen years later, in 1884.

Only one orchid has any economic importance, and that is *Vanilla fragrans (V. planifolia)* from South America, a tropical climber with fragrant seed pods. These were used by the Aztecs to flavour chocolate several centuries before America was discovered by Europeans. Like so many other natural products the high cost of production has killed the trade, and vanilla is now produced synthetically.

Soil Types

Gardening books constantly extol the benefits of good, friable, fertile and loamy soil, but this ideal does not occur automatically. It is partly a condition brought about by good cultivation and partly a blend of constituents which materially affect plants. For example, a soil has to have effective drainage, yet at the same time contain some substance or material which will retain moisture and soluble plant foods. According to the preponderance of basic particles, soils can broadly be classified as sandy loams or clay loams, for clay and sand and chalk are the main soil types in which we garden.

Since the nature of a soil affects methods of cultivation and the plants which can be grown in it, it is worth knowing a little about them.

CLAY SOILS

Clay is dirty, tenacious and hard to tackle. It sticks to the feet, clogs tools and is slow to drain.

Yet, properly handled, it is fertile soil, rich in plant foods, especially potash, with great potential for plant growth.

The stickiness of clay is associated with the fineness of its particles – which are smaller than in any other soil type – and the fact that each one of them is surrounded by an absorbent coat, called a colloid, which takes up moisture like a sponge. In wet weather the colloids swell and pack down so tightly, especially when trampled over, that they impede drainage. In a dry summer the colloids shrink, which accounts for the cracks so often seen in clay soils. In managing a clay soil, keep these points in mind:

1 Keep off the ground when it is wet. If it is deeply dug in autumn and the soil left rough all winter, the weather – and especially frost – will help to break it down. The heavy clods will then crumble more easily to a finer tilth when raked during spring cultivation once the surface is dry enough.

2 Incorporate a conditioning agent which will cause the dry particles to coagulate (flocculate) so that they become larger. This improves drainage and again creates a crumbly texture. Gypsum (sulphate of lime) or lime are often used for this purpose, but lime in particular does not suit all plants, notably rhododendrons, heathers and many gentians. Gypsum is a good soil rectifier, without increasing the alkalinity. It can be dug in at the rate of 5 lbs per square yard (2.30 kg per square metre) in spring or autumn. There are also proprietary soil conditioners, mainly based on alginates and derived originally from seaweeds.

3 Work in organic material which will keep the clay particles apart. Organic matter improves drainage, helps to maintain soil fertility, and improves the physical condition. Rotted farmyard manure, pests, leafy soil, hop manure, mushroom or garden compost are all suitable for this purpose. Annual application of organic matter, worked in during autumn cultivation will, in time, produce a friable soil.

On very heavy or wet soils the incorporation of sand, brick rubble, grit, or even weathered ashes helps to improve drainage.

Clay soils are not only potentially fertile, but they are less liable to dry out in summer than light soils. They are slow to warm up in spring, but equally retain their heat in autumn better than sandy soil. Many plants thrive in clay soils, particularly members of the rose family which includes apples, strawberries, raspberries and pyracanthas.

SANDY SOILS

Sand is practically pure silica and almost devoid of plant food. Its large particles make for quick drainage and good aeration, and sandy soils are therefore light to work, even in winter; they also warm up quicker than clays. Too much sand, however, causes such rapid drainage that water and soluble plant foods are leached out, resulting in a hungry soil.

Light soils are also inclined to be weedy, and there is a great shortage of potash, lime and soluble mineral constituents. To improve light sandy soils, liberal applications of moisture-holding materials must be regularly applied. Rotted farmyard manure and garden compost are ideal, as well as peat, leaf-mould and mushroom compost; indeed anything which will bind the soil particles together and act as a sponge in retaining water and soluble salts. Work these manures into the upper soil layer or use them as surface mulches (see also May, *Mulching*, p.119).

Potash is an element which relates to a plant's health, strengthening its resistance to disease and promoting balanced growth. On light soils where it is particularly important, potash can be supplied as a compound fertilizer or on its own as sulphate of potash. Wood ashes also contain potash and can be applied at the rate of 4-8 oz per square yard (125-250 grammes per square metre).

Quick-acting fertilizers like sulphate of ammonia and nitrate of soda are not recommended. They cause too rapid growth, with a possible susceptibility to mildew, and quickly wash away.

CHALKY SOILS

Calcareous soils are those which overlie a chalk or limestone formation; their fertility depends to a great extent on the thickness of the soil layer. If this is shallow, the ground will be poor and hungry, but if it is deep the soil can be very fertile – and, strangely, considering the underlying rock, it may not always be alkaline.

In general chalk soils are warm, but so porous that they rapidly dry out.

As a result they quickly lose plant nutrients, and organic matter and potash are frequently lacking.

Additional problems occur on chalky soils which are very alkaline; chlorosis, a yellowing of plant leaves, may develop. This is the result of the plants' inability to assimilate manganese and other essential foods and iron – the latter in association with nitrogen is responsible for the green colouring of leaves. Ample supplies of farmyard manure or compost will often correct this deficiency; if not, one or several applications of a chelated or sequestered compound applied according to the manufacturer's instructions will usually overcome the problem.

Chalky soils should therefore be regularly supplied with organic materials, initially by digging in farmyard manure, garden compost, green manures, decayed leaves and similar materials. In alternate years, spring mulches will usually maintain the moisture and food content.

Potash should also be supplied in spring in a general fertilizer or as sulphate of potash or wood ashes.

Plants which dislike limy soil include rhododendrons and azaleas, kalmias, many heathers, camellias, certain eucryphias, pieris, pernettyas and gaultherias. To compensate, many others do well – pyracanthas and cotoneasters, for example, berry well on chalk, clematis are natural plants of chalklands and dianthus, gypsophila, scabious and lupins thrive.

Vertical Gardening

Just as there is no merit in having patches of bare ground in flower borders, so views of wooden fences – especially those with the rails on your side – are hardly attractive. And aesthetic considerations apart, unclothed fences are wasted space.

Britain's bare walls must total many miles, yet along with sheds and fences they can be utilized as supports for wall shrubs, climbers and trained fruit trees.

Vertical gardening has a number of advantages. It frames the rest of the garden with a living mantle of greenery and flowers. It gives privacy, sets off house walls and masks ugly features. It enables the gardener to grow more as well as a greater range of plants – particularly important where space is limited – and it provides cutting material for the house.

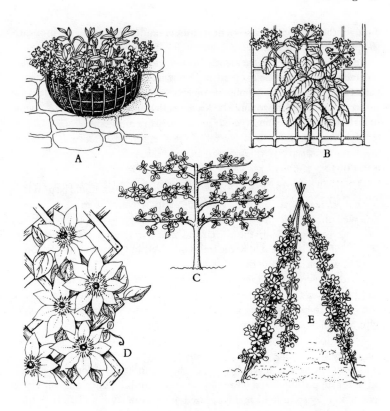

(A) a 'half' or wall basket; (B) plastic-covered wire mesh panels make an excellent support for wall shrubs; (C) an espalier-trained fruit tree; (D) clematis do well on a trellis; (E) many climbers flourish on a tripod

SOIL PREPARATION

Soil at the base of a wall often receives only half the rainfall dropping on open ground or borders, depending on aspect and the direction of wind. Accordingly, study the aspect before choosing plants. Some kinds prefer shade, others sun, some need well-drained soil while others must always have their roots moist. There are lime-tolerant plants and calcifuges which hate lime.

The soil may be poor, so work in generous quantities of rotted organic material, like garden compost, leaf soil or animal manures. This will supply food for the developing roots of new climbers and help to retain soil moisture. Be prepared to water the plants thoroughly in dry weather.

Perennial weeds are frequently found close to fences, often coming through from a neighbour's garden. Deal with these before you plant, using either a weed killer like glyphosate on the weed foliage (glyphosate does not affect the soil) and removing the leaves as they die, or by frequent hoeing which will destroy some weeds.

SUPPORTS

Few plants are self-clinging and those which need support should be provided with it *before* they are planted. Wood or plastic-covered wire trellis fastened to a wall offers good support, or short nails – vine eyes – complete with eyelet holes can be knocked into the mortar and have wires stretched between them. The plants can then be tied to the trellis or wires, and in some cases the shoots may be woven in and out of the mesh.

Plastic-covered wire mesh panels, which come in various sizes, are also ideal for fixing to fences; they can also be tied to posts to form a screen across the garden to hide eyesores, such as a compost heap, where a front barrier of climbing plants or wall shrubs can be most effective.

Not so long ago one could buy free-standing supports of 'sprogged' poles or young tree saplings 10 ft (3 m) or more high on which the side branches had been cut back to leave short stubs about 8 in. (20 cm) long. They were ideal for supporting roses, wisterias and other climbers, but along with hazel peasticks they seem to have disappeared. If you can lay your hands on three poles, push them into the soil and tie them together at the top in wigwam fashion, as a frame for climbers planted at the base. This is an effective method for climbing roses, especially when they are teamed with *Clematis* x *jackmanii*; the latter will support itself on the rose stems and come into flower after the roses have finished their first flush. Brick or wooden pillars with loops of nylon rope linking them at the top can also be used to support roses and wisterias; prefabricated wire arches and pergola sections can be bought for the same purpose.

TRAINED FRUIT TREES

Alternatively, grow climbers as standards. Wisterias, for example, can be trained in this way, as well as *Buddleia alternifolia*. Apple and pear trees trained as cordons or espaliers take up less room than bush or pyramid trees. Gooseberries and red currants can also be trained as cordons or espaliers against a wall or fence.

A great number of climbers will thrive on warm sunny walls especially if the site is sheltered. They include most of the large-flowered clematis, like those of the *C. patens* and *C.* x *jackmanii* groups, always provided that they have a cool root run. Low shrubs planted in front or paving stones laid nearby ensure the moist root coolness that clematis crave. The yellow-flowered *C. tangutica* and *C. orientalis* also relish these conditions; on really warm south-facing walls you could try the brilliant, buttercup-yellow *Fremontodendron californicum,* which flowers on and off all summer and has thick three-lobed leaves, felted underneath and with rusty brown hairs on its leaf-stalks and young branches.

Passiflora caerulea is another vigorous species for a sunny wall, remaining evergreen in mild locations and producing masses of blue, white and green flowers in high summer; in the sunny south it also fruits, bearing orange-red oval berries up to 1½ in. (4 cm) long.

Solanums do best on a high sunny wall, with a south or west aspect. The hardiest is the slender, twining *S. jasminoides* with bunches of slate-blue flowers from mid-summer onwards or its white form 'Album'. More spectacular is *S. crispum* which has rich blue, potato-like, slightly fragrant flowers 1 in. (2.5 cm) across in loose clusters. *S. crispum* will grow 12-15 ft (3.6-4.5 m) in a season, the old stems usually dying down in autumn.

Most honeysuckles flower best in sun, in spite of their reputation as woodland plants. Some are fragrant, others not; for scent choose species and cultivars of *Lonicera periclymenum,* the common woodbine of our hedgerows, *L. caprifolium, L. japonica* and the fragrant, rich yellow *L. hildebrandiana.* More colourful but scentless are the orange-scarlet *L. sempervirens* which must have a sheltered spot, *L.* x *brownii,* red and *L. henryi,* yellow and red.

Climbing roses of all kinds are suitable for south and west fences and walls. The polygonums – *P. aubertii* and *P. baldschuanicum,* both with froths of pinkish-white flowers in late summer, are ideal for rapidly covering ugly eyesores, tree stumps, old sheds and the like; they are, however, extremely rampant and should never be planted near precious or delicate plants as given half a chance the polygonums take over in a season or two. For this reason they should be cut back annually in spring.

CLIMBERS FOR NORTH- AND EAST-FACING SITES

A few climbers not only tolerate but flower well in heavy shade. Outstanding among these are *Hydrangea petiolaris* and *H. anomala*. The former will grow 50 ft (15 m) or more if allowed, but can be kept lower by pruning; the latter reaches 30-40 ft (9-12 m). Both are deciduous and self-clinging with crowded branches of yellowish-white flowers in summer. *Schizophragma hydrangeoides,* also self-clinging, has spectacular flowers with large creamy bracts, although they are more freely produced in sun.

Lonicera tragophylla needs shade and bears large clusters of golden yellow flowers in mid-summer followed by red berries; *Akebia quinata* is a slender climber with small, purple, fragrant flowers and compound hand-shaped leaves. It completely covers a north wall in our garden but sad to say rarely produces fruits, which is a pity for they are as large as sausages, dark purple and with numerous black seeds in a white pulp.

All the parthenocissus and most hederas (ivies) grow well in shade. In really sunless areas ivies are self-clinging and reliable, and there are some attractive coloured foliage forms like the bright golden *Hedera helix* 'Buttercup', 'Gold Heart', green with yellow centres and the silver and white-patterned *H. colchica* 'Dentata aurea'. *Celastrus orbiculatus,* a spiny climber, is at its best in autumn when the rounded leaves turn to gold and the yellow fruits open to display their red berries like jewels in fairy caskets.

HANGING BASKETS

Space can also be saved by growing flowering plants in window boxes, hanging baskets or half wall baskets hung on trellis against house or boundary walls (see also April, *Annuals and Bedding Plants,* p. 85). We use many half baskets on walls near our house, to hold herbs as well as flowers, thus making it easier for the cook to gather the odd sprig of parsley or sage. Since all our containers are automatically watered (see April, *Watering,* p. 95) they are trouble-free and easy to look after.

There are various types and sizes of hanging and wall baskets. Some are made of white or green plastic with a built-in saucer at the base to catch excess water; others are of galvanized or plastic-covered wire in green or white. Some kinds fold flat when not in use. Before planting any basket it should be lined with sphagnum moss (obtainable from good florists) and inside this a layer of thin plastic sheeting. The baskets are then filled with good potting compost, either John Innes No. 3 or a peat-based, loamless compost.

Pierce a few holes through the plastic lining about 2 in. (5 cm) up from the bottom to allow surplus water to drain away.

Hanging baskets, round or square, can be suspended from strong brackets screwed to a wall or fence or over a doorway or porch. Half baskets are usually hung on a couple of nails or hooks driven into a wall; better still, hang them on plastic-covered, wire-meshed panels fixed to the wall, where they can be arranged in a variety of positions.

Hanging baskets dry out quickly and need watering every day in warm weather if there is no rain (see April, *Watering*, p.95 for automatic watering of baskets, tubs and window boxes). In order to offset the loss of soluble salts through drainage we feed all our container plants once a week with a soluble fertilizer.

Some gardeners plant only the top of a basket, relying on the trailing plants finding their way down to clothe the sides. Others make holes in the plastic lining about halfway down and insert trailers in the spaces, firming the roots and building up the soil gradually.

There are numerous plants suitable for baskets and window boxes. They include most pelargoniums (geraniums) especially those with coloured leaves such as 'L'Elegante', which has green and pink leaves, and 'Golden Harry Hiover' with golden leaves surrounding a broad brown central zone. Then there are pink, red or mauve ivy-leaved trailing geraniums, and a wide range of fuchsias, upright and trailing varieties, as well as begonias.

Varieties of *Begonia pendula* which hang over the sides of baskets and the many forms of *B. semperflorens* are ideal, as are the multiflora begonias, such as 'Flamboyant', red; and 'Mrs Richard Galle', apricot-yellow. Double-flowered tuberous begonias are also suitable and if you start with a few, they can be increased the following spring by dividing the tubers so that each piece contains one or more shoots. Tuberous begonias represent good value and are easy to store through the winter in a tray covered with peat or old compost, kept slightly moist to prevent the tubers from shrivelling.

Any greenhouse or room indoors where the temperature does not fall below about 7°C (45°F) is suitable for overwintering tuberous begonias.

Petunias, marigolds *(Tagetes)*, the small yellow-flowered calceolarias, nasturtiums, alyssum, ageratums, silver-leaved plants like *Helichrysum petiolatum* and, of course, trailing lobelias are also invaluable.

A word about window boxes. They should be firmly anchored to the window-sill if there is a danger of them falling and injuring passers-by. It is surprising what a powerful gale can dislodge from a window-sill. Push several triangular wedges under the fronts of the boxes so that they tip slightly backwards.

 # MARCH

The Month in the Garden

March is usually a peak month for gardening, full of promise and as yet few disappointments. On fine days, when the air is bracing and the ground reasonably dry underfoot, most forms of cultivation are possible and there is a variety of plants ready for sowing or planting.

However, one important rule should be observed: never work the soil when it is wet and sticky. If clods of earth stick to your feet as you walk over the ground you will do more harm than good. This applies particularly to heavy soils like clays, since clay particles are smaller than those of sand or silt. Its cold sticky nature is not only due to the fineness of the grains, but to the sponge-like substances called colloids which envelop each particle. Wet conditions cause the colloids to absorb water and swell; when they dry out they shrink, forming the characteristic cracks associated with clay soils.

When a potter makes a clay pot he wets his hands repeatedly as he kneads the clay into shape. This causes the clay particles to pack tightly together, the colloids swell and the pot becomes almost watertight. The same thing happens if you trample wet clay soils. The packed down particles impede drainage and spoil the soil tilth. (See also February, *Soil Types*, p.39.) On fine days, when you can walk over the ground without your shoes becoming muddy, it is possible to kick or hoe the soil clods so that they break into fine fragments. Conditions are then right for cultivation, sowing and planting.

General Tasks Weather permitting, finish all digging especially in the vegetable garden. Rake the soil to a fine tilth. Treat paths and drives with a weedkiller; do not apply in wet or frosty weather.

WEATHER

Stronger warmth from the sun, lengthening days and shortening nights mean that soil temperatures begin to increase appreciably during March. As a result plant roots react to the warmer conditions, and signs of spring can be seen in the garden.

Spring comes first to the coastal areas in the south-west, spreading north and east along the valleys until by the end of March, in most years, it has reached most of the lower ground in England and Wales. An increase in height above sea level causes a delay in spring warmth amounting to about three days for every 100-ft rise (about one day for every 10 m); in the hills and mountains March is still a winter month.

An early spring may be a mixed blessing, especially if it is followed by a return of cold winds: 'Better late spring and bear, than early blossom and blast'.

Impatience can be consoled by the thought that 'A late spring never deceives'.

Most of all, a gardener hopes for spells of dry weather, for 'March water is worse than a stain in cloth', precisely because the adverse effects are so difficult to overcome. Far preferable is a drying topsoil which aids spring cultivation and early sowings, which is why 'a peck of dust in March is worth a king's ransom'.

March winds may help to dry out the soil, but they can be harmful to tender plants. Gardens which are well sheltered and have a southern aspect are those which show the earliest growth at this time of the year.

This rule in gardening never forget,
To sow dry and to plant wet.

planted within the next few weeks, including trees, shrubs, conifers, herbaceous plants, and rock plants. Unless the ground was manured in autumn, take out planting holes for shrubs and trees rather larger and deeper than seems necessary, then fork over the subsoil and work in plenty of well rotted organic material such as manure or garden compost or moist peat mixed with bonemeal. Cover this with soil and set each tree or shrub in place – with the roots well spread out in the case of leafless, bare-rooted deciduous specimens, but retaining the ball of soil round the rootstocks of evergreens. Fill the planting hole in with soil, firming it well with the feet; leave the soil mound slightly higher than the surrounding ground, because it always settles after a while. Standard trees should be staked at the time of planting.

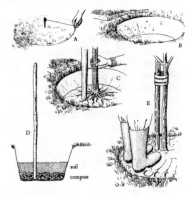

Planting a tree: (A) mark out the site; (B) take out a sufficiently large hole; (C) spread out the roots; (D) insert stake before planting; (E) return soil and tread firmly, tying tree to stake

Trees and Shrubs In the flower garden most perennials can be trans-

Shrubs damaged by frosts or snow-falls should be lightly pruned towards the end of the month. Remove the frosted tips of fuchsias, *Lavatera olbia* and *Caryopteris* species and cultivars.

Plant heathers in lime-free soil (except for lime-tolerant varieties), using pot-grown plants if possible. Space them an average 1-½ ft (30-45 cm) apart and top dress the ground liberally with moist peat.

Take root cuttings of *Rhus typhina* and romneyas.

Complete the planting of new deciduous hedges (see also December, *Hedges and Screens,* p. 263).

Remove weeds from hedge bottoms.

Prune old, overgrown hedges hard back, to spur new growth.

Climbers Plant clematis and other deciduous climbers, in planting holes prepared as for trees and shrubs. See also February, *Vertical Gardening,* p. 42.

There is still time to sow sweet peas outdoors in their flowering positions. Sow the seeds 2 in. (5 cm) deep and 4 in. (10 cm) apart in double rows, alternately spaced. Alternatively raise them in Jiffy pots, planting these out (after removing the net outer covering) when the seedlings are a few inches high. Guard against mice eating the seed by dipping them in paraffin prior to sowing.

Roses March is the recognized month for rose pruning, although some gardeners prune the bushes lightly in autumn, particularly those living in the milder parts of Britain. There are various degrees of severity applicable to March pruning, depending on the quality and quantity of flowers required, as well as the type of rose bush. Very hard pruning, for example, involves cutting each stem to within a few inches of the ground. This results in

the production of fewer, but large, well-shaped show blooms, flowering somewhat later than those treated less severely. At one time hard pruning each year was normal practice for all rose bushes, and indeed it is still necessary to cut newly planted bushes hard back in their first season. However, experiments undertaken at the Royal National Rose Society's trial grounds have shown that good roses can still be obtained by reducing the bushes to about half their height. This will also result in many more flowers. If only a third or so of the top growth is removed the bushes will produce an abundance of flowers, not perhaps of top quality, but ideal for garden display and home decoration. Moreover such lightly pruned bushes start flowering early and go on until autumn. Of course, all dead and diseased shoots must be pruned out at the base.

For more information on rose pruning, see *Roses,* p. 60.

GARDEN HINTS

Pruning for good roses **Start by removing dead, diseased and damaged branches.**

Take out weak, spindly and crossing stems, as well as sucker growths, tracing these back to their points of origin.

Always cut to an outward-pointing bud.

Do not leave 'snags' of wood above the buds or the stems will die back, encouraging diseases.

Lawns Re-seed bare areas on established lawns or repair these and broken edges with good turf (see also September, *Making Lawns,* p. 204).

Aerate the lawn with a springy wire rake so that weeds and grass stand up.

With the mower knives set high, lightly cut the grass and tidy the edges with a spade or half-moon edging iron.

Brush out wormcasts, using a switching movement.

Treat moss with a proprietary compound.

Hardy Plants Plant herbaceous perennials of all types, including *Aster amellus, Papaver orientale, Scabiosa caucasica,* pyrethrums and any other plants which move better in spring than in autumn.

Hoe the ground between established plants and to remove footprints. Mulch the soil around such hungry plants as paeonies, delphiniums and Michaelmas daisies, with decayed farmyard manure, mushroom or garden compost to encourage growth. Such top dressings not only feed the plants and keep the soil round them moist, but also suppress annual weed seedlings.

Put supports in place, using bamboo canes, branching peasticks or proprietary ring supports.

When new plants arrive from nurseries examine the roots before planting. If they are damaged trim them lightly; if dry soak them in water for half an hour before planting.

Bulbs Plant gladioli at fortnightly intervals, 3-5 in. (7.5-12.5 cm) deep according to type of soil (deepest in light ground) and 3 in. (7.5 cm) apart. In cold or exposed places wait until the end of the month to begin planting; on heavy soils, sprinkle a little sand under each corm.

Overcrowded clumps of winter aconites, snowdrops and crocuses can be lifted and divided at this time. They usually move more successfully when in leaf than when dormant.

Annuals, Biennials and Bedding Plants Sow seed of the hardier annuals outside at the end of the month. Rake the soil first, give it a light dressing of a general fertilizer and make drills in flower borders, sowing thinly. If too many seedlings come up, the thinnings can be transplanted to other areas. Hardy annuals include calendulas, annual chrysanthemums, eschscholzias, nigellas and Shirley poppies.

Rock Garden Plants Firm back any recently planted rock plants which may have been loosened by frost.

Remove weeds by hand.

Water Plants Feed fish on mild days, giving them a high protein diet.

Top up pools with fresh water.

Patio Plants Construct new patios and paved sitting areas.

Leave odd gaps in paving; fill them with good soil and plant low-growing plants like maiden pinks, *Phlox subulata* and creeping thyme.

Paint or use a wood preservative (not creosote) on the outsides of wooden troughs, tubs and window boxes.

Vegetables Many vegetable seeds can be sown this month, a week or two earlier in the south than in the north. Prepare the ground by raking it first in one direction, then the other to remove stones and to leave it level. Use a garden line when taking out seed drills.

Small seeds, like lettuces, onions and carrots, only need drills $\frac{1}{2}$ in. (1 cm) deep, taken out with a corner of a draw hoe pulled against the guiding line. Larger seeds like peas and beans need 2-in (5-cm) deep drills taken out with the whole blade of the hoe. Work backwards for both operations, keeping one foot on the line to ensure that it remains straight.

Sow vegetable seed thinly but evenly; cover the drills by scuffing the soil back over the seed with the feet or the back of a rake.

Permanent crops like rhubarb and asparagus can be planted in late March or April.

Herbs Chives make an attractive edging for a herb garden or vegetable plot. Split old clumps or plant new ones now.

Divide and replant old mint beds; to keep mint within bounds sink a bottomless bucket into the ground and plant into this. Alternatively push sheets of tin or slate down into the ground to restrain the creeping roots.

Prepare a seed bed and sow small quantities of parsley, marjoram and chervil at the end of March.

Sow basil in a pot and germinate indoors or in a greenhouse at 13°C (55°F).

Fruit Prune newly planted plums, apricots and morello cherries.

Dress the ground round blackcurrants with sulphate of ammonia at 1 oz per square yard (25 grammes per square metre) and dress raspberries similarly at half the dosage.

Plants under Glass March is a busy month in the greenhouse with many seedlings ready for potting on. Give young plants plenty of light and air in temperatures as near to 13°C (55°F) as possible. Prick out seedlings while quite small.

Sow half-hardy annuals intended in due course for the garden or greenhouse pot plants; use a proprietary seed compost. Petunias, salpiglossis, salvias, annual anchusas, ipomoeas and mesembryanthemums can all be sown now.

Sow cactus seed in light sandy compost.

Sow sweet peppers, cucumbers and courgettes; pot on tomatoes sown in January. Sow celery in a cold frame or unheated greenhouse.

Take dahlia cuttings and root in a propagator at 16°C (60°F). Take cuttings of fuchsias, marguerites, chrysanthemums, calceolarias, pelargoniums, coleus and heliotropes. Root them in small pots of sandy soil in a propagating frame or on a soil-warmed greenhouse bench. The hardier plants can be transferred to cold frames for hardening off at the end of March.

Start vines in unheated houses, lowering the rods and spraying them daily with tepid water. When growth is evident all the way down the rods tie them back into their usual place.

House Plants Check all house plants, knocking old specimens carefully from their pots. Tease away some of the old soil, prune out a few of the old roots, then repot the plants in fresh potting compost.

Wash the foliage of large-leaved plants – like ficus and philodendrons – with damp cotton wool and soft water. Small, smooth leaves can be cleaned and freshened by standing the pots in the sink and, after covering the soil with aluminium foil, spraying over the foliage. Do not wash rough-and hairy-leaved plants, such as saintpaulias. Clean off dust on these – and prickly cacti – with a soft brush.

To propagate saintpaulias, pileas and even impatiens pick individual leaves, complete with stalks, and stand the stems in a glass of water. Keep on a light warm window-sill until roots appear, then pot them individually.

PLANTS IN THEIR PRIME

Trees and Shrubs Azara; camellias; chaenomeles; *Cornus mas; Corylopsis pauciflora; Daphne laureola, D. mezereum; Erica carnea* varieties; *E. arborea;* forsythia; *Hamamelis* species and varieties; *Lonicera fragrantissima; Magnolia* x *soulangiana, M. stellata;* mahonias; parrotia; pieris; various prunus; early rhododendrons; ribes; various salix; *Spiraea thunbergii; Stachyurus praecox; Ulex europaeus; Viburnum tinus.*

Magnolia x *soulangiana*

Hardy Plants Bergenias; *Helleborus atrorubens, H. corsicus, H. orientalis* and others; *Iris unguicularis;* pansies; polyanthus; primroses; pulmonarias.

Bulbs Crocus; erythroniums; *Ipheion (Triteleia) uniflorum;* muscari; narcissus; scillas; early tulips.

Rock Garden Plants Anemones and pulsatillas; *Iris pumila;* primulas; saxifrages.

Water Plants Calthas.

CROPS TO ENJOY

Vegetables Summer-sown cabbage; kale; Brussels sprouts; sprouting broccoli; spinach and spinach beet; leeks; turnip tops.

Parsnips and other root crops in store, like swedes, carrots and onions.

Fruit Rhubarb.

PLANT ASSOCIATIONS

Purple *Erica carnea* cultivars backed by early pink rhododendrons.

Kingcups (*Caltha palustris*) and pussy willow (*Salix* sp.) with *Narcissus bulbocodium.*

Corylopsis underplanted with blue scillas.

Magnolia stellata fronted by *Pulsatilla vulgaris* or purple heathers (*Erica carnea*).

Blue and yellow polyanthus with *Daphne mezereum.*

Blue polyanthus and scillas in front of chaenomeles (Japanese quince) growing up a fence or wall.

Tulipa kaufmanniana against a green conifer background, with grape hyacinths (muscari) in the foreground.

GARDEN PROBLEMS

Loose or overtight ties on trees and climbers.

Slugs attacking young plants; protect them with slug bait laid under tiles or beneath grapefruit skins, or place topless, bottomless tins over small plants.

Weeds emerging everywhere.

Plants of the Month

PRIMROSES

The primrose (*Primula vulgaris*) is a favourite native flower, a delightful wildling but one which usually languishes and dies when brought into captivity – an excellent reason for leaving it where it does flourish, on banks, in hedgerows and light woodland. If you want primroses in the garden, raise plants from seed, or go for some of their derivatives, such as polyanthus, which are the offspring of primroses crossed with cowslips.

Primrose, *Primula vulgaris*

In the fifteenth century primrose flowers were used in cooking, particularly 'Prymerose' pottage and primrose pudding, and in later years Wakefield housewives were famous for their primrose vinegar. Today, crystallized primrose flowers are sometimes used for cake decoration, along with violets.

In Victorian times primroses became associated with Benjamin Disraeli whose favourite flower they were. At his funeral in April 1881 Queen Victoria sent a large wreath of primroses, and a society called the Primrose League was formed, which had as its object the dissemination of his Conservative principles. On the anniversary of his death each year Conservatives would wear primroses, a tradition carried on over many years in the village where I was born. As a child I remember people wearing primroses and special Primrose League badges provided by the local association.

FORSYTHIA

This popular, early-flowering shrub takes its name from William Forsyth, one-time gardener to George III and one of the seven founder members of the Horticultural Society of London, now the Royal Horticultural Society.

Forsythia

At the end of the American War of Independence the British Navy was much harassed by ships of other European nations. The position was further aggravated after Napoleon's rise to power, and good oak for new ships became of vital importance. Parliament was accordingly very disturbed to learn that a high proportion of the oak trees in the Royal Forests were so diseased as to be useless for this purpose.

About this time Forsyth was claiming to have invented a concoction which, spread over wounds, would heal decaying trees. A Parliamentary Commission, after investigating his experiments, recommended a grant of £1,500 (worth probably twenty times as much today) for the formula, promising him a similar amount when his claims had been substantiated. They never were. The formula of 'Forsyth's Plaister', as it was known, comprised a mixture of cow dung, lime rubble, wood ashes, river sand, urine and soapsuds beaten into a plaster. It had little effect on the trees and gradually fell into disrepute, but the fact that Parliament paid out such a large sum for a worthless invention gives some indication of the anxiety felt by the country at this time. Later is was claimed that the recipe was not even original, but belonged to earlier inventors.

Although he wrote a useful and popular work on the cultivation of fruit trees, Forsyth is chiefly remembered for this worthless invention, and by the lovely yellow shrub that bears his name.

Hardy Herbaceous Plants

At the beginning of this century huge flowery carpets of hardy herbaceous plants were a common feature of large gardens and estates. Some had all-season interest, others were planted so as to be at their best for specific months, usually when the family was likely to be in residence. Others again were planted in one-colour schemes, and instances of these can still be seen in the white borders at Sissinghurst and Crathes Castle and the red border at Hidcote Manor.

All but a handful of these splendid herbaceous borders have now disappeared. They belonged to the days when there were plenty of gardeners to look after them and plenty of muck and money to ensure their upkeep. Although most of the plants stayed in the borders, the earliest perennials were often lifted as they faded and replaced with later-blooming, pot-grown plants. That meant frames and greenhouses to back them up.

The vast majority of today's gardens are now tended by the owner, and, in order to cut down the work, herbaceous perennials are frequently teamed with shrubs, bulbs, annuals and bedding plants in a way which earlier generations would have deplored. The result is different, but very colourful, since early shrubs and bulbs, for instance, flower well before the bulk of the perennials. Conversely, at the other end of the year the season is prolonged by introducing dahlias, hydrangeas and winter-flowering heathers.

To the purist a true herbaceous perennial is a plant with an indefinite term of existence, but certainly more than two years. It produces flowers, stems, leaves and seeds annually, from an underground fibrous or tuberous rootstock, and loses its top growth in autumn. Within these limits plants vary enormously in height, spread, time and manner of flowering, appearance, habit and cultural requirements.

HERBACEOUS BEDS AND BORDERS

There are many places where herbaceous plants may be grown. Gardeners who wish to retain a semblance of the old-time borders may find that a practical solution is to cut small island beds in the lawn. They can be made to any size or shape, and once well manured and cultivated they can be planted in a miscellany of ways: for year-round effect, in a single colour scheme, with all low-growing or medium-sized plants or with the tall specimens in the centre and the heights decreasing towards the margins. As with large formal borders, several plants of the same kind should be planted close together so as to provide a stronger visual impact.

Another method of using herbaceous perennials is to plan interesting groupings in key positions – by a garden gate, near a flight of steps or at the side of a picture window. Some plants are impressive enough to stand alone, such as a single large acanthus or a giant fennel, *Ferula communis* (which is not a fennel at all), a rodgersia for a damp site or any large-growing hosta in a shady area.

A small border devoted entirely to two or three kinds of plants is another idea – for example, a bed of blue delphiniums interplanted with creamy *Lilium auratum* and pink astilbes; or a collection of Chinese paeonies backed by a white, double-flowered mock orange like *Philadelphus* 'Virginale'. Such beds can have a limited but spectacular period of interest and are better sited away from the main viewing points.

Then there are perennials for cutting. Pyrethrums, gaillardias, Michaelmas daisies, alstroemerias and liatris owe much of their popularity and wide-spread cultivation to the fact that they last well in water. Some low-growing perennials like *Geranium endressii* or *Dicentra eximia* may be suitable for containers surrounding, for example, a climbing rose or edging a jardiniere full of hostas. As they are permanent plants the roots of the shrubs will not be disturbed when annuals are put in or pulled out.

As herbaceous perennials remain in situ longer than annuals and bedding plants, the ground must be well prepared beforehand. Whatever its nature, it is always beneficial to dig the soil deeply and work in plenty of well-rotted compost, farmyard manure, spent mushroom compost or leaf soil. Planting can be done in early autumn or in spring; the latter period is

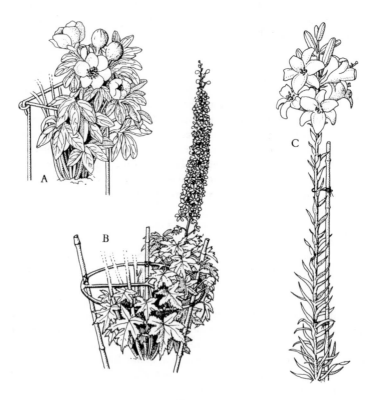

Staking perennials: (A) paeonies; (B) delphiniums; (C) lilies

advisable for such plants as oriental poppies, *Aster amellus* varieties, pyre-thrums, *Scabiosa caucasica,* as well as such early flowerers as delphiniums and lupins if the ground is very heavy.

Group the plants – using odd numbers (threes or fives) if they are naturally small or compact growers. Take care to graduate the varieties, according to height, in such a way that all can be seen. Keep the hoe going between the plants in early spring to eliminate weed seedlings. After the first season reduce the flowering stems on close plants, taking out the weaker stems from the base of the crown if many are produced. This will result in much finer flower spikes and is particularly important in the case of delphiniums, Michaelmas daisies, heliopsis and phlox.

STAKES AND SUPPORTS

Unfortunately some of the finest perennials will have to be staked, otherwise the first heavy shower or thunderstorm will bend or snap the stems and ruin the flowers. Named varieties of delphiniums, salvias, pyrethrums, oriental poppies and paeonies all require this attention. Twiggy peasticks make the best and most unobtrusive supports. The plant stems grow up and through them, and the supports can be cut to any length to fit various-sized plants. Unfortunately peasticks are not readily obtainable and are often replaced by metal ring supports which can be clipped or hooked together to take very broad plants, or used singly with small ones. Bamboo canes and green twine are also useful for staking, especially for lilies; like all types of support they must be inserted around the plants or between shoots while the growths are quite small, for once the stems become bent they will never restraighten.

DEAD-HEADING AND AUTUMN CARE

In order to keep beds colourful for as long as possible, it is advisable to prevent the plants from going to seed by frequent dead-heading – cut the faded blooms back to an unobtrusive point.

At the end of the year plants with fibrous roots can be lifted, divided and replanted if they are overgrown, otherwise most perennials can be cut back to near ground level and the soil between them lightly pricked over with a short-tined border fork. Deep digging is unnecessary and can be harmful to the roots. A few plants, like red-hot pokers (kniphofias) and border carnations should be left with the foliage intact, although tying the leaves of red-hot pokers together protects the vulnerable inner heart from getting wet and frosted.

At all seasons of the year keep a constant lookout for slugs and snails. After frosts tread back newly planted perennials that may have lifted out of the ground. A spring mulch of rotted organic material is beneficial to most plants, and particularly paeonies, delphiniums and phlox. Several foliar sprays of Phostrogen applied during the growing season can do nothing but good to all perennials. Water is important, and perennials should never be allowed to dry at the roots. A weak plant is susceptible to all kinds of ills.

PERENNIALS FOR SPECIFIC PURPOSES

Apart from the various uses already mentioned there are perennials with particular attributes like aconitum and nepetas which are attractive to bees. There are fragrant perennials, like hesperis and *Filipendula ulmaria,* to go near the house; many, including alchemilla and the tall romneyas and verbascums, never need staking – ideal for busy people. There are plants of statuesque habit which can stand alone and others with attractive fruits and seedpods as in the Chinese lantern (*Physalis alkekengi*). Some plants disappear from sight after flowering which is convenient when later blooms need to spill over into their space; also there are bad 'diers' (oriental poppies) which must *never* go in a front row position but have their dying down period artfully masked by later blooming species planted in front. Some perennials will need protection in a bad winter (agapanthus and salvia species); a few adopt a climbing habit and some are downright weedy and troublesome.

Roses

In general roses require good fertile soil, slightly on the heavy side but with good drainage, and an open position where they will receive plenty of sun. Sites to avoid include waterlogged ground, light and hungry sandy soils (although these can be greatly improved by annual manuring), very windy positions, low-lying areas in frost pockets and deep shade or other sites where the bushes receive drips from overhead trees.

It is especially important to avoid places where roses have been grown recently unless you can remove and exchange the topsoil. Rose sickness is a complex trouble which is still not completely understood. It affects the soil and consequently newly planted bushes, while established older trees have developed immunity. However, roses have a recognized term of life just like other living things, and professional growers consider ten years as their peak period. Never hang on to an old unproductive bush for it takes no more time or energy to grow a good plant than to revive a poor one.

PLANTING

To prepare the soil for roses, dig it thoroughly and deeply – two spits deep if possible, so as to break up the subsoil, and work in plenty of rotted farmyard manure, garden compost or leaf-mould. Remove all perennial weeds during cultivation, then sprinkle a general fertilizer over the surface to provide trace elements, and hoe or fork this in. Now leave the ground to settle for several weeks before planting the roses.

Roses can be planted at any time during the dormant season, weather permitting, although November is generally the most favoured month. If the plants arrive during inclement weather open the bundles – mice have been known to nest in the straw wrappings, nibbling the roots – and heel in outdoors or store in a shed with their roots kept just moist.

Before planting, soak the roots in a tub of water for an hour in case they have dried during transit. Examine the roots and trim any which are damaged.

Take out a planting hole for each bush, seemingly a little larger and deeper than seems necessary, and spread out the rose roots. Scatter a planting mixture of equal parts by bulk of moist peat and soil with a handful of bonemeal to each bucketful around the roots. Shake the bush so that the mixture gets under as well as above the roots and continue like this until each plant has been bedded in two buckets of the planting mixture. Now return the soil, treading it from time to time to make the bush firm. At the finish, the soil should be a little higher than the surrounding ground, with the graft or budded union covered; after a time the soil will settle to its old level.

PRUNING

New roses should always be hard pruned in their first season, by cutting the stems back to within three or four buds of the base. This was formerly the annual practice for all hybrid tea roses and is still employed by growers who show exhibition roses at local flower shows. However, work by the Royal National Rose Society has shown such severe pruning to be unnecessary with established bushes. Hard pruning makes for later blooms and fewer flowers than more moderate cutting, although neglected plants may occasionally benefit from severe treatment. Floribundas, however, should never be hard pruned.

Moderate pruning results in earlier flowers, including some excellent blooms early in the season. The stems are reduced by about half their length, after any weak or damaged shoots have been taken completely out. Always cut to an outward-pointing bud if possible, a method particularly appropriate for hybrid teas.

Light pruning is practised for plenty of flowers and colour and is effective in mixed borders and on floribundas. After the removal of unwanted stems, the main branches are reduced by about one-third.

Rambler roses flower on young wood and are normally pruned immediately after they have finished flowering. The old stems are either removed at ground level or, if there is a shortage of new shoots, taken back to a vigorous one lower down on the old stem. Some gardeners merely take out dead wood and shorten the old laterals that have flowered, depending on the rose variety and its ability to produce good shoots.

Climbers need little pruning beyond the removal of dead and useless wood and the occasional shortening of rampant laterals. Withered or frosted shoot tips, however, should always be cut away. Tie in new growths of rambler and climbing roses, bending them over as near as possible to the horizontal so as to encourage the production of flowering side shoots.

It is essential to have really sharp pruning tools which will not bruise or damage the young wood. Good sharp secateurs are always important, but particularly so in the case of roses.

Miniature rose

GENERAL CARE

After-care consists of keeping down weeds, watering in dry weather, disbudding over-exuberant rose varieties and dead-heading regularly as the flowers fade. Roses should also be fed from time to time, in spring with a general fertilizer applied according to the makers' instructions, and with foliar feeds about three times during the summer.

Finally, in autumn when the leaves fall, gather up as many as possible and burn them. This will do a great deal towards keeping down the dreaded black spot disease. See also August, *Plant Disorders*, p.176.

Hybrid tea, of classic shape

ROSES IN THE GARDEN

There are many ways of enjoying roses for they are free-flowering, well suited to our climate, and come in such a range of sizes, shades and textures that they have a multiplicity of uses. Few gardens in Britain are without them. There are so many situations where they can be used – in formal beds, obviously, but also as ground cover, as hedges and as climbers on walls and pergolas; shrub roses can be massed in borders or planted among other shrubs, and minature kinds grown in pots or stone sinks, even in rock gardens.

Formal rose beds This is how roses are commonly planted, especially hybrid tea roses and floribundas, now more correctly called large-flowered and cluster-flowered bush roses.

In a reasonably large garden it is possible to keep formal rose beds to one side of the house, or at any rate a reasonable distance away so that it is possible to go out and enjoy them in their season, yet where they will not offend by looking dull and unattractive from November until June. In a small garden, where the roses can be seen from the sitting or dining room every day, it is probably better to use them in conjunction with other flowers – though devoted rosarians, aiming for perfection, would call this rank heresy. For vigorous growth and first-class blooms it is easier to grow perfect roses if they have a bed to themselves where they can be fed and generally cared for without the competition of other plants.

Good roses can be grown alongside low-growing ground-cover plants – they have been doing so for many years in Queen Mary's Rose Garden in Regents Park, London. For fastidious rose growers there is a range of ground-hugging varieties which only grow about 20 in. (50 cm) high. These are known as the 'Fairy' range and all bear a profusion of small rosette flowers from July to late autumn; 'Fairyland' is rose-pink; 'Fairy Crystal' white; 'Fairy Damsel' blood-red and 'Fairy Maid' blush-pink.

If other plants are mixed with roses the beds must be fed rather more generously than for roses on their own, but with soluble fertilizers and foliar feeds this is no problem. Many years ago, when park authorities and private owners could afford plenty of labour, it was normal practice to bed out violas, which had been raised from cuttings and kept in frames all winter, under the roses. We still plant pansies under our roses, but they are the new F_1 hybrids which we raise from seed and which flower almost continuously throughout the year.

Unfortunately pansy sickness makes it difficult in many parts of the country to propagate named violas year after year by cuttings. But there are plenty of other plants to combine with roses such as crocuses, scillas, muscari, *Ipheion* (*Triteleia*) *uniflorum* and daffodils. Later come lilies like *Lilium superbum* and *L. hansonii* which welcome the shade at their roots and do not push the roses about, since they rise clear above them. Dwarf campanulas such as the purple-blue *C. portenschlagiana* (*C. muralis*) make splendid ground cover but must be cut back regularly to prevent them from clambering up the roses.

The varieties of *Ajuga reptans* are also excellent, especially *A. r.* 'Multicolor', sometimes sold as 'Rainbow', with bronze, pink and yellow-variegated leaves and blue flowers. There are also various annuals, hardy and half-hardy, to grow beneath roses: night-scented stock, alyssum and linarias may be sown direct in the site and ageratums, dwarf antirrhinums and petunias can be raised under glass, then used to edge the beds.

Floribunda roses associate well with certain herbaceous perennials; the white 'Iceberg' and crimson-scarlet 'Marlene' fit in pleasantly with delphiniums, the taller salvias and even phlox.

Moss rose

ROSE VARIETIES

When it comes to selecting rose types you must be guided to a large extent by personal preference. Some people like to keep varieties of one kind in their own bed, others mix both types and colours. There are single roses and double roses, scented kinds, and others which go on to produce handsome hips. They can be kept at an average bush height or interplanted with standards. A few very lovely ones are subject to mildew or other troubles, especially when planted near buildings. In fact, there are so many considerations to take into account that it is worthwhile to pay a visit to a good rose nursery or the Royal National Rose Society's Trial Grounds at St Albans in Hertfordshire, to study the plants as they are growing.

Unfortunately, perhaps, too many roses are introduced every year. Many of them disappear after a few seasons. What most gardeners hope for is vigour, scent and resistance to disease and the effects of bad weather. It is a useful exercise to visit an autumn rose show in a year when the weather just before the show has been stormy and wet. One can then discover which varieties have stood up best to adverse conditions.

It is only since the Second World War that the rich vermilion and salmon roses like 'Super Star' and 'Duke of Windsor' have come on the scene. Bicoloured and multicoloured roses are fairly recent introductions and include the red and gold 'Piccadilly'; 'Rose Gaujard', pink and red with a silvery reverse; 'Picasso', red streaked with white; and 'Eye Paint', an unusual shrub rose which is red with a white eye. I like, too, 'Masquerade', although some people wish it could make up its mind whether it wants to be yellow, pink or deep red, as flowers of all three shades, in different stages of development, are often out at the same time.

There are roses that are almost blue – like 'Blue Moon', a charming hybrid tea rose, strongly scented and truthfully described as lilac pink. It may not be outstanding in the garden, but shows up well in artificial light and is therefore popular with flower arrangers.

The practice of naming roses (for a fee of thousands of pounds) after a brand of cigarettes, whisky, tea, newspaper or other commodity, is a modern development and probably of little significance. Personally, I feel that Harkness & Co. deserve credit for their generosity in naming several roses after charities, such as 'Gardeners' Sunday' and 'Pacemaker', named in aid of the British Heart Foundation. Their latest rose is 'Mountbatten', in aid of the Soldiers', Sailors' and Airmen's Families' Association. Part of the retail price of each bush sold is given to the charity concerned for the first and sometimes the second year.

ROSE TROUBLES

It is interesting to note that while some rose growers indicate if a variety is subject to mildew or black spot, others do not. Personally I am not keen on spending a lot of money and time spraying plants against diseases. Pests I accept that we will almost certainly have to deal with, but I discarded 'Super Star' and 'Frensham' years ago when they became susceptible to mildew. Strangely enough, both these varieties started life with immunity to mildew, but presumably a strain of mildew (of which there are dozens) came along to which they had no resistance. Both are certainly good roses, provided you are prepared to spray them against mildew; fungicides such as bupirimate and triforine are excellent for the control of mildew and black spot.

In our garden there is a thriving specimen of the lovely double, carmine, scented climbing thornless 'Zephirine Drouhin', now a venerable but still vigorous old lady having been introduced in 1868 of unknown parentage. It is the first of our roses to bloom and the first to become affected by mildew. As soon as we see the tell-tale signs we spray *all* the roses and repeat the dose two or three times at two-week intervals.

ROSES FOR SMALL PLACES

Apart from the obvious uses of roses in beds and borders, as wall climbers and as specimen shrubs, there are a number of more unusual ideas, some of which would be suitable for small and even roof top gardens:

Make a rose hedge, either against a low garden fence or wall or as a free-standing divider between the vegetable and flower garden. It will not make a dense screen, but will be highly attractive during the flowering season. For a hedge 2-4 ft (60-120 cm) high, choose 'Frau Dagmar Hastrup', a single pink with fine hips in autumn; 'Yesterday', semi-double, magenta; or any of the 'Fairy' range already mentioned. For a taller hedge of 4-8 ft (1.2-2.4 m) there is the lovely pink 'Queen Elizabeth', the single crimson 'Frank Naylor', the single primrose-yellow 'Golden Wings' or the fragrant purplish 'Roseraie de l'Hay'.

Make a rose pot by planting miniature roses in a strawberry pot with openings round the sides. The terracotta kinds are best as they have broad lips to retain the soil. Stand such a pot in a large, deep saucer and water the roses by filling the saucer. With plastic pots make a tube about 2 in. (5 cm) across of 1-in. (2.5-cm) wire netting and insert this in the centre. Fill it with pebbles and pack soil all round it, planting the side openings with roses as the pot is filled up. Finally set one or two little roses in the top. Water into the tube so that it can filter out and moisten all the soil.

Make a rose wigwam by fashioning a framework of light but strong wooden or metal poles 6-8 ft (1.8-2.4 m) high. Lash them together at the top and plant a climbing rose at the base of each pole, but leave space for an entrance. The wigwam can be of any size – large enough to make a shady bower for a sitting area or composed simply of three poles.

Make a rose trough by planting up a trough or stone sink with miniature roses. It can be formal or informal, with little paths and standards as well as small rose bushes. Mount the container on bricks to bring it near eye level. This is especially suitable in limited spaces and on paved areas. Miniature roses can also be grown in window boxes and tubs.

Make a rose tree by growing roses up trees, especially old neglected fruit trees, or even over dead trees which cannot easily be grubbed out. Choose robust varieties like 'Albertine', light salmon and pink; 'François Juranville', rose; 'Wedding Day', yellowish-white; or that particularly vigorous rose for special situations, the single white 'Kiftsgate' which will attain a height of 50 ft (15 m) or more.

Rosa xanthina, 'Canary Bird'

Make a mix of roses and climbers by combining *Clematis* x *jackmanii* with pink or red climbing roses; the former will flower when the roses are past their best. Try yellow *Clematis tangutica* behind a small bed of orange roses or mix blue wisterias with red roses.

Make a rose bank with climbing or rambler roses, training the young growths down horizontally instead of letting them run upwards. They will need careful pruning to maintain the young wood, but in flower will be a picture with blooms all along their lengths. I first saw roses treated in this manner at Sissinghurst Castle in Kent, when Vita Sackville-West was alive; the branches were kept about 1½ ft (45 cm) above the ground so that the soil beneath could be kept weedfree.

ROSES: HOMELY USES

The historical background of roses is described in June, *Plants of the Month,* (p. 133). Almost as interesting are some of the recipes for food and drinks made from the blooms, not to mention perfumes and sweet waters. Our great-grandmothers used rose petals freely in the making of syrups, cordials, jams and jellies, while generations earlier nosegays, perfumes and pot-pourris figured prominently in the housewife's collection of simples.

Today there is a revived interest in these pleasant confections of a more leisurely age, and I have therefore included a few recipes taken from old books and records.

First perfumery, and here rose petals are a basic ingredient of many scents. In Elizabethan days they were preserved whole in sand, which retained their colour and unwrinkled appearance. Layers of sand and rose petals were spread alternately in boxes and placed in a warm corner by the fireplace until the petals became quite dry. A hot airing cupboard would be a more appropriate drying place today. The petals were taken out of the sand and stored in airtight jars to prevent them from reabsorbing moisture. I gather the petals early in the day, when the dew is off them but before the sun has had a chance to bleach the colours. They are spread on wire sieves in a cool but airy place to dry, and I then put them in airtight bottles with bay salt (to absorb any remaining moisture) or rub them down to a powder and store this in an airtight jar. Either way the petals are at hand for various recipes.

Pot-pourris are of two kinds: those consisting entirely of dried flowers, which have a faint elusive scent; and the more potent mixtures which owe their stronger perfume to the presence of added essential oils. Bought pot-pourri has usually been sprayed with a mixture of scents and when this wears off little perfume is discernible. Old-fashioned pot-pourris rely on such ingredients as scented rose petals, honeysuckle and jasmine flowers, lavender, philadelphus, carnations and pinks, the powdered dried leaves of woodruff – which has the scent of new mown hay – lemon verbena, sweet briar, southernwood, balm and various mints. Powdered orris root, grated orange rind or lemon peel are sometimes added, as well as the leaves of the rose geranium (*Pelargonium capitatum*) when a stronger scent is required.

Pot-Pourri (1)

2 oz (50 g) ground orris root	3 oz (75 g) brown sugar
1 oz (25 g) gum benzoin	1 fl oz (25 ml) brandy or pure
(These are fixatives, without	alcohol (optional)
which the fragrance will not last.)	1 oz (25 g) whole cloves
4 drops attar of roses (if available)	2 oz (50 g) allspice
or a slightly larger quantity of a	1 oz (25 g) stick cinnamon
synthetic rose perfume	4 pt (approx. 2 l) dried rose petals

Grind the spices together and mix with the fixatives – if these are difficult to obtain, a commercial pot-pourri mix can be bought from some chemists. Add the sugar and the dried rose petals and mix thoroughly in a large bowl. Cover the bowl and set aside to ferment for three to four weeks, stirring the mixture daily. Finally add the attar of roses and, if the mixture seems dry, a little brandy. Fill the mixture into airtight jars and use in small decorative bowls as required. After a few years the addition of brandy and rose essence can be repeated, when the fragrance will be revived.

Pot-Pourri (2)

2 oz (50 g) cloves	8 grains of musk
2 oz (50 g) bay salt	½ oz (15 g) gum benzoin or
½ oz (15 g) orris root	1 oz (25 g) of commercial pot-
A little sugar	pourri mix can be substituted for
½ oz (15 g) gum storax	the previous three ingredients.

Pound all the ingredients well and mix thoroughly. Spread in alternate layers with dried rose petals, in small jars.

Cooking with Roses

Most garden roses are suitable for cooking; those which have the strongest perfume (usually red roses) producing the best flavours and scents. Do not eat any which have been sprayed with a poisonous insecticide or have had systemic poisons applied to the roots. If in doubt, obtain dried rose petals from a herbalist.

Honey of Roses

4 oz (100 g) dried rose petals 5 lb (2¼ kg) honey
3 pt (1.7 l) boiling water

Remove the white bases from the rose petals if this was not done before drying; pour boiling water over them. Leave for six hours, then strain and boil up the liquid with the honey until it becomes a thick syrup. Bottle and store. (*Seventeenth-century recipe.*)

Rose petal jam Use any fruit with a high pectin content, such as gooseberry or apple, adding the juice of one lemon and 1 lb (500 g) sugar to each 1 lb (500 g) of prepared fruit. Mix together in a bowl and leave overnight. Chop up two handfuls of rose petals (which can be fresh) for each 1 lb (500 g) of fruit and cook together until the jam sets. Red petals give the best colour, especially with ripe gooseberries or even rhubarb.

Rose Petal Wine

4 pt (2 l) scented rose petals 3 lb (1.4 kg) white sugar
1 gall. (4.5 l) boiling water Yeast

Put the petals in a bowl and add 2 pt (1 l) of boiling water; crush well with a wooden spoon. When cool, strain the liquid into a jar. Return the petals to the bowl and add another 2 pt (1 l) of boiling water; repeat the process of crushing and straining. Mix the two liquids. Dissolve the sugar in the remaining water and pour into the fermenting jar with the yeast.

Thereafter proceed as for other wines; there are many methods, one of which continues as follows. Keep in a cool place for fourteen days, then filter. Bottle, but before corking add two large chopped raisins to each bottle. Cork, wire or tie down and leave the bottles on their sides for six months in a cool, dark place.

Rose-hip marmalade Collect the hips after the first frost, but do not use them if they have been sprayed with poisonous insecticides. Place in a heavy pan, with one cup of water to each 1 lb (500 g) of rose hips and simmer until fruit is tender. Rub the fruit through a fine sieve. Add 1 lb (500 g) of warmed preserving sugar to each 1 lb (500 g) of pulp, with three teaspoons of lemon juice to increase the setting power. Simmer until thick, then bottle.

Rose petal jelly Make apple or gooseberry jelly in the usual way by cutting up the washed fruit (without peeling or coring) and just cover with water. Simmer slowly to a pulp and strain through a jelly bag. For each pint ($\frac{1}{2}$ l) of liquid allow 1 lb (500 g) of preserving sugar; heat and stir until dissolved. Add as many dried rose petals as the liquid will take. Bring to the boil, test in the usual way and strain before potting. An added leaf of rose geranium increases the flavour.

Rose Hip Syrup

1 lb (500 g) rose hips	2 pt (1 l) water
$\frac{1}{2}$ lb (250 g) white sugar	

Chop the rose hips finely and drop them into a preserving pan containing $1\frac{1}{2}$ pts (750 ml) boiling water. Bring to the boil again and leave on one side for fifteen minutes. Strain through a jelly bag. Return the pulp to the pan with the rest of the water and reboil. Remove from the heat and leave for fifteen minutes as before and strain. Mix the two lots of liquid and simmer for half an hour, then add the sugar and boil until the syrup thickens.

Rose Drops

1 oz (25 g) dried red roses	Lemon juice
1 lb (500 g) sugar	

Beat the roses and sugar separately to a fine powder (or use an electric mixer). Sift and mix together, with enough lemon juice to make a thick paste. Place over low heat in a double saucepan and stir. When very hot remove from the heat and drop tiny portions on oiled greaseproof paper. Place in a very cool oven until set.

Rose and Coconut Candies

1 lb (500 g) sugar	A few drops of cochineal
$\frac{1}{4}$ pt (150 ml) water	2 tablespoons evaporated milk
2 tablespoons rose-water	3 oz (75 g) desiccated coconut

Put the sugar in a strong heavy-based pan and dissolve in the water, stirring well. Place over gentle heat and add the rose-water and cochineal. Allow to boil steadily until the syrup forms a soft ball when a little is dropped in cold water. Remove the pan from the heat and allow to cool slightly. Beat well, adding the evaporated milk and coconut; continue heating until sugary. When cold, form into small balls and coat with coconut.

Coping with Weeds

All gardeners have weed problems. Some types are more difficult to deal with than others because much depends on the soil type, the locality and the part of the garden where the weeds grow. Broadly speaking, there are three main ways of coping with weeds: mechanical (pulling them out by hand or chopping them off with a hoe); smothering them by mulching; and by using chemicals.

You can soon detect the difference between seedlings of plants you have sown – be they flowers or vegetables – and those of weeds, because sown seedlings are usually visible in considerable numbers, either in the rows or on the spot where they were broadcast.

In general, weeds in fruit and vegetable plots, in rose beds, and in borders and beds of hardy and half-hardy plants may be controlled by hoeing, mulching and chemicals. The golden rule is to hoe when no weeds are visible, and there never will be any weeds. This is, of course, a counsel of perfection because either we do not have time to do all the hoeing at exactly the right moment, or the weather prevents us from doing so.

Very tiny weeds will shrivel in a few hours of sunshine once they are sliced off with the hoe, while larger weeds are more difficult to hoe off, and they will probably have to be raked up and carted to the compost heap. Left on the ground, weeds may root again if the weather is wet and some, like grasses and groundsel, will ripen their seeds even if the plants have been cut off at the roots.

For mulching as a form of weed control, see May, *Mulching,* p. 119.

CHEMICAL WEEDKILLERS

Commercial growers rely heavily on chemical weed control, and many formulations are available to farmers, market gardeners and nurserymen. There is also a good selection in small packs for amateur gardeners.

Chemical weedkillers fall into three main categories: total, implying that they will kill virtually all vegetation they come in contact with: systemic, meaning that the chemical is absorbed by the plants through stems and foliage to be translocated throughout the plant; and pre-emergent, meaning that chemicals are applied to the ground once it has been cleared of annual and perennial weeds; a pre-emergent weedkiller will keep the ground clean for periods of up to three months by inhibiting the growth of weed seeds.

Within these broad categories are certain sub-divisions. For example total weedkillers, such as sodium chlorate, dichlobenil and simazine, remain active in the soil for a year or more, thus preventing any planting being done during that time.

However, simazine and dichlobenil can be used at lower rates to control weeds under shrubs and roses and are, indeed, used extensively in public parks – the southern approach road to Aberdeen, with thousands of roses planted for miles on either side and on the central reservation, is kept weed-free by these chemicals.

Newer formulations based on paraquat and diquat or on glyphosate are total weedkillers but do not affect the soil. They can be applied one day, with sowing or planting taking place the next day if desired. These weed-killers are useful for lawns that have been allowed to become heavily weed-infested, and in which the grasses are coarse native types like rye grass. One may be tempted to dig the whole lawn over and start again, but if the surface is smooth there is little point in digging the whole lawn up. The whole weary business of raking the soil, treading it firm and raking it again before sowing or turfing must be gone through, with the very real danger that any perennial weeds on the site will come through again.

It is a better idea to let grass and weeds grow to a height of 4-6 in. (10-15cm) and then lightly spray or water them with one of these total weedkillers. Leave it for about seven days, then chop off grass and weeds. The site can now be lightly forked over to a depth of 4 in. (10cm), and sown with a good lawn seed mixture or the new dwarf, slow-growing variety of rye grass called 'Hunter' which is becoming very popular both for play areas which have hard wear and for ornamental lawns.

SELECTIVE WEEDKILLERS

Shortly before the Second World War the first hormone-type, selective weedkiller appeared. When applied to lawns, it destroyed almost all weeds but did not harm the grass. There are now several chemicals, in various formulations, such as 2,4-D, mecoprop, fenoprop and others, which kill specific lawn weeds.

Several firms offer combined mixtures of herbicides (weedkillers) and fertilizers for lawn application. They are quite useful, but very weedy lawns are better treated with a dressing of lawn fertilizer, rich in nitrogen, in early April, say, followed in May by a selective weedkiller.

A fertilizer application will stimulate the growth of both grass and weeds. When the weedkiller is applied it will be absorbed by a large leaf area on the weeds, to be translocated to the roots; in a very short time the weeds will die.

When a lawn is full of weeds in early spring we are tempted to apply selective weedkillers in March or April. But they do not work well until the weather warms up to a minimum night temperature of 10°C (50°F), which usually occurs towards the end of May in the south of the country or after the first week of June in the north. Thereafter the weeds will begin to shrivel in a matter of days.

Few of the selective weedkillers and even fewer of the pre-emergent weed-killers are used by amateur gardeners. Yet they are tremendously useful, keeping clean ground clean and free of annual weeds for up to twelve weeks or for up to a year in the case of simazine under roses.

Two selective weedkillers have been found very effective in keeping clean ground clean without harming established border plants. One is based on propachlor and the other is a formulation of CIPC, diuron and IPC. There is now a new selective weedkiller which destroys twitch (couch grass); very useful in herbaceous borders and shrubberies. Avoid using it near lawns, sweet corn or bamboos, but elsewhere it is harmless.

A useful publication for those who seek chemical aids to weed destruction is the *Directory of Garden Chemicals,* a new edition of which was published in 1982 by the British Agrochemicals Association, Alembic House, 93 Albert Embankment, London SE1 7TU. It not only gives the chemical names and functions of various insecticides, fungicides, herbicides and other garden chemicals, but also the trade names under which they are sold.

THE DANGER OF CHEMICALS

A few words of warning about chemicals. Always use them strictly according to the maker's instructions without 'another teaspoonful for luck'.

Always wash watering cans and sprayers thoroughly after use; rinse once with hot water plus a dash of detergent, followed by two rinses with clear cold water. Even then it may not be possible to remove all traces of hormone weedkillers, and ideally separate equipment should be reserved for chemical application.

Much trouble can be avoided if a separate can or sprayer is kept for total weedkillers such as glyphosate and paraquat, that do not affect the soil, and a third for selective lawn weedkillers. Then the only rinsing necessary is through the rose or sprinkler bar to clear any clogged holes.

Obviously a separate can must be kept for ordinary watering or for applying soluble fertilizer. Plastic watering cans are not very expensive, and sprinkler bars can be fitted to any can. They consist of a horizontal plastic tube or bar, up to 2 ft (60cm) long, punctured with small holes which makes it easy to apply weedkiller or any other chemical exactly where it is needed. There are also short bars, about 4 in. (10 cm), for spot treatment of small weed patches on lawns, paths or among plants.

Apply chemicals preferably in the evening when the bees have gone to bed.

SELF-SEEDING

There are gardens, such as ours, where self-sown seedlings – to us known affectionately as volunteers – are a much valued asset in beds, borders or in the rock garden. We greatly value the self-sown seedlings of variegated honesty (*Lunaria annua* 'Variegata'), and the yellow- and orange-flowered Welsh poppy, *Meconopsis cambrica*. With us the latter is a little too exuberant and has to be thinned out in some parts of the garden, but it gives valuable colour in wild garden settings and shrubberies at the end of May and well into June.

Limnanthes douglasii, the poached egg plant, with gold and white blossoms, also seeds itself regularly, but is not invasive. *Eryngium giganteum* is another self-seeder, affectionately known as 'Miss Willmot's ghost' because all parts – leaves, stems and flowers – are silvery-blue and appear in August when blue-flowering herbaceous plants are not so plentiful.

Small bulbs like crocuses, winter aconites, muscari and others will increase by self-sown seed, but the single seed leaf of bulbous flowers is easily confused with grass seed leaves. If you value self-sown seedlings do not be in a hurry to weed until you can determine which is which. Chemical weedkillers cannot be used where self-sown seedlings are to be encouraged, when hand-weeding is the only answer.

 APRIL

The Month in the Garden

April is a month of contradictions. It can be fine and sunny one minute and rainy the next, and sometimes both at the same time. Occasionally there are severe frosts or snow, as in 1981; at other times hot sun wilts early flowers or strong winds bring down the blossoms from flowering trees.

General Tasks April is above all a good growing month, for weeds as well as cultivated plants, so work round the garden systematically, removing weeds, staking, mulching and generally tidying everything ready for summer.

Preparing the ground for planting and sowing is now urgent, but do not be tempted to plant tender bedding plants outside for another month. Some garden centres display petunias, tagetes, geraniums and even tomatoes as early as March, but unless you can keep them under glass, resist the temptation to buy until May.

Trees and Shrubs Together with early autumn, April is generally considered an ideal month for transplanting evergreens. Unlike deciduous trees and shrubs which move best when dormant, winter is not a good time to move evergreens, except for container-

grown plants. With evergreens, transpiration losses through retained foliage continue, which put a strain on the roots when they are disturbed. To avoid any risk of flagging, evergreens should be moved when conditions are favourable to the early development of new roots, as in spring.

Always retain a ball of soil round the roots of evergreens (although damaged roots should be trimmed with a knife, making slanting cuts on their undersides). Plant firmly, staking if necessary, and water the plants afterwards.

Apart from the general run of evergreens – conifers, rhododendrons, hollies and the like – the practice of lifting shrubs with a ball of soil or planting out from pots should be extended to cistus, cytisus (brooms) and the evergreen berberis, all of which resent root disturbance.

There are, however, new techniques which enable gardeners to move evergreens at any season. Container-grown specimens can be transferred to open ground whenever the weather and soil conditions are suitable; an anti-desiccant spray over the foliage checks transpiration until the roots settle in. This spray is often used on Christmas trees to prevent the needles from dropping.

Layering Many deciduous and evergreen shrubs, like rhododendrons, wisterias, magnolias, and even climbing roses, increase freely from layers, a useful propagation method from a solitary specimen. Choose supple young branches fairly low down on the plant, make an upward incision through one of the joints (nodes) and press this portion down into good soil – or into a pot of compost sunk into the ground nearby. It is important to pin or peg the shoot down in such a way that the cut remains opens. In some cases a heavy stone will hold it firm. Keep the layer well watered; and detach it from the parent plant when roots have formed at the cut area, and plant out.

Air layering can also be practised at this season. See July, *New Plants from Old*, p. 154

Prune forsythias by cutting out, at the base, some of the older branches and shortening back the flowering branches to near the older wood. Retain strong unflowered shoots as these will carry next season's blooms.

Cut stems of *Hydrangea paniculata* 'Grandiflora' back almost to the old wood; they will flower later in the year on new shoots produced from these areas.

Propagate heathers by layers and heel cuttings; shear off old flowered shoots to keep the plants compact.

Sow broom (*Cytisus scoparius*) seeds where they are to flower.

WEATHER

In the opinion of the French 'April is gentle, but when she is angry, the worse for all'.

Gentleness is a feature not often experienced in a British April, which is far more likely to be a tomboy in behaviour, with rain and sunshine – both together!

From the gardener's point of view, the typical April showers are welcome because they provide the ideal treatment for young plants whose roots are still shallow and which need frequent refreshment with small amounts of rain.

Careful watering in late spring can work wonders in the garden: 'The top two inches of soil are most important, look after them'. And if April showers are not sufficient to keep the topsoil moist, follow the advice 'Although it rain, throw not away thy watering-pot'.

A garden will lose more than two gallons per square yard (almost ten litres per square metre) each week by evaporation and transpiration in April – and more in later months.

The main weather danger in April is a spell of cold weather such as the 'blackthorn winter', and few areas escape night frosts except those very close to the coast. Such frosts will always be more severe over dry ground, and again frequent watering is good gardening practice.

The consolation for inclement spring weather is that better days must follow: 'What March will not, April brings alway: What April cannot do, May will do all day'.

Most of our summer visitors, the migratory birds, arrive this month, and 15 April is known as Swallows' Day for this reason: 'When martins appear, winter has broken'.

Plant evergreen hedges – conifers, laurels and hollies – (see December, *Hedges and Screens,* p. 263).

In dry spells, water continuously new hedges planted in autumn; also firm plants lifted by frost.

Climbers There is still time to plant deciduous climbers such as clematis, honeysuckle and wisteria. At this time of year they transplant best as pot-grown specimens; water the root area thoroughly afterwards.

Roses Complete all pruning and feed established plants with a soluble fertilizer or proprietary rose feed.

Water newly planted bushes whenever the weather is dry for several days running, allowing 1-1½ gallons (4-6 l) to each plant. Mulch round established bushes if this was omitted earlier (see also May, *Mulching,* p. 119).

Lawns Sow grass seed for new lawns or to repair and patch old ones.

Lawns now need more frequent cutting; the mower blades can be lowered towards the middle of the month.

Apply a spring fertilizer to established lawns; ten days later apply a selective weedkiller (see also March, *Coping with Weeds,* p. 73).

Level humps in lawns by lifting the turf; remove enough of the subsoil to level the turf when firmed back. Conversely, fill hollows with good potting soil, adding a little at a time as the grass grows through the new soil.

Hardy Plants There is still time to plant or divide many herbaceous perennials, but try to complete this job as soon as possible; water them freely in dry weather.

Staking should receive high priority,

while the new growths are still short and sturdy; once kinked or bowed down by wind and rain delphiniums, lupins and other tall plants with hollow stems never recover fully. Use twiggy peasticks if possible, otherwise canes and green twine or metal ring stakes and various attachments can be purchased from garden centres. Insert support canes *behind* the stems of tall plants to make them as unobtrusive as possible. They should not be visible when the plants are in flower.

Make good winter losses with new plants to fill any gaps.

Plant hardy ferns in moist shade, adding leaf-mould or damp peat to the existing soil.

Bulbs Old bulbs in containers which have finished flowering can now be planted outside, perhaps near ordinary outdoor bulbs. Turn them out of the containers and plant them in one clump if possible; give them a good watering with an added soluble fertilizer.

Dead-head tulips and other large-flowered bulbs to maintain a neat display. Leave small bulbs like snowdrops, scillas and crocuses to set seed and form new colonies.

Annuals, Biennials and Bedding Plants Sow hardy annuals where they are to flower; leave the half-hardy kinds until next month.

Plant out and stake sweet peas which have been raised under glass, but harden them off in a cold frame first. March-sown sweet peas, raised outdoors, will also need staking.

Rock Garden Plants Hand weed between plants.

Replace dead plants and fill any gaps with new, preferably from pots.

Give the rock garden a light dressing of soluble fertilizer.

Lift and replant any alpines which have pulled their way upwards and out of the ground.

Water Plants Construct new pools using PVC liners or prefabricated ponds (Seę May, *Water Gardens,* p. 112). Immediately after being filled with water, prefabricated pools can be planted with water lilies, marginal and floating aquatics as well as submerged oxygenators.

Recently made concrete pools should be filled with water and left until May.

Patio Plants Sow hardy annuals in some containers and prepare others for tender bedding plants which will go out next month. Fill these and window boxes with fresh soil.

Finish any construction work.

Plant hardy climbers from pots to cover pillars and trellis. Clematis and climbing roses grown together look particularly attractive.

Vegetables In the south, sow dwarf beans midway through the month, two weeks later in the north. For an early crop, sow also in small pots under glass; plant out when all danger of frost is over.

Sow globe beetroot in sheltered beds.

Plant second early and late potatoes, allowing 15 in. (38 cm) between the tubers and 3 ft (90 cm) between rows. Cover with 3 in. (7.5 cm) of soil.

Protect early potatoes, now showing their shoots, with plastic, or dry straw, or earth them up with soil when frost threatens.

Plant asparagus.

Sow salsify and various winter greens – Brussels sprouts, broccoli, cabbages and kale in a seed bed. Protect against birds.

Plant onion sets.

Sow spinach beet, lettuce and radishes.

Sow maincrop carrots, later thinning seedlings to 6in. (15 cm) apart.

Plant late summer cabbages 1½ ft (45 cm) apart in rows 2 ft (60 cm) apart, in firm ground, first dusting the roots with calomel as a precaution against club root.

Stake peas.

Thin spinach and lettuce.

Sow kohl rabi outdoors.

Herbs Plant out mint, sage and thyme as rooted plants, and other herbs from pots.

Layer thyme for new plants; after rooting separate the layers from the parent stock and plant out.

Plant a lavender hedge, setting young plants 10–12 in. (25-30 cm) apart.

Fruit Spray apple and pear trees attacked by scab disease last season, using Bordeaux mixture.

Remove blossom from recently planted strawberries.

Spray fruit bushes and trees against aphids directly these appear. Do *not* spray when the plants are in flower as this may harm bees and other beneficial insects.

Plants under Glass Give greenhouse plants more air and water.

Feed established plants with a soluble fertilizer; repeat the dose two weeks later.

Dampen down floors and benches in warm weather.

Harden off half-hardy plants in a cold frame, ready for planting out next month; keep the frame lights open during sunny days.

Sow seeds of *Campanula pyramidalis* and *Solanum capsicastrum*.

Rest freesias and lachenalias which have finished flowering by gradually reducing the water supply; keep the pots near the glass.

Continue taking cuttings and pricking off seedlings (see March, p. 52).

Pot on overcrowded plants.

Repot azaleas and camellias in a loam and moss peat compost, with a little sand, or use a proprietary loamless compost with added John Innes base fertilizer. Keep the plants in the greenhouse for a time and syringe daily with soft, lime-free water.

Stop early-flowering chrysanthemums by pinching out the growing tips when the plants are about 6 in. (15 cm) high.

Pot cyclamen seedlings.

Start old dahlia tubers into growth in an unheated frame.

Thin peaches under glass so as to leave one fruit every 8 in. (22.5 cm).

Plant tomatoes for fruiting under glass in beds or pots.

House Plants Increase the rate of watering for foliage plants and give cacti their first good drink since last autumn.

Propagate ivies, tradescantias, chlorophytums, saintpaulias, impatiens, rhoicissus and philodendrons from leaf and stem cuttings. All will root if placed in small containers of water or inserted in potting compost and kept in a light warm place.

Divide and repot ferns.

Air-layer ficus plants, fatshederas and fatsias (see July, *New Plants from Old*, p. 154).

Propagate *Begonia rex* and peperomias by leaf cuttings; slash the intersections of veins on the back of the leaves and pin these down with hairpins on a base of sand and peat (equal parts). Keep in a closed frame or in a box covered with glass or plastic, placed in a container of moist peat and stood on top of a radiator.

PLANTS IN THEIR PRIME

Trees and Shrubs Deciduous: Acers; *Amelanchier canadensis*; chaenomeles; corylopsis; *Cytisus* x *praecox*; forsythias, magnolias including *M. campbelli*, *M. denudata*, *M.* x *soulangiana*, *M.* x *soulangiana* 'Lennei', and *M. stellata*; *Prunus* species and varieties including *P. padus* (bird cherry), *P. persica* (peach), and the near related almonds and ornamental cherries, as well as various crab apples like *Malus floribunda* and *M.* x *purpurea* 'Eleyi'; *Ribes sanguineum*, (flowering currant); *Robinia pseudoacacia*; *Spiraea* x *arguta*; *S. prunifolia* and *S. thunbergii*.

Evergreen: Berberis, many kinds; *Ceanothus rigidus* (in sheltered places); *Choisya ternata*; *Coronilla glauca*; *Erica arborea*, *E. australis* (sheltered places), *E. carnea* forms, *E.* x *darleyensis*, *E. mediterranea*; *Osmanthus delavayi*; *Osmarea* 'Burkwoodii'; *Phillyrea decora*; *Pieris* sp.; *Rhododendron* species and varieties; *Skimmia japonica*, *S. reevesiana*; *Viburnum* x *burkwoodii*; and vincas.

Climbers *Abelia lobata*; *Clematis armandii*, *C. alpina*.

Roses *Rosa hugonis*

Hardy Plants *Achillea herba-rota*, *A. rupestris*; adonis; bergenias; *Brunnera macrophylla*; *Doronicum plantagineum*; hellebores; polyanthus; polygonatum (Solomon's seal); *Primula*, many forms; pulmonarias; *Ranunculus ficaria* forms.

Bulbs *Anemone coronaria* and varieties; chionodoxas; convallarias; crocuses (Dutch forms); *Cyclamen repandum*; erythroniums, various; *Fritillaria imperalis, F. meleagris* and other species; hyacinths; *Ipheion uniflorum*; leucojums; muscari; narcissus, many; scillas (bluebells); *Trillium erectum, T. grandiflorum* and others; tulips, many.

Annuals and Biennials Wallflowers, including Siberian wallflowers (*Cheiranthus* sp.); *Bellis perennis* 'Monstrosa'; *Lunaria annua*; myosotis.

Rock Garden Plants Aethionemas; *Alyssum saxatile*; androsace; *Anemone appennina, A. ranunculoides, A. sylvestris*; arabis; *Armeria caespitosa*; aubrietas; *Cornus canadensis*; *Corydalis* species; *Cotyledon simplicifolia*; daphnes, various; *Dicentra eximia*; drabas; epimediums; *Gentiana acaulis, G. verna*; *Geum montanum*; *Iberis sempervirens*; *Iris cristata*; omphalodes; *Primula auricula, P. juliana* and others; *Pulsatilla vulgaris*; mossy saxifrages; tiarellas; violas.

Water Plants Calthas; *Cardamine pratensis* 'Plena'; *Peltiphyllum peltata*.

CROPS TO ENJOY

Vegetables Cabbage; kale; sprouting broccoli; leeks; salad onions; turnip tops.

Mustard and cress; lettuces and radishes (under glass).

Fruit Rhubarb
Strawberries (under glass).

PLANT ASSOCIATIONS

Bold groupings of variegated-leaved honesty (*Lunaria annua* 'Variegata') against a dark green conifer and in a shady corner.

Amelanchier canadensis underplanted with red hyacinths or blue muscari.

Dutch crocuses beneath corylopsis.

Scarlet chaenomeles on a white wall with pulsatillas and Solomon's seal.

Alyssum saxatile with aubrietas on a sunny wall or rock garden.

Cornus canadensis under *Magnolia stellata*.

Brunnera and polyanthus beneath white flowering cherry.

Siberian wallflowers with pale yellow wallflowers and white pheasant-eye narcissus.

Pink Darwin tulips with blue forget-me-nots.

GARDEN PROBLEMS

Slugs and snails attacking young crops and soft growths, particularly lettuces, delphiniums and hostas.
  Aphids on strawberries.
  Mildew on roses.
  Weeds on lawns.

Plants of the Month

CROWN IMPERIAL

Fritillaria imperialis, the stately crown imperial, was a favourite plant with the old Dutch Masters, who included it in many of their floral compositions. At 3-4 ft (1-1.2m) it is the tallest of the early-flowering bulbs, traditionally starting to bloom on 18 March, which is the anniversary of the death of Edward the Martyr, the tenth-century English King who was murdered by his stepmother, Elfrida, while drinking a stirrup cup.

Crown imperial, *Fritillaria imperialis*

Legend also has it that the pendent, orange-red flowers, growing in whorls beneath a topknot of leaves on thick stems, were once white and looked upwards. When our Lord passed through the Garden of Gethsemane, the crown imperial, alone of all the flowers, failed to bow its head, whereupon our Lord gently rebuked it, so that the blooms hung their heads, blushed a rosy-red and tears came into their eyes. Turn one of the flowers upwards and six pearly drops of nectar will be revealed. They will not drip even when the flower is roughly shaken, and although they can be removed with blotting paper, they rapidly reform.

The plant has a strange foxy smell which comes and goes in the air, a scent which the late E. A. Bowles described as 'a mixture of mangy fox, dirty dog kennel, the small cats' house at the zoo and Exeter railway station'. There is a variety with yellow flowers and others with gold and silver leaf-variegations. White, pink and red forms have been seen in its native Iran, but these have yet to reach our gardens.

TULIPS

Tulips came to Europe from Turkey in the sixteenth century and almost immediately gardeners were attracted to their stately habit and brilliant colours. They quickly achieved great popularity, particularly in The Netherlands, where an urge to grow tulips swept the country around the 1630s and *Tulipomania* was born. Everyone joined in, rich and poor, aristocrats, merchants and artisans; fortunes were made – and lost – by speculating in bulbs which many of the gamblers probably never even saw.

Striped varieties were particularly admired, and in the seventeenth century bulbs changed hands at the equivalent of £400 apiece, while a simple specimen of one called 'Viceroy' was exchanged for:

2 lasts (loads) of wheat	4 fat oxen
4 lasts (loads) of rye	8 fat swine
12 fat sheep	4 tuns of beer
2 hogsheads of wine	2 tuns of butter
1 complete bed	1 silver drinking horn
1 suit of clothes	1000 lb of cheese

The whole being valued at 3,500 guilders.

Eventually the gambling in tulip bulbs became so reckless that the Dutch government stepped in to regulate transactions, and as the bottom fell out of the market many speculators went bankrupt or were subjected to legal action on account of broken contracts. Even then tulip interest remained and in the nineteenth century a single bulb of 'Citadel of Antwerp' was sold for £690. In the meantime, the Dutch had discovered one important fact – their soil had proved ideal for the growing of tulips, and so in due course Holland became the bulb nursery of the world.

Three varieties of tulip: early single (left); Darwin (centre); lily-flowered (right)

Annuals and Bedding Plants

The correct definition of an annual is a plant which completes its life cycle, from seed to seed, in one growing season and then dies. Normally annuals are sown in spring to flower the same year, and some, like the hardy larkspurs, calendulas and cornflowers, may be sown in autumn to flower the following year. Yet others, like antirrhinums, are really quick-growing perennials, but are nevertheless grown as annuals.

Annuals almost without exception have vivid, eye-catching flowers and seem to compensate for their short life by bright and cheerful colours. Many are of tropical origin, and as comparatively few of them have much scent, nature presumably endowed them with brilliant colours to attract pollinating insects.

Be all this as it may, annual flowers provide the cheapest plants to clothe a garden with colour in summer and early autumn. It is a strange reflection on our times that sales of hardy annual flower seeds have slumped in recent years while sales of boxes of half-hardy annuals like petunias and marigolds have rocketed. Presumably people prefer to buy young tender plants rather than sowing hardy annuals in situ at a fraction of the cost for a stunning display.

ANNUALS IN BORDERS AND BEDS

Few people have the time or inclination to make a complete annual border, although splendid examples can be seen each year at the Royal Horticultural Society's garden at Wisley in Surrey. In order to achieve a balanced effect it is necessary to make a rough plan on paper first. Graph paper is best for assessing distances and determining how much room should be allotted to each variety. Draw irregular patches on the plan, rather like the pieces of a jigsaw puzzle, and mark them with the names of the plants. Height, colour, flowering season and other details must all be considered while the plan is being worked out, and it is easier to do this on paper and alter it if necessary than to work directly on the border itself.

After the ground has been adequately prepared by digging, manuring, weeding and raking, sowing will be easier if the jigsaw shapes are reproduced on the border by scratch marks made with a pointed stick or with outlines of sand. If a label with the name of each occupant is then inserted in each segment it becomes an easy matter to find the appropriate places when sowing or planting out.

Annuals should not be sown in straight lines if they are grown in decorative borders. Nor should they be sown too deeply. Make irregular drills, about $\frac{1}{2}$ in. (12mm) deep or according to instructions on the seed packet, using a pointed stick or the edge of a hoe. Sow the seed thinly and cover it lightly with soil. Thin the seedlings while they are quite small.

Some patches may be left for half-hardy annuals to be planted towards the end of May, or early in June in the colder north: petunias, lobelias, ageratums, marigolds, salvias, and asters, for example.

Four types of annuals: (A) *Nigella damascena*, 'love in the mist'; (B) *Eschscholzia californica*, Californian poppy; (C) *Tagetes*, African marigold; (D) *Limnanthes douglasii*, poached egg plant

Generally, the half-hardy kinds are longer-lasting in bloom than hardy annuals, although some of the latter, like calendulas, sweet alyssum and linaria, will produce a second or even a third show of flowers if they are trimmed hard back after flowering and before they have had time to set seeds.

In recent years several desirable new strains of annual flowers have appeared notably dwarf sweet peas, such as 'Snoopea' which produces quite large flowers on plants only 1-2 ft (30-60 cm) high and needs no support. Also quite charming are *Lavatera* 'Mont Blanc', pure white, and *L.* 'Silver Cup', rose-pink; both make bushy plants, 2-2½ ft (60-75cm) high which are smothered with mallow-like flowers from June onwards. Sow the seeds in the open in March or April or raise them in late winter under glass to obtain larger plants for earlier flowering. The old deep pink *Lavatera* 'Loveliness' is still a good plant and like the newer lavateras is good for cutting.

UNDERPLANTING AND FILLERS

In a small garden there is rarely room to devote beds or borders exclusively to roses. The temptation to underplant them with low-growing plants is strong, and as this need not be detrimental to the roses, annual flowers may fit in very well. Annuals are also useful for growing in bare patches in shrub borders, especially in new borders or where old shrubs have been removed and young small ones are struggling to take their place. It will be some years before they will fill their allotted space, and even then many shrubs would look better with an underplanting of annual flowers, bulbs or ground-covering plants.

For purposes such as these, hardy or tender annuals, such as nasturtiums, may be sown in situ among the roses. Other choices are sweet alyssum, candytuft, clarkias, dwarf godetias, *Convolvulus minor* in mixture, esch-scholzias, linarias, linums, night-scented stocks and mignonette. *Phacelia campanularia,* perhaps the best blue annual flower, the poached egg plant, *Limnanthes douglasii,* and Virginian stocks are others.

HALF-HARDY ANNUALS

Among the half-hardy annuals which must be raised under glass or purchased there is a splendid selection of neat dwarf and very floriferous plants which will flower all summer long. Perhaps the most rewarding are ageratums, lobelias, dwarf or carpeting antirrhinums, and begonias of all kinds but especially the newer varieties of *B. semperflorens* which flower all summer. I like especially those varieties of *B. semperflorens* with bronze foliage which can be obtained either in separate flower colours or in a mixture of shades, for their foliage is attractive even before the plants start to flower.

Then there are dwarf busy Lizzies, varieties of *Impatiens wallerana* (*I. sultani*), which flower right on into the autumn, even in partial shade. Probably the most effective plants to cover the ground under roses or shrubs, or indeed anywhere else, are petunias and dwarf French and African marigolds.

Pansies and violas are easily raised from seed and some of the new F_1 hybrids flower for many months of the year, even fitfully in winter and early spring. They may be sown outdoors in a well-prepared seed bed, but as the seed is expensive and as there are only a few in each packet, I prefer to sow them in a pot in the greenhouse. Later I prick the seedlings off into pots or Jiffy 7s, thus making sure that every seed produces a plant. Pansies and violas, of course, are not annuals; they will persist for two years although they may have to be trimmed a little in the second season as they tend to sprawl.

SCENTED ANNUALS

Perhaps because annual flowers with brilliantly coloured flowers can attract and are pollinated by insects they do not need much scent. The colour of the flowers is sufficient. Those whose powerful fragrance springs most readily to mind – like mignonette and sweet alyssum – are certainly not flamboyant flowers nor are night-scented stocks or nicotianas, the tobacco plants.

Sweet peas are both attractive and usually strongly fragrant, including many of the newer varieties. Some firms offer a mixture of very strongly scented sweet peas made up of types derived from the original 'Grandiflora' varieties which were popular before the large-flowered, waved or 'Spencer' sweet peas came along. The blooms of these are smaller, but so richly fragrant that it is worth growing a few to mix with the new large-flowered varieties, in bowls indoors or to enjoy in the garden.

Sweet sultan, which resembles a cornflower and comes in a variety of colours, is sweetly scented, and so, too, are the many varieties of double stocks; candytuft has a sweet honey scent. I like the tangy aroma of nasturtiums, but loathe that of the unpleasantly tainted tagetes or African marigold.

Wallflowers, of course, are delicious in spring, with annual lupins as well as several biennials or perennials normally grown as annuals like sweet rocket, *Hesperis matronalis,* and *Oenothera odorata* and *O. biennis,* the evening primroses.

CLIMBING ANNUALS

There are not many climbing annuals. Sweet peas come at the top of the list, and there are tall or climbing nasturtiums which will ramble up a trellis or sprawl over an ugly rubbish heap to a height of up to 6 ft (1.8 m). The half-hardy cup-and-saucer plant, *Cobaea scandens,* will grow rapidly against a sunny wall. Seed should be sown in February or March in a heated greenhouse to give it an early start; after potting-on the plants can be put outside when all risk of frost is past. It has bell-shaped flowers which are green when young, then develop to purple. When happy the plants will grow up to 10 ft (3 m).

The loveliest of climbing annuals, though also half-hardy, is the vivid-blue morning glory, *Ipomoea rubro-coerulea* 'Heavenly Blue'. It will climb to 8-10 ft (1.4-3 m) and may either be planted against a sunny wall or trellis, or three or four plants can be grouped in a large pot or tub and grown up a wigwam of bamboo canes. It is very important to avoid a check to growth by cold nights, so morning glory should be kept in a warm greenhouse, sun lounge or cold frame until the weather has warmed up, often not until the end of the first week in June. Subjected to cold nights, the foliage will turn yellow and the plants become stunted and fail to grow properly.

The black-eyed Susan, *Thunbergia alata,* will grow to about 4 ft (1.2 m) up a trellis or a wigwam of canes and it may also be used in hanging baskets and allowed to trail. It needs a warm sunny spot and like cobaeas and morning glories is really best grown in a cool greenhouse, conservatory or sun lounge. The original black-eyed Susan was orange with a black eye but there are now white and yellow forms with or without the black centre.

The canary creeper, *Tropaeolum peregrinum* (*T. canariense*), with its lavish display of fringed yellow flowers, is not often seen these days, but it is a useful climber for a fence or trellis, reaching a height of 12 ft (3.5 m). It may be sown in the open in April or May, but seed sown under glass in February or March will provide plants that bloom much earlier. It does quite well in shade but is happier in full sun.

Curiously, runner beans are not grown for their edible pods in the United States nor in certain Scandinavian countries, but for their red or white flowers. The first plants grown in Britain were also used as ornamentals, and there really is no reason why we should not grow a few clumps at the back of a border. In one garden, I saw them growing up poles on opposite sides of a path and then trained over the path to a linking half circle of canes. They not only looked attractive, but the pods were easy to pick. Many people grow ornamental, but still edible, variegated creamy, pink or purple-foliaged cabbages in borders, so why not runner beans?

Always certain to attract comment are ornamental gourds which will also climb over a trellis or other support up to 4 ft (1.2 m) or so. A packet of mixed seed will produce gourds of many shapes and colourings: white pear-shaped fruits that look like a row of electric light bulbs strung along a fence, apple and orange-like gourds, others with wart-like protuberances all over them or serpent-like kinds with long necks. All are best started off in peat pots or Jiffy 7s in a greenhouse or cold frame and planted out at the end of May. Alternatively, they may be sown in the open at the end of April for smaller and later fruits. These are inedible, but can be dried off and varnished for use in winter flower arragements.

TUBS, WINDOW BOXES AND HANGING BASKETS

Many annuals, biennials and perennials normally grown as annuals are eminently suitable for growing in tubs and other containers. Again the simplest method is to sow hardy annuals, such as sweet alyssum, dwarf godetias, clarkias, mignonettes, dwarf calendula 'Fiesta Gitana', dwarf or semi-dwarf nasturtiums and pansies in situ. Among the half-hardy kinds, petunias, dwarf marigolds, *Begonia semperflorens* varieties, dwarf asters, ageratums, antirrhinums, busy Lizzies (*Impatiens*), salvias, and the almost obligatory trailing lobelias, are all excellent. These complement admirably the white marguerites, fuchsias, geraniums, and tuberous begonias which usually form the mainstay of such containers.

ANNUALS FOR CUTTING

Many annuals, both hardy and half-hardy, make good cut flowers. Once more sweet peas must be near the top of the list. Everybody has his or her preference for colours, and I think men in the main prefer stronger colours while women go more for pastel shades. However, much depends on the occasion and where the flowers are to be placed. If you want predominantly bold colours it is no use relying on a packet of mixed sweet peas. Much better to buy half a dozen packets of named varieties and if this produces rather more seed than you need, share it with a friend. Stocks, zinnias, asters, gypsophila and the very large-flowered varieties of *Rudbeckia hirta,* the gloriosa daisies such as 'Marmalade', are all excellent for cutting. For later on, in summer and early autumn, we have a good range of China aster varieties. For small posy-type arrangements nasturtiums are highly effective and last well in water as do antirrhinums, larkspurs, calendulas, annual carnations in the 'Chabaud' range or 'Marguerite' varieties, cosmeas, annual chrysanthemums, nigellas, clarkias, wallflowers, cornflowers, gaillardias and lavateras.

Some people use African and French marigolds in arrangements, and as long as they are not handled, the pungent aroma of the foliage, repulsive to many people, is no problem. I must admit that they are not great favourites of mine, and we never have them in the garden or in the house.

EVERLASTING FLOWERS FOR DRYING

Many flowers may be dried in silica gel or by other techniques, for use in winter arrangements, but there are also everlasting flowers which only need cutting in their prime – that is just before they have fully developed, when there is usually enough sap in the stems to finish the opening of the flowers. They can then be tied in small bunches to hang in an airy, but not sunny, place to dry. These so-called everlastings are the simplest to deal with. One of my favourites is the silvery *Eryngium giganteum;* it is really a biennial:

Everlasting flowers for drying: (A) *Eryngium giganteum;* (B) *Achillea filipendulina;* (C) *Physalis alkekengi,* Chinese lanterns

you sow it one year to gather its splendid silvery flower heads the next year. It seeds itself freely, and when we cut the flower stems to dry for winter, we simply shake them around and are then assured of a regular crop of self-sown seedlings. It is a simple matter to pull up any unwanted seedlings in the spring.

Everlastings raised from seed are usually half-hardy annuals and probably the best value is found in the varieties of *Helichrysum*. Most seedsmen offer a mixture, but it is also possible to buy golden, rose, salmon-rose, terracotta and white varieties separately, and the new tetraploid varieties are very vigorous with extra large flowers. Next I would put the acrocliniums, now more correctly called helipterums. They bear their daisy flowers in clusters and there are golden, white, rose and red varieties. Gomphrenas are like purple, papery-flowered clovers.

Statice (*Limonium sinuatum*) is a popular and colourful everlasting, with blue, rose, white or yellow flowers, and one of my favourites, *L. suworowii*, the candlewick statice, has long fluffy-looking spikes of pink flowers.

Honesty is a biennial, but once established seeds itself freely and is well worth growing for its purple flowers – good for cutting – in early spring when there is little colour in the garden, and for its white papery seed pods which are so useful for winter arrangements.

Ornamental grasses are also useful for winter decoration and are sold either in mixtures or as separate species. *Briza maxima,* quaking grass; *Lagurus ovatus,* hare's-tail; and the squirrel's-tail grass, *Hordeum jubatum,* are particularly attractive. The perennial *Achillea filipendulina* flowers and seed cases of the Chinese lantern (*Physalis alkekengi*) may also be dried for winter arrangements.

Seaside Gardening

The greatest hazards for gardeners in coastal areas are strong winds and salt- and sand-laden breezes. Not many plants can tolerate such conditions, and the first priority for people who live near the shore is to form a protective barrier against the elements.

Ideally a barrier should be of several thicknesses: one set of shrubs behind another so as to foil winds and consequent spray. Start with a fence, of laths or wattle, then plant an evergreen tree or shrub screen of *Cupressus macrocarpa* or its golden form 'Lutea'; *Quercus ilex,* the evergreen oak; or the Austrian pine (*Pinus nigra*). A natural candidate is the sea buckthorn, *Hippophae rhamnoides;* it is a tall, deciduous shrub with outstanding orange-yellow berries clustered in winter along the spiny branches. Male and female plants must be planted together. Next plant an ornamental hedge to form a pleasing background inside the garden. Suitable hedging includes, *Arundinaria japonica,* a wind-filtering bamboo; escallonias; *Griselinia littoralis,* a splendid evergreen with thick, oval, bright green leaves, very salt-tolerant and especially suitable for south and south-west gardens; hebes and tamarisks.

Within this protective belt a tremendous number of plants can be grown, and the construction of rock gardens, pools, herbaceous borders and vegetable plots are all possible.

However, for plants to grow satisfactorily they must have good soil, and beach gardens are notoriously poor, owing to their salt content and sharp drainage, which leaches out plant foods as well as water. Both sand and shingle are devoid of nourishment and it is essential to provide humus. This can either be dug into the ground or added as a mulch. Rotted manure, garden compost, leaf-mould and peat are the most suitable kinds of humus, and seaweed is just as good. Additionally, when establishing new plants, put rotted compost or moist peat in the planting holes.

pH VALUES

Another environmental factor is soil acidity. Most coastal soils are highly alkaline, and although humus tends to correct this condition it is not unusual for certain plants to fail. To grow the lime-hating rhododendrons, azaleas and some ericas satisfactorily, it is usually necessary to use a chelated chemical so that iron and other minerals inhibited by lime become available to the plants. A pH of 5-6 is acid and ideal for rhododendrons; pH7 is neutral; above that, alkaline.

Problems can also be caused by bright sun in a hot, dry summer. This not only dries out the soil, but can scorch the leaves of plants not resistant to salt. The solution is to spray the foliage with soft water in the evenings and to use plenty of ground-cover mulches to keep the soil shady and moist.

SEASIDE PLANTS

Natural denizens of seashores are the plants most likely to succeed. Strangely, many of these come from New Zealand, among them the wind-resistant, sun-loving olearias and the long-flowering hebes. Most Mediterranean shrubs, like lavender, cistus, rosemary and cotton lavender (santolina) also do well.

Olearia x *haastii* is the best known of the daisy bushes, probably because it is the hardiest and grows inland as well as near the coast. It attains a height of 4-5 ft (1.2-1.5 m), with small, evergreen, oval grey-green leaves, which like those of most olearias are white and woolly underneath, and clusters of small white daisies in July and August. *O. macrodonta,* 4-6 ft (1.2-1.8 m) high, usually known as New Zealand holly, has toothed leaves and larger flower trusses in June. *O. ilicifolia,* one of the best, has grey-green, toothed leaves and fragrant white flowers in June; the Tasmanian *O. stellulata* 'Splendens' has blue, pink and lavender-flowered forms.

Hebes persist in flower for weeks and are much more dependable near the coast than inland. They are medium-sized, evergreen shrubs with long racemes of variously coloured flowers. 'Autumn Glory' is a particularly free-flowering, violet variety; 'Midsummer Beauty' is lavender; 'Lindsayi', pink; 'Blue Gem', bright blue; and 'White Star', white.

High gloss on the foliage enables plants to throw off sand and salt spray, and the green-flowered, evergreen *Bupleurum fruticosum* and most euonymus and pittosporums thrive. Gorse, genista, brooms and the green-stemmed, almost leafless *Spartium junceum,* with long sprays of yellow, fragrant, pea-shaped flowers all summer, are others to plant.

Silver-foliaged plants also do well, such as *Santolina pinnata* and *S. chamaecyparissus,* pinks and border carnations, aubrietas, and *Senecio* 'Sunshine' and *S. bicolor* 'Silver Dust' and 'White Diamond'.

Sea pinks (armerias), sea lavenders (limoniums), dimorphothecas (the beautiful daisy plants from South Africa), ice plants (mesembryanthemums and dorotheanthus), echinops, sea hollies (eryngiums) and red-hot pokers (kniphofias) are all easy and natural plants for coastal gardens. As the protected garden develops, bulbs, roses and herbaceous perennials will also give a good account of themselves.

Watering

We British pride ourselves on our gardens, and with some justification for our equable climate allows us to grow a wider range of plants than any other country in the world.

Admittedly we have been gardening for five centuries and know a lot about it, but if we are honest we must admit that most of the credit for our wonderful lawns and beautiful gardens is due to our weather and particularly to our usually adequate rainfall.

In this country we do not suffer from typhoons, cyclones or hurricanes, nor, in average years, from prolonged periods of severe frost or torrid drought. Perhaps once in every ten years we have a wicked winter with prolonged snow and temperatures below freezing and about once in every ten years we have a hot dry summer. In between the seasons are usually gentle and kind to gardeners, but in most parts of Britain there are certain periods in every year, be they spring, summer or autumn, when insufficient rain falls for optimum growth, or even for the survival of young plants and newly germinated seedlings.

The three basic requirements for plant life are soil, sunshine and water. Of sunshine we have a sufficiency. Soils vary enormously but even the poorest can be improved with regard to the water needs of plants. Mulching and the digging in of moisture-holding materials, such as peat or compost, reduce the adverse effects of short dry spells and put off the moment when watering should be commenced in order to ensure continued growth.

Amateurs often do not realize how important it is to start watering *before* plants begin to suffer and receive growth checks. Sometimes such checks are not serious, but with certain crops, such as summer cauliflowers, a check in the young stages may well lead to a total failure. With others, the plants will continue to grow but will never make the same healthy, vigorous growth that they would have done if they had not received a check. Too often gardeners wait until plants show signs of distress by flagging; and by that time much damage may have been done.

I think this reluctance to start watering originated with those old-time private gardeners who did not have hose pipes or ring main watering systems, but had to push huge galvanized water barrows, on metal wheels without tyres, around the garden. They would naturally be reluctant to start watering and therefore invented a rule that once it was started it would have to continue. This attitude to irrigation has been handed down through generations of professional gardeners, some of whom will still spread this heresy.

Watering should *start before plants show stress* and continue for as long as necessary. With plastic pipes and hoses and a multiplicity of plastic couplings we can make watering a garden the simplest of jobs. The important thing is to start watering immediately plants are in danger of suffering from water shortage, and to keep on watering until the rains come.

HOW MUCH TO WATER?

I have pointed out the importance of watering plants before they suffer from a shortage, and the question now arises of how much water to apply.

Research based on work done by scientists such as Dr H. L. Penman and L. P. Smith on this subject has resulted in the publication of brilliant advice to farmers, market gardeners and seed growers. As gardeners we can profit by the spin off. Briefly, Smith and Penman realized that water leaves the soil by evaporation and transpiration through the plant foliage and that the rate of such loss is determined by the amount of sunlight received. Accordingly they were able to work out a formula, by which the rainfall is measured against the average hours of sunshine received in each month, from April to September inclusive, the significant periods for applying water.

It was then possible to calculate to a very reasonable degree the amount of water to be applied in given parts of the country when insufficient rain has fallen, so as to replace water lost by evaporation and transpiration.

Gardeners may with advantage carry out their irrigation programmes by following the advice contained in Bulletin No. 138 'Irrigation' of the Ministry of Agriculture, Fisheries and Food. For the amateur, the simple guide overleaf, if acted upon intelligently, will ensure steady growth and satisfying results in the garden.

WHEN TO WATER

Whether you water the garden by rule of thumb, by intuition born of long experience in your own garden, or whether you decide to follow the guide lines set out below, there still remains the question of when to water. In areas with a heavy demand for water in the evenings during dry spells, the water pressure often falls below that needed to operate sprinklers at their maximum efficiency. It often pays to set the sprinklers to work early in the morning.

Many gardeners are afraid to water during the day because they think that the sun's rays focussing through the droplets will scorch the plant leaves. In practice there is little danger of this, and nurserymen and market gardeners water quite happily by day or night. On balance it is probably better to water in the evening.

HOW TO WATER

Obviously water can be carried in a can from a tap *ad infinitum* or supplied through a hose, but both operations are tedious and time-consuming. A wide range of sprinklers is available, from quite small ones with a short spike for

WATER LOSS IN THE UK

The water lost from a garden, by evaporation from the soil and transpiration from the plants, varies from day to day and from place to place.

Approximate *weekly* losses (in inches and millimetres) are shown in the following table.

AREA	APRIL SEPTEMBER	MAY AUGUST	JUNE JULY
North of Glasgow or Edinburgh	0.35 in. (9 mm)	0.5 in. (12 mm)	0.7 in. (18 mm)
South of Glasgow or Edinburgh North of Hull or Liverpool (including N. Ireland)	0.4 in. (10 mm)	0.55 in. (14 mm)	0.8 in. (20 mm)
South of Hull or Liverpool North of Bristol or London (including Wales)	0.45 in. (11 mm)	0.65 in. (16 mm)	0.9 in. (22 mm)
South of Bristol or London	0.5 in. (12 mm)	0.7 in. (18 mm)	1.0 in. (25 mm)

If the weekly rainfall is less than these amounts, it is likely that water reserves in the soil have *decreased*. If this is the case, watering may be necessary, by amounts not exceeding the difference.

If the weekly rainfall is greater than these amounts, it is likely that water has been *added* to the soil.

1 inch of rain is approximately 25 mm, and is equivalent to about $4\frac{1}{2}$ gallons per square yard (20 litres per square metre).

Any garden over 500 ft (150 m) above sea level should be regarded as being in the previous (more northerly) category.

---

inserting in the soil or lawn, to oscillating sprinklers which – according to the water pressure – can water a rectangle of more than 200 square yards (167 sq. metres), and there are rotating sprinklers capable of watering a circle of over 250 square yards (209 sq. metres).

Sprinklers There are also several ingenious travelling sprinklers which are invaluable in a large garden. A hosepipe is laid out along the length of a lawn or path in a straight or winding line, the sprinkler is attached and when the water is turned on two sprinkler arms rotate and almost imperceptibly propel the sprinkler along the length of the hose.

When it reaches the end it automatically shuts the water off. It can thus be set to work at odd times, although, again, the area covered will depend on water pressure and the length and diameter of the hose.

Oscillating sprinklers are much favoured by gardeners because they deliver the water in fine gentle droplets and do not unduly weigh down the plant foliage. The 'flip-flap' or impulse sprinklers which flip round, driven by the water pressure, are also excellent although the droplets are larger than those of oscillating sprinklers. They can be mounted on a pole – a long length of old 1-in. (2.5-cm) water pipe driven firmly into the ground is ideal – and thus throw the water well above tall crops such as raspberries and runner beans.

It is possible to buy a flip-flap sprinkler mounted on an adjustable portable tripod which will raise it 2-3 ft (60–90 cm) above the ground. In a large garden, however, it is preferable to install several permanent fixed flip-flap sprinklers which are operated simply by turning a tap.

Ring mains When Roy Hay and I were married he cheerfully admitted his fundamental idleness and hence preoccupation with labour-saving gadgets. He promptly set about installing what he calls a 'ring main' round the garden.

Our plot is a large rectangle with the house in the middle so there is garden on all four sides. We have a garden water supply from the main with a tap in front of the house, and from there we took alkathene pipes round two sides and the rear of the house and fitted three taps. With a Y-shaped adaptor we then laid lengths of plastic hose all round the garden on each side of the house and at the rear installed a hose on a through-feed reel.

Y-shaped plastic joints were fitted to the two taps at the sides of the house and from one we took lengths of plastic hose (the ring mains) right round the garden on either side of the house. We simply laid the hose on the surface in the 'gutter' between lawn and soil in the borders. We could, of course, have buried it 1 in. (2.5 cm) or so deep but it is hardly noticeable lying on the surface.

The advantage of these semi-rigid alkathene plastic pipes and flexible thin plastic hoses is that if water inside them freezes they will expand but not burst. In any case, we turn the water off at the main in November and open all the taps so that there is no danger of bursts.

In the ring mains we inserted T joints, and into these sockets which are in fact taps. Then we fitted a length of very lightweight plastic hose with a male connector at one end and an oscillating sprinkler at the other. We are now able simply to plug the hose into any one of the tap sockets and instantly the sprinkler delivers water. The length of hose – some 20 ft (6 m) – is enough to reach all parts of the garden from the various tap sockets and it is so light that it can be lifted in seconds with one hand.

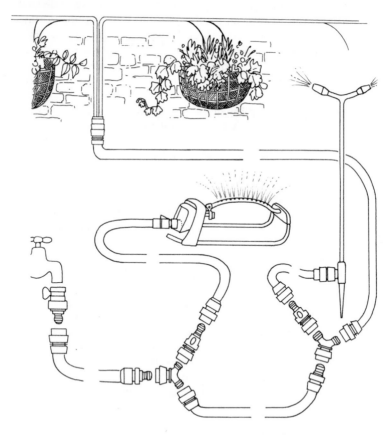

A ring main system for watering a garden. With modern connectors and sprinklers, water can be applied to any part of the garden with the minimum of trouble

Oscillating sprinklers are excellent for another reason. They can be set to water a complete rectangle or only part of one, making it possible to water a border without wasting it on a path or drive. For many areas of a garden they are therefore better than rotating sprinklers. On the other hand, rotating flip-flap sprinklers set in a permanent position are a great boon for fruit and vegetable plots.

A through-feed hose-reel is another time- and effort-saver. A short length of hose connects the reel to the main water supply which is conducted through the centre of the reel to the hose coiled round it. You just pull off enough hose to reach the area you wish to water and when you have finished you wind it back again. If you have several taps in the garden there are hose reels on wheels which make it easier to move the hose from one point to another. A through-feed hose-reel connected to an outside tap also makes a splendid piece of fire-fighting equipment.

There are many types of plastic hose, and as with most things the more you pay the better the article. Some plastic hoses become stiff and unmanageable in cold weather while others remain pliable. The type to look for is braided plastic hose, and the best makes carry a five-year guarantee.

TUBS, WINDOW BOXES AND HANGING BASKETS

Hanging baskets and half-baskets attached to walls or fences are attractive in any garden, but, like window boxes and tubs, they need regular watering, once or even twice a day in hot weather. There are ingenious pulleys by means of which hanging baskets can be lowered and raised, and a twitch of the cord anchors them at any height. Easier and better is a new system which delivers water through very thin tubes to tubs, window boxes, hanging baskets, stone sinks and other containers – all without the aid of hoses or watering cans. The system comprises a kit with a metering valve which allows the same amount of water to pass through to up to four separate $\frac{3}{8}$-in. (9-mm) plastic tubes no matter what the pressure is. The tubes are taken to the various containers and either laid on the ground nearby or clipped to the wall or fence for hanging and wall baskets.

Plastic clips which electricians use to nail cables to walls are exactly the right size for attaching these tubes to any kind of wall, fence or trellis; their black colour can be disguised, if desired, with paint to match the surrounds. At an appropriate spot above or near the various containers holes are made with a small tool – a nail is provided in the kit – and into these holes are inserted short lengths of very thin plastic tubing, about the thickness of a

No. 12 knitting needle. These feeder tubes are then pushed into the top ½ in. (1 cm) of soil in the container.

One feeder tube is enough for a small container, but two or more may be needed for a window box or large tub. The idea is to insert enough tubes so that when the water is turned on each container will receive sufficient water during the same period, perhaps ten to twenty minutes.

The metering valve, which is in effect a plug, fits into a socket on the end of a length of hose connected to the water main. Simply turn on the tap and when water begins to seep through the bottom of the basket or container, turn the tap off. The system can be adapted to water rows of plants such as strawberries or runner beans, and in greenhouses.

Such saturated watering may leach out plant food, but this is easily replaced by a weekly feed with a soluble fertilizer.

 MAY

The Month in the Garden

The opening days of May are usually delightful, with clear washed skies, lengthening days, tender young leaves on burgeoning trees and a wealth of flowers. Yet there can be unpredictable factors. High day temperatures followed by sharp night frosts first induce new growths, then damage those which are tender. Strong winds, storms or even snow are possibilities, and it is difficult to guard against all these eventualities.

General Tasks There are various precautions we can take against the weather, such as refraining from planting out tender perennials and half-hardy subjects before the end of the month, a week or two later in the north. Many garden centres offer such plants far too early, sometimes in April and straight from a greenhouse. If you do buy early, keep the plants in a frame or cold greenhouse until planting is safe so as to avoid the risk of costly, disappointing failures. Home-raised plants should be similarly treated: harden off early in the month by transferring them to cold frames, keeping the frame lights open whenever possible during the day and closing them in the evening; remove them altogether a few days before planting out.

Another good idea is to plant early bloomers subject to frost damage, such as paeonies, in positions where they miss the early morning sun. If valued plants are frosted and the morning is bright and sunny, spray them with cold water and lay a newspaper over the flowers. This may save the blooms as thawing will be gradual.

Lengthening days may mean longer hours spent outdoors, when the ornamental garden becomes increasingly important. Prepare for the change from spring to summer bedding plants about the middle of the month, starting with the removal of bulbs which have finished flowering. Lift them, preferably with the leaves still attached, and lay them in shallow trenches in a spare corner of the garden. Fill in with soil and firm this so that the bulbs are anchored, then water them well and apply a soluble fertilizer. This will feed the new bulbs developing under ground and they ultimately die down in good condition, ready for planting elsewhere in the garden during autumn.

Polyanthus can also be kept for a second year, but meantime they should be lifted, divided if the clumps are very large, and replanted in a shady spot. Keep them watered in dry weather, sprinkle a little general fertilizer over the ground and leave them until autumn (see *Annuals, Biennials and Bedding Plants,* opposite).

Forget-me-nots and wallflowers are useless a second time around so consign them to the compost heap. If forget-me-nots are vigorously shaken so that the seeds drop over a piece of spare ground, the resultant seedlings will provide plenty of new stock for planting out in autumn, saving a separate sowing.

Dig over the empty beds and borders and give these a dressing of general fertilizer if the soil is otherwise in good condition. On poor or impoverished soil dig in well-rotted organic material (farmyard manure, garden compost, hop manure and the like). Display beds lose a vast amount of plant nutrients in a season; they are expected to provide at least two shows a year and cannot give good results indefinitely unless some food is returned to the soil.

Towards the end of the month window boxes, hanging baskets and containers of various kinds should also receive attention. Some of these will have been used for spring bedding and the contents should be treated as suggested for display beds. I like to renew all or half of the soil at this time in order to achieve good results, the amount changed depending on the length of time it has been in the container and on the degree of impoverishment.

WEATHER

'April and May are the keys of the year', may be a true saying in more than one sense. The weather during these two months often seems to influence conditions over the rest of the year, and cold wet weather, in particular, presages a poor summer. In the garden, if all is going well by the end of May, with annual plants well established and the first signs of pests and diseases under control, then well begun is indeed more than half done.

Seeds germinate quickly and plants grow vigorously as summer approaches, always provided that soil moisture supplies are adequate. However, it must be remembered that, 'In the middle of May comes the tail of the winter' and the Ice Saints, St Pancratius, St Servatius and St Boniface, hold sway on 12, 13 and 14 May.

Late May frosts, dreaded by all fruit growers, occur most frequently when the weather has been dry; a wet spring is more favourable and most English gardens, except those in notorious frost-hollows, can hope to escape serious damage.

An old belief in Gloucestershire is that when the mulberry has shown green leaves, there will be no more frost, but as far south as France they say that 'No vine grower is happy until St Orban's Day (25 May) is past.' No cautious British gardener would risk planting out the more tender plants until the end of May.

For those who believe in omens, 1 May may provide an encouraging forecast: 'If it rains on St Philip and St Jacob's Day (1 May) a fertile year may be expected', but if the weather is fine, 'First of May, first of May, Hedgerow loving starts today'.

Trees and Shrubs Most heaths (*Erica*

species) have now finished flowering and will benefit from being cut back to points just above the old wood. If this procedure is practised annually the plants will remain sturdy and compact.

Continue pruning (see April) of those spring-flowering shrubs and trees which carry their blooms on new wood and have now finished flowering. This may not be necessary every year but is advisable on a regular basis to control size or improve shape. Philadelphus and deutzias are examples of shrubs which flower on the previous year's shoots, but at the same time they also throw up new stems in the growing season which often results in dense masses of twiggy growths. Here the procedure is to leave most of the new shoots intact and remove the crowded or badly placed shoots so as to let more light and air into the shrubs. (See also November, *Pruning,* p. 235.)

Give strong-growing hedges like privet and *Lonicera nitida* their first trim of the season.

Prune to shape informal hedges of forsythia and flowering currants as soon as the blooms have faded.

In dry weather, water freely hedges planted during the previous autumn and winter (see December, *Hedges and Screens,* p. 263).

Control weeds in hedge bottoms.

Climbers Prune *Clematis armandii* grown in restricted spaces, as soon as flowering is finished.

Tie in new shoots of clematis and jasmine.

Check honeysuckles for greenfly and spray as soon as noticed (see August, *Plant Disorders,* p. 176).

Plant passion flower (*Passiflora cae-*

rulea) against sheltered, sunny walls, on strong trellis supports.

Roses Keep a careful watch for the first signs of greenfly, mildew and black spot and apply the appropriate sprays. (See August, *Plant Disorders,* p. 176.)

Lawns Continue regular mowing and edge trimming.

Apply a selective weedkiller if necessary.

Water when required.

Hardy Plants Hoe between plants to keep down weeds and remove footprints. Stake floppy plants like delphiniums, erigerons, paeonies and aconitums before the new shoots grow too tall, using peasticks for preference, canes and twine or wire plant-supports.

Thin out shoots of such plants as delphiniums and phlox which benefit from plenty of light and air, removing entirely all weaklings, especially near the inside of the clumps, and reducing the remainder by up to half.

Water newly planted perennials if the weather turns dry and apply a liquid feed towards the end of the month.

Bulbs Remove dead flower heads from daffodils and early tulips to prevent seeding and especially the spread of tulip diseases.

Lift bulbs used for spring bedding and lay in trenches as already described under General Tasks.

Annuals, Biennials and Bedding Plants Towards the end of the month plant out half-hardy annuals raised under glass.

Work out plans for annual borders, outlining each section with sand, then plant out or sow each kind in its allotted space and label it clearly.

Sow hardy biennials, like wall-flowers, sweet williams and foxgloves, in drills in a nursery bed or in boxes left in a cold frame.

Rock Garden Plants Hand-weed between plants and trim back trailers like aubrieta quite severely to prevent indiscriminate seeding and their tendency to smother other plants.

Water Plants Plant water-lilies and other aquatics, as well as submerged oxygenators and moisture-loving perennials for the waterside (see *Water Gardens*, p. 112).

Remove algae by hand, with a net or by twisting it round a forked stick.

Thin and divide old, overgrown aquatics, and keep pools filled with water.

Feed established water-lilies with bonemeal pills, at the rate of one per basket. Make them from bonemeal and damp clay to tennis-ball size and push them down into the soil.

Patio Plants Remove spring bedding from containers and window boxes and replant. (See February, *Vertical Gardening*, p. 42.)

Plant up hanging baskets towards the end of the month, lining them first with moss or green polythene. If the weather turns cool, keep the baskets in a sheltered place for a few days before hanging them outside.

Tie in climbing plants and put out tender bedding plants towards the end of the month. Water frequently in hot weather.

Vegetables Plant trench celery 9 in. (23 cm) apart and water in well.

Earth up early potatoes.

Stake broad beans. Prepare the ground and install climbing frames for runner beans.

Hoe regularly between crops.

Sow summer spinach and salad crops; also sea kale, beet, swedes, French beans and peas.

Prepare a site in a sunny sheltered place for outdoor tomatoes.

Sow vegetable marrows at the end of the month in a prepared site, in good rich soil.

Thin these and all other crops as they grow large enough to handle.

Herbs Sow basil, chervil, dill, fennel, sweet marjoram and a second batch of parsley.

Plant out herbs in new herb gardens (see June, *A Home for Herbs*, p. 140).

Divide mint which has become straggly.

Fruit Harvest the first strawberries (under cloches) and gooseberries; put down slug pellets and protect berry fruit against birds with fine-mesh netting or fruit cages.

Plant out alpine strawberries.

Control weeds around bush and tree fruit and feed established plants.

Thin fruits on wall trees if these grow too close together.

Remove unwanted raspberry canes as they appear; water fruiting canes freely if necessary.

Thin out shoots of newly planted peaches and nectarines until a framework is established.

Remove fruit tree suckers.

Plants under Glass Repot azaleas and heaths that have flowered indoors, using a lime-free compost; cut back old flowered shoots.

Pot on early rooted cuttings and seedlings of ornamental and food plants.

Plant gloxinias and tuberous begonias in their flowering pots, using a light rich compost. Keep them away from strong sunlight.

Damp down greenhouse floors and benches in the morning, and repeat in early afternoon if the weather turns warm.

Apply shading to the glass if the house is exposed to full sun, particularly for ferns, bromeliads, cinerarias and gloxinias.

Sow sweet corn for planting outside next month.

Feed and water liberally greenhouse plants in full growth.

Feed tomatoes in heated houses every seven to ten days and pinch out side shoots.

Plant tomatoes in cold greenhouse borders, in large pots, or in bottomless rings stood on a shingle bed.

Feed greenhouse vines and thin out berries in developing fruit clusters.

House Plants Keep all plants well watered and every other week feed with liquid fertilizer at half the recommended strength.

Remove old flowered bromeliad stems and carefully cut off any new side shoots growing close to the base. Pot them up separately and grow on.

Repot plants as necessary.

Remove plants from hot windowsills in direct sun and place in a good west or north light, or shade them with net curtaining or blinds during the midday hours.

PLANTS IN THEIR PRIME

Shrubs and Trees Aesculus (horse chestnut); amelanchiers; *Buddleia globosa*; ceratostigma; *Cercis siliquastrum* (Judas tree); flowering cherries; cotoneasters; crataegus (various kinds); *Cytisus* varieties; deutzias; *Fremontodendron californicum*; *Hebe hulkeana*; *Kerria japonica* and varieties; *Kolkwitzia amabilis*; laburnums; magnolias; *Malus* varieties; *Rhododendron* in variety; ribes; *Robinia pseudoacacia*; sorbus (whitebeam); *Spirea* x *arguta*; syringas (lilac); *Tamarix tetrandra*; viburnums; vincas; weigelas.

Climbers *Akebia quinata*; *Clematis montana*, *C. patens*; wisterias.

Hardy Plants Aquilegias; *Brunnera myostidiflora*; convallaria (lily of the valley); *Dicentra spectabilis*; *Doronicum plantagineum*; eremurus; iris (intermediates and dwarfs); *Lupinus polyphyllus*; *Meconopsis cambrica*; *Paeonia officinalis*; polygonatum (Solomon's seal); *Trollius europaeus*; violas (pansies and violas).

Bulbs Alliums (various); *Cyclamen repandum*; erythroniums; *Fritillaria imperialis* and others; *Ipheion uniflorum*; leucojum; muscaris; *Narcissus poeticus*; scillas (including bluebells); trilliums; tulips (particularly cottage, Darwins and parrots).

Annuals, Biennials and Bedding Plants *Bellis perennis* (daisy); *Cheiranthus allionii* (*Erysimum* x *allionii*); Siberian wallflowers; myosotis (forget-me-not).

Rock Garden Plants *Alyssum saxatile*; androsace; armeria; aubrieta; *Campanula garganica*; *Gentiana acaulis* and *G. verna*; helianthemum; iberis; irises; lithospernum; *Phlox subulata*; *Pulsatilla vulgaris* (pasque flower); saxifrages (mossy types).

Water Plants Calthas; *Menyanthes trifoliata;* primulas (candelabra types); *Ranunculus aquatilis.*

CROPS TO ENJOY

Vegetables Asparagus; broad beans; cabbages; carrots (early kind); lettuce; radishes; salad onions; spinach (summer); turnips.

Fruit Gooseberries; rhubarb; strawberries (under glass).

PLANT ASSOCIATIONS

In a moist shady glade receiving sunshine for only part of the day, group pink and red candelabra primulas, like *P. pulverulenta* 'Bartley Strain' with blue meconopsis and the feathery fronds of hardy ferns.

In borders, *Fritillaria imperialis* (yellow or orange) look attractive with *Meconopsis cambrica* in similar shades and yellow pansies or Siberian wallflowers in front.

Set bluebells (*Scilla hispanica*) and Solomon's seal beneath a purple lilac.

Mass red helianthemums, golden *Alyssum saxatile* and purple aubrieta to tumble over rocks or low brick walls.

A rosy purple Judas tree (*Cercis siliquastrum*) associates well with variously coloured intermediate irises and an edging of blue pansies.

Naturalize blue muscari with white spring snowflakes (*Leucojum vernum*) in short grass with *Narcissus poeticus.*

Mauve wisteria is stunning fronted by mainly pink lupins and an edging of muscari or ipheion.

GARDEN PROBLEMS

Suckers on roses, lilacs and fruit trees; remove where they arise with a hard pull or a sharp knife. Lawn clippings piled round lilacs inhibit suckers.

Blackfly and greenfly on many plants, particularly broad beans and spinach, roses, honeysuckles, and plums.

Slugs and snails attacking plants and seedlings.

Sawfly caterpillar on gooseberries; spray with derris.

Frost damage to tender plants.

Algae in pools.

Plants of the Month

IRISES

Irises have a long history of cultivation, not only as garden plants but in very early times as a source of drugs. Dykes in *The Genus Iris* mentions that iris preparations were used in the second century AD for a variety of purposes, such as the removal of freckles, fastening loose teeth, curing ulcers, inducing sleep, easing the pains of childbirth and treating snake-bites.

Orris root, derived from the rhizomes of *I. florentina* (a form of *I. germanica*), is still valued as the source of orris oil – one of the rare spices of Ancient Egypt. The plant was taken there from Syria by Thutmosis III (1501-1447 BC) and is clearly represented in bas relief in his temple at Karnak. Today, powdered orris, which smells like violets, is still used in various toilet preparations. The full fragrance does not develop until the dried rhizome is two years old.

Iris pseudacorus, yellow flag

The *fleur-de-lis* of France is generally accepted as being derived from the yellow flag *Iris pseudacorus*, a moisture-loving plant native to Europe, including Britain. According to legend, in the sixth century AD, Clovis I, King of the Franks, was hemmed in by Goths in a bend of the Rhine near Cologne. Seeking a way of escape he noted masses of yellow irises growing in the river bed and realized that the water at that point must be fairly shallow. Accordingly the army escaped over this ford and in gratitude Clovis adopted the flower as his emblem. In the twelfth century Louis VII revived the emblem as *fleur-de-Louis,* later corrupted to *fleur-de-lis* or *fleur-de-lys.* The seeds have been used as a coffee substitute and the leaves for thatching chairs. Eton College (founded by Henry VI) still flies the Plantagenet standard which included the *fleur-de-lis* through their claim to the French throne, and uses it in its coat of arms.

Opium poppies (*Papaver somniferum*) are both a friend and foe to man. On the credit side, the latex which exudes from scratched green seed pods becomes, when refined, high grade opium or morphine – a bringer of sleep and a drug against pain. But against this, when improperly administered opium becomes a mind-destroying addiction. Its misuse has brought ruin and degradation to millions.

The type plant has silvery stems and leaves and commonly white flowers but scarlet, pink, mauve and even maroon flowers, both singles and doubles, are common in garden varieties, all easily raised from seed.

In Europe opium was known and used in prehistoric times. Remnants of seed pods have been found in Stone Age lake dwellings in Switzerland, and we know it was recognized by the Sumerians six thousand years ago as a 'plant of joy'. The Ancient Egyptians were aware of its properties, as their murals show, and in more recent times it reached China and the Far East, as well as the New World. Strangely the seeds do not contain the drug and they are frequently sprinkled on bread and cakes. This practice was inherited from the Greeks, who also looked upon the capsule juice as a symbol of forgetfulness, one which could also be used as a poison – an unobtrusive murder weapon!

The scarlet field poppy of Britain, with black blotches at the base of the petals, is *P. rhoeas,* the well-known annual weed of cornfields. In 1880 the Rev. W. Wilks of Shirley, near Croydon in Surrey, found in the vicarage glebelands a poppy which had white-based flowers instead of black. Intrigued, he marked the plant and in due course collected and sowed the seed, producing many black-based seedlings but also a few white. Continuing through the years to rogue and sow seed from the white-based forms, Wilks began to obtain petal colours other than scarlet – including pink, rose, carmine, crimson and even white. Eventually he produced double-flowered forms as well. Now grown all over the world, Shirley poppies – which must have white bases or they are not true – are among the most charming of our summer-flowering annuals.

P. *orientale* is a large-flowered perennial from south-east Europe, much grown in permanent borders. Until 1903 the flowers were always scarlet but in that year my late father-in-law, Amos Perry, discovered a rich pink form among his seedlings. He named it 'Mrs Perry' and then strove for many years, unsuccessfully, to produce a white form. One day in 1912 he suddenly received an irate letter from a client complaining that seed he had purchased as 'Mrs Perry' for his all-pink border had produced one which was white, thus spoiling the effect. Amos Perry replied that in all probability seed of an opium poppy had got into the garden; there were no white oriental poppies. The client wrote again, saying that he knew an opium poppy from an oriental poppy and what did Mr Perry intend to do about it. He also sent petals of the intruder.

Papaver orientale 'Mrs Perry'

As the garden was in the vicinity Amos Perry went to appease an angry customer, and there, sure enough, in the pink border grew a white poppy! Enraptured, he crooned over the plant while the owner again asked what my father-in-law intended to do about it. 'I have some good pot-grown plants of *Montbretia rosea* which will fit in well with your colour scheme,' was the reply. 'I'll send you some down.' At last everyone was satisfied, and Amos Perry went home hugging his precious new poppy, which ultimately became 'Perry's White'.

Water Gardens

Never in the history of gardening has there been greater interest in water gardening than during the past twenty-five years. Thousands of ponds are installed every year, largely because of easy DIY methods.

At its simplest you can build a water garden by sinking a sawn-down cask, old bath or cistern in the ground: fill it with water and put in a few plants. This takes an hour or two. Alternatively, you can go in for elaborate rock and stream gardens and large concrete pools, expensive in materials and labour. Easier and less expensive, you can install a pre-fabricated pool made of resin-bonded glass fibre or line a cavity with heavy-duty PVC or butyl rubber plastic sheeting. Whatever its type and regardless of scale, an ornamental pool should be sited in sun, and away from overhanging trees.

POND LINERS

The easiest and cheapest method of pool making is a liner made from heavy-duty PVC; all that is necessary is to excavate soil to the required shape and depth (or series of depths) and line the hole with a waterproof sheet. Spread the sheeting tautly over the excavation and hold it firm at the edges with bricks or pieces of rock. Use a hose to run water into the centre of the sheet.

As the weight builds up and the pool fills, the sheeting will stretch and take on the contours of the excavation. Finally fold back any surplus material – nick it if necessary so that it lies flat or cut away all but 6 in. (15 cm) round the edges and tuck it away out of sight under soil, rock or turf.

On rough stony ground it is advisable to line the hole first with sand or sifted ashes so that stones will not pierce the fabric.

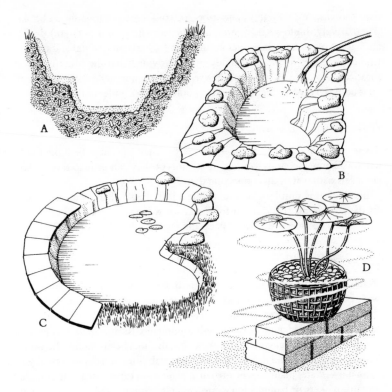

Making a pool: (A) take out soil to the depth and size required; (B) anchor plastic liner over the pool with stones, and fill with water; (C) hide plastic with an edging of turf or paving; (D) mount lilies on bricks in deep water

CONCRETE POOLS

Traditional and solid, a concrete pool stands up to hard knocks and can be made to any shape and depth or to a series of depths and size. The sides can be raised or sunken. Do not economize with the materials – a leaking pool is not a pool. The Cement and Concrete Marketing Association will advise on mixes for pools, or ready mixed concrete can usually be obtained and certainly reduces labour. A depth of $2\frac{1}{2}$ ft (75 cm) allows for 6 in. (15 cm) of concrete, the minimum requirements against leakage, 6 in. (15 cm) of soil or the depth of a planting basket and 18 in. (45 cm) of water.

Shallow-water aquatics need no more than 3 in. (7.5 cm) of water above their crowns, and they must either be grown in pots or raised up on bricks. Alternatively, build shallow troughs, approximately 10 in. (25 cm) deep – allowing for 4 in. (10 cm) concrete and 3 in. (7.5 cm) each of soil and water – round the edges of the deeper lily pool. Provided that the inner edges of these troughs are 1 in. (2.5 cm) lower than the outer edges, water can spill over between the two sections and the pool takes on a wider outline.

PRE-FABRICATED POOLS

These come in a variety of shapes and sizes. They can often be linked with narrow channel sections to simulate streams or they can be placed on different levels with waterfalls connecting them.

Installation is simple: excavate a hole a little larger than seems necessary, set the pool in place and test it for levels – it will annoy you for years if the water runs to one end – then pack the excavated soil firmly round it.

PLANTING A POND

Water-lilies are best planted in aquatic baskets which are made of plastic with lattice work sides. Use fibre-free heavy loam enriched with a handful of bonemeal to a basket, and plant very firmly. Top dress the soil with clean washed shingle which will prevent fish rooting into the mud and discolouring the water. Prop the baskets on bricks so that the lilies lie just under the water; lower them to the pool floor when they are established and begin growing.

Shallow-water plants can be grown in plain loam top dressed with shingle – in pans, baskets or troughs built into concrete. Submerged oxygenators are essential to ensure water clarity as they starve out green algae and also produce oxygen. Oxygenators need little planting; just clip several stems together with a narrow lead strip and throw them into the pool. Floating plants are simply placed on the water surface.

Ornamental fish are not only attractive to look at but also keep down mosquito larvae, caddis worms, aphids and other pests. Water snails are not essential, but if you do decide to add some, introduce ramshorns (*Planorbis corneus*) or freshwater winkles (*Paludina vivipara*) – never the plant-eating freshwater whelks (*Limnaea stagnalis*).

AQUATIC PLANTS

There are about seventy varieties of hardy water-lilies, some very large with flowers the size of a dessert plate, others small enough to slip through a wedding ring. They can be fragrant or scentless and come in various colours – from white and cream to pink, rose, yellow or coppery-red. Before buying tell the nurseryman which colours you prefer and the depth of your pool so that he can advise you regarding suitable kinds. There are many decorative aquatics for shallow water including the following:

White-flowered *Calla palustris* (bog arum), creeping habit, 9 in. (23 cm) high, white arums followed by scarlet berries. *Iris laevigata* 'Alba', 2½ ft (75 cm) high. *Sagittaria sagittifolia* 'Flore Pleno' 3 ft (90 cm), like a double-flowered stock with arrow-shaped leaves.

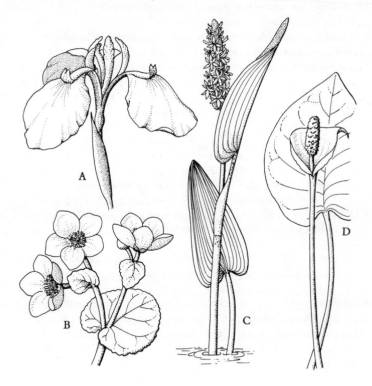

Water and bog plants: (A) *Iris Kaempferi;* (B) *Caltha palustris,* kingcup; (C) *Pontederia cordata,* pickerel weed; (D) *Calla palustris,* bog arum

Pink-flowered *Butomus umbellatus* (flowering rush), 2½ ft (75 cm) bronze-green, strap-shaped leaves, umbels of three-petalled flowers. *Baldellia (Echinodorus) ranunculoides* (lesser water plantain) 6-8 in. (15-20 cm), lance-shaped leaves, small purplish-pink flowers in loose sprays. *Iris laevigata* 'Rose Queen', 2-2½ ft (60-75 cm), broad-petalled flowers.

Blue-flowered There are several good *laevigata* irises in this group, including the type species, as well as 'Atropurpurea', dark blue, 'Colchesteri', blue and white, and 'Variegata' which has cream-striped foliage. *Pontederia cordata* (pickerel weed), 2 ft (60 cm), heart-shaped leaves and poker-like spikes of soft blue flowers. *Myosotis palustris* (water forget-me-not), 9 in. (23 cm), bright blue. *Iris kaempferi* come in a variety of shades.

Gold and yellow-flowered Glorious kingcups, *Caltha palustris*, 1½ ft (45 cm), single or double are a must for spring. The large curious arums of *Lysichitum americanum,* 2 ft (60 cm), thrive in the shallows and have large heart-shaped leaves. There are also golden spearworts (*Ranunculus lingua* 'Grandiflora') with buttercup-like flowers on 2½-ft (75-cm) stems, and gold-striped rushes (*Juncus* species) for connoisseurs.

THE PRINCIPLES OF WATER GARDENING

Water discoloration and green slime are the bugbears of the water gardener. Avoid such problems from the start by following these rules:

1 Use heavy-loam planting compost, free of plant roots and fibre. A little bonemeal may be added, but no other fertilizer.

2 Plant water-lilies in baskets, just covering them with water until they throw out new leaves. Top dress with shingle.

3 Introduce plenty of submerged oxygenating plants, such as elodeas, lagarosiphons and callitriches. They feed on the salts which nourish algae, while oxygenating the water and casting shade – algae must have plenty of light. A pool 6 ft x 4ft (1.8 x 1.2 m) wide and 2 ft (60 cm) deep will need about twenty oxygenators.

4 Flood the pool over occasionally to rid it of floating debris and scum; do not keep emptying a pool.

5 Fish ensure the absence of mosquitos as they feed on the larvae. Goldfish or golden orfe are best. A pool of the size referred to above would need about eight fish.

6 Never introduce duckweed, pondweed (*Potamogeton natans*) or the giant reedmace (*Typha latifolia*) or indeed any rampageous plants.

7 Dredge out or trap fallen leaves.

Children's Gardens

Surely the summers of childhood were longer and hotter, and the flowers more fragrant? I remember long days in a sunny garden where I made flower dolls and held dolls' tea parties, with poppy seedheads for jellies and the blossoms of mullein (verbascum) representing custard. There were many other fantasies to amuse my brothers and me in those long lazy days of the past.

On the whole, gardening is taken seriously by most people only when they have a home and garden of their own. Still, the natural curiosity of children can be the foundation of an interest in growing things, and parents can do a great deal to start their children on what can become a lifetime's hobby. My own sons' began in their prams, when we made a game of recognizing trees in the same way as other youngsters spot makes of cars and aeroplanes.

At the age of four they knew the names of all common trees, in winter as well as summer, and yet never consciously learnt them by rule.

The smallest child is interested in stories about plants, and nearly every plant has one – its discovery, use, or association with the Bible, science, art or history.

If you encourage children to garden give them a small area to start with; it is better for them to cultivate their own small garden properly than to have their spirit broken trying to cope with an over-large plot. Select an open sunny place, dig the ground over and level it for children under the age of ten. Older children will probably be able and willing to do this themselves, and there are small tools with which they can dig, hoe and rake.

In the beginning guide the children's choice with suitable plants, selecting those which germinate quickly, including such annuals as Shirley poppies, marigolds, forget-me-nots, lupins and eschscholzias. Encourage them to grow vegetables – lettuce, radish and the ever-popular mustard and cress, which can be grown in a variety of ways, indoors on a damp piece of flannel or from May onwards outside. Instead of regular rows, suggest they make shallow drills in the shape of their names, sowing and covering the seeds with soil. Then they can watch a developing Joan or James. Scratching their names on a young marrow is another possibility.

Cacti, too, are easy plants for children because they will not flag if they are allowed to become dry – after all they are adapted for desert conditions. Overwatering will kill them in time; indeed, more house plants are killed by overwatering than by underwatering.

Ideas for children's gardens: (A) mustard and cress sown on a piece of flannel or paper towelling; (B) avocado pear stone set on a jar of water and potted after germination; (C) growing a pineapple from an old top; (D) scratching a name on a marrow

Although children can begin with easy, undemanding plants like cacti, they should be taught how to water pot plants, how to tell by lifting the pot whether it needs water or not.

A child of ten or eleven is not too young to raise and look after a black-currant bush or layer a shrub. He will grow the burning bush (*Dictamnus albus*) with enthusiasm if you explain that it gives off a volatile oil which can be lit without injuring the plant.

FUN PLANTS

There is a particular appeal in growing things by methods that adults normally do not attempt. On a warm window sill it is possible to raise from seed the sensitive plant *Mimosa pudica* and later watch the leaves droop within seconds of being touched. A large turnip, with the centre scooped out and hung upside down, will sprout from the base if the centre is kept full of water. Carrot tops grow feathery leaves on moist stones in a saucer. Pineapple tops dried for twenty-four hours and then planted in sandy soil usually grow easily in a warm place (make sure that the growing centre has not been removed when you buy the pineapple).

A peach stone lightly cracked in the centre and planted outdoors or in a pot of soil will usually sprout and grow. Other fruits such as dates, oranges, lemons and avocado pears can also be grown in pots, too, but the stones of these should not be cracked.

Fresh ground (monkey) nuts can be planted about 1 in. (2.5 cm) deep in compost in a box from which one side has been removed and replaced with glass. Cover it with black polythene to keep the soil in darkness. As the plants grow they will produce pinnate leaves and bright yellow, pea-shaped flowers which turn into the soil as they die. Later remove the polythene to watch the developing new 'nuts' under the soil.

Mulching

Among the many horticultural terms which gardeners have to learn sooner or later if they take their hobby seriously is the word *mulch*. Quite simply a mulch is a layer, usually of organic material, but also including black plastic sheeting, which is spread over the ground between and around plants. Wisely used, a mulch has many advantages – and some disadvantages.

Let us consider first the materials we can use and how to apply them, then the pros and cons and the conclusions we can draw on how to make the most valuable use of mulches on different soils, for different purposes and for different crops.

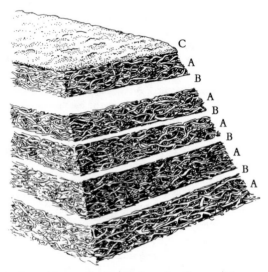

Making a compost heap: (A) grass clippings, garden refuse (but no sticks or straw), tealeaves, eggshells, animal manure, etc. in 9-in. (22.5-dm) layers, with a good dusting of sulphate of ammonia or a proprietary accelerator; (B) lime; (C) soil covering the complete heap. Keep the heap moist and turn once. Cover with polythene in heavy rain.

The most commonly used mulching materials are decayed leaves, well-rotted garden compost, spent mushroom compost and hops, peat, sawdust, pulverized bark, seaweed, bracken, straw – either long or chopped – and grass mowings. Black plastic sheeting has also been found useful for certain purposes.

My own preferences are for well-made garden compost, peat – expensive unless you can buy it in bulk quantities and have room to store it – half-decayed leaves, mushroom compost, sawdust and spent hops.

Unfortunately, whenever somebody finds a use for a waste commodity, such as bark, sawdust or wood chippings, which at one time could be bought for the cost of carriage, up goes the price. Once a lorry load of sawdust could be had for a pittance in the Greater London area, but as soon as it was discovered that sawdust could be compressed into hardboard the price shot up skyhigh. There are no doubt still areas where sawdust and maybe bark can be bought cheaply, and these materials are worth looking for. Spent hops, formerly a splendid, cheap mulch material, have now virtually disappeared.

Another valuable mulching material is used compost from mushroom farms. It is sometimes referred to as 'spent' mushroom compost, but it is far from spent! It consists of horse manure that has produced several crops of mushrooms and during this process has become thoroughly decomposed, although its value as manure is estimated to be about half that of fresh horse manure.

MULCHING, FOR AND AGAINST

When and how to apply organic mulching materials depends on the type of soil and the type of plants involved, the purpose of the mulch and the kind of materials used.

There are several advantages to be gained from mulches. For one thing, they tend to retain moisture in the soil by blanketing the area, thus reducing evaporation losses. Also they help to reduce time spent on weeding and hoeing as they prevent the germination of annual weed seeds in the soil. Unfortunately perennial weeds, like couch grass and convolvulus, will come up through a mulch several inches thick so these should be eliminated before a mulch is applied. Mulches can also help to prevent surface soil on a sloping garden from being washed away by torrential rains.

Some mulching materials, such as well-decayed farmyard or horse manure and well-made garden compost, are also sources of food for the plants, not only while they lie on the surface, but later when they are dug into the soil.

The disadvantages of a mulch are mainly due to the effects mulching has on the temperature of the soil and therefore on the plants growing in it. In addition, a really thick mulch, such as is favoured by some soft fruit growers who are able to obtain cheap mulching materials, may absorb light showers and thereby prevent rain from reaching the roots of plants.

As regards soil temperatures, a mulch acts like a blanket to the soil. It prevents it from warming up quickly in the spring and by the same token prevents any heat stored in the soil during the day from rising at night to warm the air around plants. This is particularly important with frost-tender plants such as strawberries when these are in flower. If a soil is kept moist, compact and free from weeds the sun will warm it during the day and heat rising from it at night may well ward off the few degrees of frost that would otherwise blacken the flowers. This is because water is a good conductor of heat while air is not. A loose mulch, however, or even a layer of dry hoed soil, acts like a cellular blanket, keeping the air spaces between soil particles cooler by day and the air round the plants colder at night.

A mulch should therefore not be applied to plants like strawberries and others, which are susceptible to frost or retarded by low night temperatures, until the end of May or early June. The same applies to putting down straw, plastic sheeting or protective mats round strawberry plants while they are in flower.

On most garden areas where plants' susceptibility to frost is not a consideration the point is unimportant. On herbaceous and shrub borders and under soft fruit bushes a mulch can be left in position all the time, or it may be dug into the soil during autumn or spring cultivation and a fresh mulch applied before weed seedlings can germinate.

On light soils where mulching is particularly helpful in conserving moisture and minimizing the effects of drought, mulches can be applied in early April provided that the ground is thoroughly *moist*.

Heavy soils, once they have warmed up, also benefit from mulching. A good ground cover of organic material will usually prevent clay soils from cracking in hot dry spells. But on areas that have to be dug over every year, like vegetable plots, it is normal practice to turn heavy clay soils over in autumn and leave them rough. Winter frosts will help to break the tenacious clods into friable fragments and make it easier to work the soil into a fine tilth in spring. In such cases, mulches or organic materials would be dug in during the autumn, and a fresh surface mulch applied in spring – remember that clay soils take longer to warm up than light soils.

Obviously the thickness of a mulch will be determined by the availability and cost of the material. If bracken, straw, pulverized bark or sawdust, which flatten down considerably after rain, are available cheaply they may be applied about 6 in. (15 cm) deep. Peat and mushroom compost mulches, 2-3 in. (1-7.5 cm) deep, will give excellent results.

Straw may be teased out and spread, as it comes from the packing, round soft fruit bushes, but if dried bracken is available this is preferable because it clings together and does not blow about as easily as straw.

While some materials, such as hop manure (not to be confused with spent hops from a brewery which have little manurial value), horse and farmyard manure, garden compost and mushroom compost have considerable value as plant food, others, like bark fibre, sawdust, straw and bracken, have very little. Indeed, when they are used for mulching and, more particularly, if they are later dug into the soil, they may cause a denitrification problem. Where such waste materials are present, soil bacteria start to work to decompose them. During the various processes the bacteria need nitrogen which they take from the soil, causing a temporary nitrogen deficiency for the plants. Eventually, after such mulches have been rotted down by soil bacteria, nitrogen will reappear as nitrates and will then be available to the plants, but in the meantime there will be a nitrogen shortage. This can be overcome by applying sulphate of ammonia on top of the mulch as a ready supply of the nitrogen needed during the breakdown processes.

A great deal of work on this problem has been carried out in the United States where vast quantities of corn husks are dug into the soil annually. From various experiments it was found that one hundredweight (50 kg) of sulphate of ammonia applied to one ton of sawdust, straw or similar material would take care of the nitrogen requirements of soil bacteria during the breakdown process.

Whenever I have used sawdust or bark fibre as a mulch I have always scattered a handful of sulphate of ammonia on each square yard (metre) of a 2-3 in. (5-7.5 cm) thick mulch, and I have never experienced soil nutrition problems. Normally in herbaceous borders, on the vegetable plot and among roses I fork the broken down mulches into the top layer of soil the following autumn.

On shrub borders the work of weed control can be practically eliminated by spreading a thick mulch of dead leaves over the ground in autumn, adding to it every year, which is what happens in natural woodland.

Plastic sheeting is useful where shrubs and roses are being underplanted. It takes at least a year or two for small ground-cover plants like ivies, periwinkles, hypericums, ajugas and the like to become established and grow together to form a thick cover. In the meantime the ground between them has to be kept free of weeds – no small problem. If the area is covered with black plastic, ground-cover plants can be planted through holes cut in the sheeting, and they will establish themselves firmly without any weed competition. Thereafter the plastic must be removed to allow the plants to spread. Thus one might say – without being too fanciful – that an artificial mulch can be used to establish a live mulch of ground-cover plants.

Thin black plastic sheeting is used increasingly, with the scarcity and expense of organic materials. It is excellent for spreading over the soil under strawberry plants, where it suppresses weed growth and protects the fruits from mud splashes after heavy rains which often occur in June when the fruits are swelling and ripening. Plastic sheeting also deters slugs from attacking the berries as they do not like slithering over the plastic surface.

Old newspapers also make a good mulch, particularly for newly planted roses and other shrubs in sunny situations. When the bushes are in place, lay several thicknesses of newsprint all over the bare ground between them in spring and soak them with water. Spread garden soil over the top, to mask the paper and hold it down, then water the ground again. Not only will this mulch help to keep the soil damp, it will also inhibit weed seedlings; by autumn the paper will have broken down and can be dug in to help feed the roots for it is an organic material. Repeat the process the following spring.

Finally there are the 'living mulches' provided by what are commonly known as ground-cover plants. They will achieve at least some of the results that we seek to obtain by organic or plastic mulches. It is often said that ground-cover planting helps to conserve moisture by shading the soil, thereby minimizing soil evaporation. This is not quite true because a living mulch must use water to keep alive, but close ground cover, as for example that provided by ivy, suppresses weeds and eliminates or reduces time-consuming weeding. It also prevents cracking, overheating of the soil and panning of the surface after heavy summer storms. Added to that a living mulch looks more attractive than bare ground.

Sometimes roots of plants covered with paving or concrete grow more strongly than in the open ground, presumably because the soil beneath keeps moist and cool. This particularly applies to clematis cultivars which in dry soils and sunny situations do benefit from a loose covering over the root area.

Although it is not true mulching, as the gardener understands the term, large pebbles or stones are often used in tropical countries for conserving soil moisture. The soil beneath a large stone, brick or paving slab is invariably moister than bare open soil although it can also harbour woodlice and other pests.

Yet another type of 'mulching', much favoured by local authorities, is the technique of spraying bitumen on steep banks that have been sown with grass seed to stabilize loose surface soil and prevent it from being washed away by rain. The grass seed germinates safe from birds or erosion, and the seedlings push their way through the layer of bitumen.

Where climbers and shrubs against a wall or fence do not seem to be growing as strongly as they might, the cause may be lack of moisture at the roots. A border at the foot of a wall or fence receives much less rain than a bed in the open garden and needs thorough and frequent watering (see also February, *Vertical Gardening*, p. 42).

 JUNE

The Month in the Garden

June – traditionally the month of roses, of heady scents, warm days and balmy nights – does not always live up to expectations as L. P. Smith's weather notes for the month indicate.

Nevertheless, it is usually a delightful time of year, with our gardens a riot of colour, for as fast as one group of flowers passes from bloom another takes its place. Warm June nights have a spell-binding attraction. It is then that summer scents grow more marked – honeysuckle becomes more noticeable, while such plants as evening primroses, night scented stocks and tobacco plants are at their most fragrant when the sun goes down.

General Tasks It is important to water the garden if there are many fine days in a row. Plants take up and transpire great quantities of water through their leaves at this time of year, and if you wait until the plants start to flag you can give them a nasty check. Further details concerning how much and when to water are given in April, *Watering*, p. 95.

Even the smallest garden can be brightened by standing containers full of showy annuals or bedding plants at strategic points; window boxes and hanging baskets also bring colour to the scene – sometimes serving a double purpose if they can be viewed from the house as well as the garden. They can

be put outside early in the month and if watered by the automatic drip device, will grow in beauty, yet demand little further attention until summer's end.

Tender bedding plants can also be used to fill up gaps in borders, but unless the weather is showery water the area the night before, and again when the plants are in position. Sometimes gardeners devote a whole bed to frost-tender or subtropical bedding. In such cases it is advisable to start in the centre and work outwards. A few plants somewhat taller than the rest and known as 'dot plants' create more pleasing effects when positioned between the others and take away the bed's flat outline. Standard fuchsias and heliotropes, young eucalyptus plants, dracaenas and cannas are popular as dot plants. They should be planted first or positioned on the bed so that an asymmetrical effect is obtained. If the soil is loose or has recently been dug over, stand on a board to prevent unnecessary trampling.

Use a trowel for making the holes and after inserting the plants exert moderate pressure, using both hands, to settle each plant comfortably in its new position. If planting out from boxes water the contents first so that the plants come out with a good soil ball. Bought bedding plants should be selected with care. Plenty of flowers and buds on the plants may not be an indication of quality; quite often the opposite. Look for strong stocky plants with healthy, bright green leaves. Yellowing leaves, spindly habit or stunted growth indicate poor cultivation.

Trees and Shrubs Prune philadelphus as soon as the flowers fade, not too drastically, but to cut out weak, dead or diseased wood, and to reduce a few of the old flowered branches down to strong young growths lower on the stems. This will keep a compact sturdy shape.

Deutzias, spiraeas and weigelas can also be trimmed to shape.

Cut brooms back after flowering, almost but not quite to the old wood. Do not cut into this or the stems will die.

Start propagating shrubs, particularly chaenomeles and clematis, by means of layers into pots of sandy soil sunk into the ground near the mother plants. Soft cuttings of rosemary, lavender, santolina, caryopteris and weigela can be rooted in a propagating frame. Taken with a heel as half-ripe

cuttings at the end of the month, they can be rooted in sandy soil in an open cold frame in a north situation or a frame which can be shaded against sun. See also July, *New Plants from Old*, p. 154.

Climbers Plant out tender annual climbers for summer display, such as *Cobaea scandens,* morning glories (quamoclits or ipomoeas), and canary creeper (*Tropaeolum peregrinum*), all raised under glass.

Roses For large quality blooms, disbud roses by removing all secondary buds from the flower stems. Deadhead regularly.

Keep down weeds and briar suckers; spray against aphids with a systemic insecticide. Control mildew with dinocap, black spot with captan or triforine.

Lawns Continue regular mowing. If the weather is dry, raise the mower blades and dispense with the box, leaving the mowings on the lawn. Give a light feed if this was omitted in May and continue with selective weedkillers against weeds and clover, except during a drought.

Hardy Plants Cut back early flowering herbaceous perennials as they finish blooming, to give other plants more light and air and also to produce a second later crop of flowers. On paeonies, cut off the faded flower heads, but remove the whole stems on delphiniums and oriental poppies.

Pinch out the growing points of early-flowering chrysanthemums.

Continue staking tall perennials.

Apply a mulch of rotted compost to paeonies and delphiniums.

Cut back as necessary overgrown

perennials threatening to smother low growers.

Trim the foliage of *Iris unguicularis* with shears. This tidies the clumps and lets sun and air in to ripen the roots.

Paeony

Bulbs Most spring bulbs will have yellowing leaves or have died down by the end of the month. The majority can be left in the ground, but those removed from display beds and left to ripen in trenches elsewhere can now be lifted, cleaned of dead leaves and skins and placed in trays or open boxes in a cool, dry shed until early autumn.

Annuals, Biennials and Bedding Plants Sow hardy biennials, sweet williams and wallflowers outdoors (see May).

Thin earlier seedlings and transplant the thinnings to nursery beds, 6–9 in. (15–23 cm) apart to grow on.

Finish planting out dahlias, cannas, pelargoniums and other tender bedding plants. Two or three weeks after planting, pinch out the tip of the leading shoots of dahlias; stake the plants when 12 in. (30 cm) high.

WEATHER

'Before St John's Day (24 June), we pray for rain; After that we get it anyhow' is an old saying which neatly expresses the average distribution of summer rainfall in the British Isles – the earlier months of April, May and June are generally drier than the following July, August and September – and also emphasizes that garden plants need frequent rain (or watering) in their early stages of development.

'A good leak in June, sets all things in tune'. The rate at which fully growing gardens extract moisture from the soil and transpire it into the atmosphere is far greater than most people realize. In June and July it amounts to some four to five gallons per square yard (eighteen to twenty-three litres per square metre) per week.

Although June brings the longest days and the strongest sunshine, it is not often the warmest month of the summer, because the soil and surrounding seas are still cool and do not reach their annual maximum until July.

If winds frequently blow from a northerly quarter, the weather can be both cool and wet with frequent showers, and 'A cold and wet June spoils the rest of the year'.

A south-westerly wind is more welcome, bringing both warmth and occasional refreshing rain which is kinder to gardens than heavy showers.

The type of summer weather that a gardener would prefer is not always the first choice of others: 'The peasant longs for rain, the traveller longs for sunshine, but God gives each what is best'.

There are very few years when Britain has to endure long dry spells: 'such arid months as only exiles know, with longing for the smell of English rains'.

Stake tall-growing annuals in display beds with peasticks, thin canes and twine or wire supports. Summer storms can do a great deal of damage to the fragile stems.

Hoe between plants in display areas and complete all planting by the middle of the month.

Dead-head sweet peas and other annuals regularly to prevent seeding and to encourage further blooming.

Water sweet peas in dry weather and support the plants with ties and stakes. On cordon-grown plants remove side shoots and tendrils as they appear.

There is still time to sow the sweetly fragrant night-scented stock close to the house.

Rock Garden Plants Continue weeding and lightly pricking over the soil between plants.

Trim hard back old flowered stems of aubrietas, rock phlox and similar trailers to prevent seeding and to keep the plants compact.

Water if necessary, preferably with a sprinkler.

Water Plants Plant up new pools (see May, *Water Gardens,* p. 112). Use fibre-free loam for planting, covered with a top dressing of washed shingle. Add more oxygenators if the water remains cloudy.

Divide overgrown water-lilies and aquatics in old pools. Remove algae regularly, using a net, notched stick or the hands. Chemical methods should only be used as a last resort; it is very easy to upset the balance between fish and plants.

Patio Plants Keep everything fresh looking by regular dead-heading and removal of old leaves and stems. Sweep paved areas.

Water containers regularly and replace faded, untidy plants.

Vegetables Continue successional sowings of quick-maturing crops like lettuce, radishes, French beans and beet.

Plant young leek seedlings, transplanting only the thickest and sturdiest. Trim the tops, as well as long roots, and plant in rows; drop the leeks singly into holes made with a dibber at 6-in. (15-cm) intervals. Do not return the soil, but fill the holes with water so that soil washes over the roots.

Plant marrows if this was not done at the end of May.

Plant Brussels sprouts, savoys and 'Drumhead' and 'January King' cabbages for winter use; keep the ground as firm as possible.

Plant outdoor tomatoes, leaving a slight depression for watering. Better still, at planting time insert a 4-in. (10-cm) pot in the ground near each plant with its top at soil level. Fill the pots regularly with water, and the moisture will go directly to the roots rather than over the top soil; diluted fertilizer can also be given through the pots. Stake and water the plants in; bush varieties do not require staking.

Sow swedes for a winter crop, dusting the $\frac{1}{2}$-in. (12-mm) deep drills with calomel as a precaution against club root.

Stop cutting asparagus by the middle of the month.

Herbs Many herbs will be at their best for drying or freezing this month. Pick the young fresh leaves of sage, thyme and fennel and dry on trays in a cool oven with the door left open. When dry and brittle rub them down to fine crumbs, pack into small airtight bottles and store in a dark cupboard.

For freezing, blanch the herbs (including parsley) for a minute in boiling water. Rinse in cold water, pack into small labelled plastic bags or cartons and freeze. Chives and parsley should be chopped beforehand. Frozen herbs are useful for flavouring but will not become crisp again, so are not suitable for garnishes.

Fruit Keep harvesting strawberries and raspberries or the young fruits will spoil after coming into contact with overripe berries.

Mulch soft-fruit bushes with rotted farmyard manure or ripe garden compost.

Net fruit against birds and watch out for slugs.

Tie in new blackberry shoots.

Remove raspberry suckers coming up in paths and other unwanted places; some may be used, if required, to fill gaps in the rows.

Remove runners from young strawberry plants and restrict the numbers retained on older plants to three or four.

Thin fruits on wall-trained stone fruits.

Plants under Glass Empty cool greenhouses of as many plants as possible. Many older specimens of azaleas, hydrangeas, regal pelargoniums and resting house plants will be all the better for a sojourn outdoors. Plunge them, in their pots, up to their rims in soil, ashes or peat in a semi-shady place. Water as required.

The shoots of regal pelargoniums should be shortened by about half when flowering is finished. Some of the young removed shoots can be used for cuttings.

Shade pot-grown camellias and ficus from hot sun which will burn young shoots and leaves. If possible, stand them in a north-facing position.

Sow cinerarias and *Primula malacoides* for winter and spring flowering.

Feed actively growing plants at fortnightly intervals. Remove dead leaves and flowers regularly.

An electric fan kept going in the greenhouse creates a constant movement of air and is a sure deterrent to mildew and other diseases.

Dampen down greenhouse floors twice daily in hot weather and the benches too unless they are linked with a self-watering system. See also January, *Greenhouse Gardening*, p. 18.

Admit as much air as possible, but be guided by weather and temperature.

House Plants Continue watering, feeding and removing old leaves.

Move the hardier plants outside for a few months (see *Plants under Glass* above), but keep them in partial shade in a north-facing site. Keep the leaves of indoor plants clean; watch out for aphids.

PLANTS IN THEIR PRIME

Trees and Shrubs Abelias; *Abutilon vitifolium;* aesculus, various kinds including the red horse chestnut *A. x carnea; Buddleia alternifolia, B. globosa; Ceanothus dentatus, C. veitchianus* (both evergreen); *Calycanthus floridus; Chionanthus virginicus; Colutea arborescens;* cistus; cotoneasters; *Cytisus scoparius* (brooms); deutzias; ericas (various); *Fraxinus ornus* (flowering ash); genistas; hebes (various); kalmias; *Kolkwitzia amabilis;* laburnums; magnolias (various); philadelphus; *Potentilla fruticosa;* robinias; rhododendrons; roses; sorbus (various, including whitebeam and mountain

ash); spiraeas; syringa (lilacs);
Viburnum tomentosum and others;
weigela.

Laburnum

Climbers Clematis (various);
*Hydrangea petiolaris; Jasminum
officinale;* lonicera (honeysuckles);
roses; wisteria.

Hardy Plants *Acanthus mollis;
Achillea ptarmica;* aconitums; anchusas;
Anthericum liliago; aquilegias; aruncus;
asphodelus; astrantias; *Campanula
glomerata, C. persicifolia* and others;
centaureas; *Chrysanthemum
leucanthemum;* delphiniums; dianthus;
dicentras; eremurus; erigerons;
Galega officinalis; geraniums;
heucheras; incarvilleas; irises;
kniphofias; linums; lupins; *Lychnis
coronaria, L. viscosa;* meconopsis;
nepeta; paeonies; *Papaver orientale;
Penstemon heterophyllus;* polygonatum
(Solomon's seal); potentillas;
pyrethrums; *Ranunculus aconitifolius*
'Flore Pleno' and others; *Saxifraga
umbrosa* (London pride); *Thermopsis
montana;* trollius; *Tropaeolum
polyphyllum.*

Bulbs Alliums; camassias;
Gladiolus byzantinus, G. x *colvillei*
hybrids; irises (English and Spanish);
Lilium martagon, L. regale and others;
ornithogalums; *Scilla peruviana.*

**Annuals, Biennials and Bedding
Plants** Ageratums; *Akebia quinata;*
alyssum; antirrhinums; begonias;
calceolarias; candytuft; Canterbury
bells; fuchsias; *Limnanthes douglasii;*
lobelias; marguerites; nasturtiums;
pelargoniums; poppies; sweet peas;
sweet williams.

Rock Garden Plants
Acantholimons; achilleas;
aethionemas; *Alyssum saxatile;*
androsace; armerias; asperulas;
campanulas (various); codonopsis;
corydalis; dianthus; *Dryas octopetala;*
geraniums; geums; globularia;
helianthemums; lewisia; *Linum
arboreum* and others; lithospermums;
oenotheras; oxalis; penstemons
(various); potentilla (various);
primulas; ramonda; *Roscoea cautleoides.*

Water Plants *Acorus calamus;* alisma;
aponogeton; butomus; *Hottonia
palustris; Iris kaempferi, I. laevigata,
I. pseudacorus; Menyanthes trifoliata;*
nymphaeas (water-lilies); bog
primulas.

CROPS TO ENJOY

Vegetables Asparagus; broad
beans; early carrots; cauliflowers;
lettuce; salad onions; early varieties of
peas; early potatoes; radishes; spinach;
turnips.

Fruit Cherries ('Early Rivers', 'May
Duke', 'Waterloo' etc); green
gooseberries; strawberries.
    Raspberries towards end of month.

PLANT ASSOCIATIONS

Pink double paeonies with deep blue delphiniums behind, and in front the greenish-yellow flowers of *Alchemilla mollis*.

Lilium regale with pale blue delphiniums; in front generous clusters of blue *Penstemon heterophyllus*.

For partial shade, deep blue aconitums at the back, white *Iris sibirica* and good gold- and green-leaved hostas in front. For brighter colour substitute the iris with the magenta-pink *Geranium psilostemon*.

Aruncus dioicus with deep red paeonies, singles or doubles.

For hanging baskets, pink ivy-leaved geraniums and blue trailing lobelia at the sides, with large-flowered, double tuberous begonias of deep rose or red, at the top.

For a strawberry pot: mixed petunias of pink, blue and red shades; exclude white.

For a container: silver-leaved *Heli-chrysum petiolatum* with blue bedding plants, such as petunias, heliotropes, or harmonizing fuchsias.

Yellow calceolarias and marguerites with blue trailing lobelia.

GARDEN PROBLEMS

Blackfly on beans, spinach and globe artichokes.

Greenfly on roses, campanulas and other garden plants. Apply appropriate sprays.

Summer storms, with damage to poorly staked perennials, annuals and climbers.

Weeds everywhere!

Drought; water in time.

Bird damage to soft fruits; slugs and snails on young plants.

Black spot on roses, mildew on these and other plants.

Plants of the Month

LEWISIA

Alpine growers are always intrigued by the diversity of colours and free-flowering habit of the spring- and summer-flowering lewisias. They are greedy feeders and dislike equally lime and water settling in their flat leaf rosettes. For these reasons lewisias are usually planted vertically in rock crevices, and kept fairly dry after flowering so as to rest the thick roots.

Their discovery occurred on one of the most important expeditions in American history. In 1803 President Jefferson commissioned Captain Merriwether Lewis and Captain William Clark, a botanist, to explore the practically unknown North West territory, ownership of which was in dispute between the British and American governments. It was a long and arduous journey up the Missouri River, across the Divide and down the Columbia to the Pacific.

They were frequently short of food, and one autumn day while Lewis was scouting around for game, he came across an Indian encampment. Noticing some roots drying in the sun, which he was told were edible, he acquired some. He was informed that the plants grew in dry and stony ground at high altitudes, that the skins were bitter but that the white starchy roots after boiling made good eating. The result, he later wrote, was 'a very bitter taste that was nauseous to my palate', but for lack of anything else they sometimes had to eat these roots.

Lewisia rediviva, bitterroot

Soon the explorers found a suitable pass through these mountains, which they named Bitterroot Mountains, and pushed on, navigating various rivers until they descended to the coast. For the first time America had been crossed from east to west, and all that land was acquired by the United States.

But the story does not end there. The explorers returned with many plant specimens which, after various vicissitudes, were given by President Jefferson to a German botanist called Frederick Pursh. When, in 1814, Pursh was writing his *Flora of North America,* he had only some dry-looking bitterroots to study. With a botanist's curiosity he planted one and to his amazement it sprouted and grew. Pursh therefore called the plant *Lewisia rediviva* – after its finder and the fact that it grew again. The other member of the expedition is commemorated by the well-known annual, *Clarkia.* Other plants discovered on the expedition include *Mimulus luteus, Gaillardia aristata, Erythronium grandiflorum* and *Holodiscus discolor.*

ROSES

Roses are undoubtedly of ancient lineage, always much loved and lavishly used. All are native to the northern hemisphere, though Biblical references such as 'the desert shall blossom like the rose' are thought to refer to other flowers. Cleopatra apparently spread rose petals inches deep on the palace floors when entertaining Mark Antony. Nero spent tremendous sums on the flowers for lavish banquets, while one emperor called Elagabalus is reputed to have had so many dropped through apertures in the ceiling at one feast that several of his guests were suffocated.

In Greek the rose is called *rhodon* and gave its name to the Island of Rhodes because so many roses grew there. Roses were portayed on the coins of Rhodes just as Tudor roses are on British coins.

It has always been the flower of luxury. After bathing, wealthy Romans would powder their bodies with dried rose petals and anoint themselves with rose oil. They drank rose wine, while the luxury-loving Sybarites went one better and made mattresses of rose petals – hence the saying 'a bed of roses'.

The Romans grew roses in great quantities and obtained out-of-season blooms by keeping the buds in sealed containers in cold cellars. They were taken out as required and the stems placed in hot water or in an oven lately used for baking bread, to open up.

The custom of hanging a rose from the ceiling is said to commemorate Cupid's gift of a rose to Harpocrates, the god of silence, to bribe him into not revealing the amorous indiscretions of Aphrodite. In Roman times, after-dinner gossip was sacrosanct, and suspending a rose from the ceiling or wearing a chaplet of roses (a common custom) indicated that everything said was *sub rosa* and not to be repeated. Apparently this idea was copied by supporters of Bonnie Prince Charlie during the Jacobite rebellion.

The rose has long been a British favourite, figuring prominently in English heraldry since the fifteenth century. Henry VI and his Lancastrian supporters adopted the red rose, while Edward IV and his Yorkist supporters adopted a white rose. When Henry VII's marriage to Elizabeth of York brought an end to the wearying Wars of the Roses, he joined the two roses together to form the Tudor Rose, and it has become our national flower.

Rose 'Frühlingsgold'

Roses provide work for hundreds of thousands, particularly in south-east Europe, which is the source of more than three-quarters of the world's supply of attar of roses, the essential ingredient or base of almost every perfume. One ton of rose petals is required to yield one pound of attar.

Roses have also been used as rent quits. 'Red Rose Rent Day' in the

United States falls in September, with a celebration based on a deed executed for the family of William Penn. In 1731 the founder of Pennsylvania rented a few hundred acres to a rose grower, based in part on the payment of one red rose each year. Roses are still grown on this land, and the rose rent is paid annually.

The first rosaries were made from chopped rose petals simmered in a little water – without boiling – for several days. The mixture eventually became a stiff paste and was turned deep black by warming it in a rusty pan. The beads were moulded to shape with the fingers, pierced with a sharp instrument to make the holes and left to dry before being threaded. When held in a warm hand for a few moments such beads give out a pleasing fragrance.

Another unusual use for rose petals was their employment as substitutes for cork tips on cigarettes. Apparently an old pink variety called 'Richmond' was used, but the trade was short-lived, presumably because of the cost and labour involved.

Fertilizers and Feeds

It should be self-evident that to grow plants successfully, whether in the open ground, in containers such as tubs or window boxes, in pots indoors or in a greenhouse, they will need adequate supplies of plant nutrients. Soil preparation and fertility in the open garden is discussed in February, *Soil Types*, p. 39, but here I am concerned with supplementing the plant food which is available in the soil with liquid or soluble fertilizers, applied either to the soil or to the plant foliage.

There are organic and inorganic – or chemical – fertilizers. Some people are against man-made chemical fertilizers for various reasons, and while I do not propose to enter into lengthy discussions about the pros and cons of the so-called natural gardening methods, I find many of the ideas held by the non-chemical enthusiasts difficult to understand. I am not convinced that plants grown with 'artificial' fertilizers are less nourishing and flavoursome than those grown with 'natural' manures or fertilizers. I do not understand why soot, which man makes when he burns coal, is acceptable, but not sulphate of ammonia, which is made in a factory. As the late H. V. Taylor of the Ministry of Agriculture once said, 'A nitrate is a nitrate whether it comes from rotted down humus or nitrate of soda'.

FOLIAR FEEDING

For many years it was believed that plants absorbed nutrients only through their roots, but now foliar feeding is a practice accepted by many commercial and amateur growers. Before the Second World War the late F. A. Secrett, a well-known market gardener, used to apply foliar feeds to his crops, long before it became accepted practice. He obtained a piece of equipment used by textile manufacturers for injecting varying quantities of dye in water, and fitted this into his overhead irrigation system with excellent results. However, it was not until the late 1960s that the chemical industry set about producing foliar feeds in handy packs for amateur gardeners.

Foliar feeds are recommended for use *in addition* to whatever feeding is given to the roots. There is no doubt that nutrients absorbed through the leaves have a very beneficial effect on plant development, particularly on root growth. A plant with a large root system is obviously better able to draw up water and food than one with less well-developed roots.

The benefits of leaf feeding are particularly noticeable in summers when rainfall is less than the plants require for optimum growth. Leaf-fed plants always perform better in a drought as I have seen demonstrated on trials with runner beans. Foliar feeding also helps plants which have received a check to growth, for example due to cold nights after planting in the case of runner beans, marrows, tomatoes and the like, or after a pest or disease attack which has been arrested by appropriate spraying.

Foliar feeding also assists newly planted shrubs, such as roses, to establish a good root system quickly. It is also beneficial when applied to bulb foliage after flowering. The only time daffodils, crocuses and other small bulbs have a chance to fatten up their new replacement bulbs for another year is between the fading of the flowers and the dying-down of the leaves. I have found spraying them with a foliar feed three times between the middle of April and the middle of June works wonders. Watering of the bulbs during this period is also very important. Most narcissi are native to mountain-sides and valleys and as the snows melt in spring the bulbs are bathed in water to the extent that they even sit in water for short periods.

Tulips, on the other hand, are native to hot countries in the Near East, and are accustomed to hot dry conditions after flowering. Nevertheless I am sure that several foliar feeds help such tulips as the hybrids or varieties of

Tulipa kaufmanniana, T. greigii and *T. fosterana.* If these and other species are happy in a warm sunny border they will live for years.

CHEMICAL FERTILIZERS

There are many different formulations of chemical (inorganic) fertilizers. Some come in granular form, others are sold as soluble powders and others again as a concentrated liquid. The basic foods necessary for plant growth are nitrogen, phosphorus (provided by phosphates), and potassium or potash. Some formulations also contain added trace elements such as iron or magnesium. Growmore, a formula first recommended by the Ministry of Agriculture more than forty years ago, is still compounded by a number of manufacturers. It is a good balanced fertilizer for many crops and contains 7 per cent each of nitrogen, phosphorus and potash. Some growers prefer a 10:10:10 formulation, but one of the most popular compound fertilizers, used for all kinds of crops, lawns and pot plants – both for root and foliar feeding – has an analysis of 10 per cent nitrogen, 10 per cent phosphorus and 27 per cent potash, with added trace elements. It seems that the reason this particular formulation is so successful is because the very high potash content greatly stimulates root action, hence excellent growth above ground.

Soluble fertilizers are equally beneficial for plants growing in pots in homes or greenhouses, and for plants in tubs, window boxes and hanging baskets. I find that in the summer months it is often better to apply fertilizers to container plants twice as often, but at half the strength, as recommended by the makers. I am not sure why plants respond better to this technique, but possibly a full-strength dose can be leached out and lost when the next application of water is applied. If the fertilizer is applied in two half-strength doses, at an interval of three or four days, it will not be washed down and lost so rapidly.

Never apply a liquid feed to dry soil. It should be already moist, otherwise the fertilizer may work in reverse, drawing water from the roots, thus causing the plants to wilt. If this should occur, water the container copiously to redress the damage. This may be another reason why two half-strength applications are frequently more successful than one strong dose.

WEATHER-RELATED GROWTH

It is not generally realized that the weather can affect plants in much the same way as different types of fertilizer. This is particularly noticeable with tomatoes grown under glass. A period of two or three weeks of dull weather can have the same effect as an overdose of nitrogen, resulting in the plants becoming soft with lush growth. The condition can be corrected by applying potash – at the rate of about $\frac{1}{4}$ oz (7 g) of sulphate of potash watered in for each plant.

Conversely a period of abundant sunshine has the same effect as an overdose of potash: the plants become hard and slow to grow; this is corrected by the application of a quick-acting nitrogenous fertilizer, such as soluble dried blood, at the rate of 4 oz to the square yard (100 g to the square metre) either watered in or applied in solution. This technique of feeding in tune with the weather applies to many other crops, apart from tomatoes.

POINTS TO REMEMBER

Whenever plants have received a check to growth give them a foliar feed.

Water plants in containers before applying a fertilizer solution. Never exceed the recommended dosage.

Rock Gardens

Alpine plants can be grown in various ways. Given the space, time and money, plus the opportunity to obtain sizeable pieces of rock – now increasingly difficult since some authorities prohibit its removal from natural sites – a large, good-looking replica of the real thing can be constructed, complete with pools, waterfalls and streams. The commonest stones used for these large constructions are Westmorland limestone, sandstone, tufa or granite. Although artificial fibreglass rocks can be bought, they are frowned upon by purists.

Where space is restricted, similar but less ambitious gardens can be made using smaller pieces of stone. Rock plants can also be grown in raised beds constructed in frames with hard path surrounds – very convenient for disabled people and easily protected with polythene sheeting in severe winters. Smaller alpines can be grown in stone sinks, raised on bricks for convenience, or on a dry wall, with trailers planted here and there between the stones, plus a few upright kinds on top. Some people segregate alpine species and varieties in separate pans, housing these in winter on a bench in an unheated greenhouse. Here they may be enjoyed and kept dry at the crowns –

most important for some species – in the coldest and wettest weather. During the summer they can be stood in a frame or an odd corner outside.

Some common rock garden plants: (A) *Gentiana sino-ornata*, which flowers in September; (B) *Sempervivum*, house leek; (C) *Leontopodium alpinum*, edelweiss, which flowers in June or July

Not all rock plants have the same requirements, although nearly all demand sharp drainage and freedom from draughts. The majority are sun lovers but a few, like ramondas and haberleas, must have shade, so are usually grown behind a south-facing rock. Many rock plants appreciate lime in the soil, but there are gentians and other plants which cannot tolerate lime and will quickly die under alkaline conditions. These must be given an acid or peaty compost and since most alpines are fairly expensive to buy, it is sensible to check on their likes and dislikes before purchase.

Many rock plants are low-growing, so easily smothered by weeds. Keep these down by hand weeding and as a further deterrent top dress the soil around your plants with granite chips or crushed brick. These will also keep standing water from rotting the collars of fleshy-leaved plants – like cushion (Kabschia) saxifrages and androsaces.

TIPS FOR THE ROCK GARDEN

Start with easy plants and, as your interest grows, expand your collection.

The danger period for rock plants is when dry weather occurs in late spring and early summer; water is then necessary.

Plants in the north can tolerate more hot sun than those in the south, usually needing less water.

Cut back straggly growths from aubrietas, alyssum and helianthemums to keep the plants shapely and in good health.

Ensure good drainage by raising beds above ground level, putting in plants appreciating arid conditions at the top.

Renew old plants from time to time by means of seed, cuttings, or root division.

Small bulbs associate pleasingly with rock plants.

A Home for Herbs

Today herbs seem to be appreciated as much as they were in Edwardian times, and they deserve better attention than the odd clump of mint or parsley here, or a thyme bush there. Make the herb garden into a distinctive feature in an open position where the subtle differences in leaf textures, shades and shapes can be appreciated.

Herbs come from a variety of climates, altitudes and conditions, and some thrive better than others in certain soils. In clays, for example, angelica, parsley, chamomile and all the mints flourish, while in lighter soils, which have sharp drainage and warmer soil conditions, Mediterranean plants such as rosemary, sage, marjoram, savory, thyme and lavender do particularly well. Angelica, lovage, mint, chervil and chives will tolerate some shade, but thyme, sage and marjoram need sun. These differences can be met by growing each type in its own pocket of soil, adding peat or sand to suit individual needs.

Herbs are often relegated to the vegetable plot, which may be at the far end of the garden, although most cooks would prefer to have them closer to the kitchen. Ideally the site should face south-east or south-west, and it must, of course, be free of perennial weeds.

Some common herbs: (A) tarragon; (B) applemint; (C) chives; (D) sage; (E) thyme; (F) parsley

CHECKERBOARDS AND CARTWHEELS

There are various means of keeping herb varieties separate. Paving stones (or bricks) can be laid with pockets of soil in checkerboard fashion so that soil spaces alternate with paving. This makes it easy to fill the soil gaps with different plants without fear of them encroaching on one another; it also makes it more pleasant and dryer underfoot.

Another idea is to make the plot circular, like a wheel, with 'spokes' of wood, bricks or narrow courses of stone. Slates or thick sheets of plastic set upright into the soil will ensure that the roots of each herb stay in its allotted territory. A taller, more permanent herb like lavender, rosemary or a small bay tree can be planted in the centre. The rim of the wheel can be edged with chives or parsley – both in constant demand in the kitchen and looking fresh and green all summer; in addition chives have pretty round heads of mauve flowers.

MINIATURE HERB GARDENS

Herbs can also be grown in window boxes and in strawberry pots – a different kind in each hole; pots of mint and parsley can flourish on a sunny window-sill, and thyme and sage can sprout from hanging bottles. For the last use wine bottles, preferably those with an inward-pointing dome at the base. Using a diamond cutter, make a hole in the centre of the dome about $\frac{3}{4}$ in. (2 cm) across. Fasten a wire round the neck or, if it has no pronounced rim, push a piece of flexible wire through the bottle, hooking one end round the base and bending the other end at the top to form a hook.

Half fill the bottle with potting compost and push two or three rooted cuttings of sage or thyme through the small opening at the base. Turn the bottle the right way up and hang it in a light window. Water from the top as necessary, and soon the plants will grow downwards a little way, then turn upwards towards the light all round the outside of the bottle.

Annual herbs can be raised from seed, the half-hardy types sown under glass and hardened off before planting out. Hardy herbs – dill, chervil and parsley – are sown directly in their growing sites. Parsley is notoriously slow to germinate, but boiling water poured on the ground before sowing will hasten germination. Perennial herbs like mint and chives can be divided, while woody evergreen herbs such as rosemary, sage and thyme are easily increased from cuttings.

USING HERBS

For drying, foliage herbs should be gathered *just before* they reach their prime. Dry them in a cool oven, then crumble the leaves and store them in airtight jars in a dark place. Seeds (dill and fennel) are ready for drying when they turn brown; hang the stems upside down in an airy place and, when completely dry, shake out the seeds.

Mint for sauce can be kept all winter if the leaves are chopped in the ordinary way then stirred into a jar of honey or golden syrup and stored in a refrigerator. The jar will hold a surprising amount of mint; when needed, dilute a little of the mint mixture with vinegar.

Flowers for Food

The edible parts of cauliflowers, sprouting broccoli and calabrese are all immature flower heads. Like other vegetable greens (cabbage and Brussels sprouts), these plants all derive from a yellow-flowered British crucifer called *Brassica oleracea.*

No one can be sure when and where the flower forms evolved, although according to Pliny the Romans knew and grew sprouting broccoli in the first century AD, and the oldest record of cauliflowers dates back to the sixth century BC. When cauliflowers first reached England from Cyprus around 1619, they were referred to as Cyprus coleworts.

The globe artichoke (*Cynara scolymus*), another immature flower head, is a staple food in the Mediterranean and North Africa, where, from early times, it seems to have been appreciated by the Greeks and Romans. The similar-looking cardoons (*C. cardunculus*) are not held in such esteem by gourmets; the flowers are not very tasty and the plants are grown primarily for their blanched stems.

Another immature flower that may not be recognized as such is the green fig. In its young state, it is a flower reversed, that is to say it has the essential flower parts of stamens and stigmas inside. It only becomes a fruit after pollination, by a minute fig wasp, which crawls inside through an opening at the top of the fig to lay its eggs. These wasps are, perhaps fortunately, not hardy in the British Isles. All figs grown here remain soft and greenish, which is one reason why they do not travel well and cost a lot.

Cloves are the dried flower buds of *Syzygium aromaticum* (*Eugenia caryophyllus*), a tropical tree from Indonesia, which grows about 40 ft (12 m) high; the buds are sun-dried to cure them. Capers are the unopened flower heads of a Mediterranean spiny shrub called *Capparis spinosa.* If allowed to open, they make very beautiful 2-in (5-cm) white or pinkish flowers filled with yellow stamens.

The saffron crocus (*Crocus sativus*) yields a most important textile dye and spice in the three-branched stigmas of its open flowers. Long known and jealously guarded in Asia Minor, it reached England in the fourteenth century, as described in October's *Plants of the Month*, p. 216. The saffron industry flourished in Essex for some five hundred years until synthetics provided a cheaper means of obtaining the spice.

Red roses have a long history of imparting a delicate flavour and scent to jams, wines and other preserves. Crystallized rose petals have been popular since Elizabethan times, while rose butter is made by blending three cups of fresh rose petals, dried in an oven, with 1 lb (500 g) of butter. After three days the butter absorbs the rose flavour and fragrance. Rose petals are an attractive adjunct to green salads and can also be used to flavour vinegar if steeped in it for two or three weeks. Rose ice-cream, rose lozenges and pickled rosebuds are other delights (see also March, *Roses,* p.60).

Violet, mimosa and borage flowers are also crystallized for cake and confectionery decorations. Violet flowers can be made into syrups and marmalade, using apple pulp to help setting, and for violet vinegar and violets in jelly.

The stuffed flowers of vegetable marrows are the dolmas of Turkish cookery. After packing the blooms with a preparation of minced mutton, spices and other ingredients, the dolmas are gently cooked in a flat pan with a little broth.

When we were young, my mother used to make primrose or paigle (cowslip) puddings. They had a suet crust and were filled with cowslip flowers, sugar, dried fruits, cherries, nuts and other ingredients, then steamed for two hours. Alas, cowslips have been so denuded by agricultural ploughing and careless cultivation that we cannot try such recipes today. Marigold pudding can be made in the same way, but the flavour is rather strong so use the flowers sparingly.

I still use a few bergamot and nasturtium flowers to give mixed salads colour and a tangy flavour. There are countless other possibilities, notably wines, made from elderflowers, lavender, marigolds, clary, carnations, dandelions and cowslips to name but a few. Elderflower fritters, chrysanthemum soup, and pickled broom buds (popular with the Plantagenets) are other old recipes, not to mention the importance of hop flowers in beer-making.

 JULY

The Month in the Garden

In July the brightest flowers are found among the annuals, biennials and bedding plants, particularly those grouped closely together in beds, window boxes and containers. There should still be plenty of interesting perennials in herbaceous and mixed borders, and the water garden is usually at its best at this time of year with elegant, cup-shaped water-lilies floating on the water, and dragonflies hovering over waterside irises and aquatics.

General Tasks Carry on with the routine jobs of watering, dead-heading and weeding. July is a good propagating month, particularly for shrubs, rock plants, border carnations and pinks. Continue taking heel cuttings from shrubs as suggested in June, but layer choice shrubs which are normally difficult to root by other methods.

Among a host of plants which can be increased from cuttings in July are heathers, ceanothus, helianthemums, penstemons, lavenders, santolinas and philadelphus. Even *Viburnum farreri* and ribes can often be induced to root without the aid of a greenhouse. Instead cold frames, belljars, cloches or even large sweet jars may prove helpful, although they should all be sited in a north-facing position or the glass will need shading when the sun shines. Rake the soil in the cuttings bed before any

cuttings are inserted and cover it with ½ in. (12 mm) of coarse sand to stimulate rooting.

Take the cuttings from young pieces of the current season's growth, 2-4 in. (5-10 cm) long and either with a heel (for woody plants) or cut just below a joint on soft shoots. First dip the cut ends in water and then in a hormone-rooting compound to accelerate their rooting.

Hydrangeas can also be propagated now, but in their case cut the leafy young shoots *between* two joints rather than immediately below them; for some reason hydrangea cuttings root more readily from these parts. Insert each cutting separately in a small pot of compost or a Jiffy 7 and root in a closed frame shaded from sun.

Garden pinks and border carnations are always welcome, for they make excellent edgings to borders and the sweetly scented blooms are favourites for cut flowers. Apart from propagating pinks by slips (see *New Plants from Old,* p. 154) border carnations can be increased from layers. Select strong, non-flowered, young basal shoots and strip away some of the leaves a little way up from the base. With a sharp knife cut halfway through the stem, turn the blade and run it up through the stem to just beyond one of the joints. This makes a tongue cut. Peg the layer down in the soil nearby or in a small pot with gritty compost sunk to its rim; but keep the tongue open as you peg the layer down, holding it firm with a hairpin or bent piece of wire. Keep the ground moist, and by September stocky new plants should have developed from the layers. They can now be separated from the parent plants and planted elsewhere in the garden.

Trees and Shrubs Propagate shrubs by layers and cuttings (see above).

Complete any necessary summer pruning of ornamental – and domestic – plum and cherry trees. There is less risk of them contracting silver leaf disease through wounds at this time of the year than in the later winter months.

Trim privet and other hedges as well as topiary specimens.

If beech hedges are pruned in July they produce fresh young leaves which turn russet brown in autumn and remain on the hedge all through the winter.

Hoe and weed hedge bottoms.

Climbers Water sweet peas frequently and apply a soluble fertilizer at least once a fortnight. Cordon-grown plants which have reached the top of their supports can be carefully untied, the lower parts of the stems turned to run horizontally up to the second support, then tied upright again. If all the plants are treated in this way, they will produce new flowering stems. All sweet pea blooms must be picked regularly or they will set seed and stop flowering.

Tie in new clematis shoots. It may be necessary to cut back very vigorous kinds like *Clematis tangutica* and *C. orientalis,* both yellow-flowered and apt to climb over everything, as well as the spring-flowering *C. montana* and *C. macropetala.*

Roses Dead-heading and sucker removal are the main tasks this month. When cutting out faded blooms remove the stem down to the nearest strong bud joint. New flowers will usually appear from this part later in the season.

Bud roses on suitable rootstocks.

Lawns Keep lawns watered in dry weather and apply a selective weed-killer if necessary.

Trim edges.

Hardy Plants Lift and divide June-flowering irises which have been in the same site for three or more years. Retain a fan of new leaves and several inches of rhizome to each division and shorten the foliage to about 6 in. (15 cm) to prevent wind rocking. Dust the rhizome cuts with charcoal and plant, preferably, in a fresh site.

Sow hardy perennials like lupins, delphiniums, geums and polyanthus during showery weather, in an outdoor nursery bed. Keep the seed rows watered.

Plan new borders while weak spots in the present layout can be recognized.

Aim for a continuity of blooms over as long a season as possible.

Reduce the shoots on outdoor-flowering chrysanthemums in order to obtain better flowers. Spray varieties should be left alone.

Trim edging plants which have finished flowering.

Bulbs Finish lifting and storing tulips and bedding hyacinths.

Stake tall gladioli and give them a soluble feed.

When available, plant autumn crocuses – *Crocus sativus* and *C. speciosus* – 2-3 in. (5-7.5 cm) deep in rock garden pockets or in groups at the front of shrub and perennial borders, or in grass for September flowering. Colchicums, which look like large white or reddish-purple crocuses but are quite different in habit and belong to another family, are best kept in shrubberies or round the base of island trees as they produce large fleshy leaves and seedpods in spring – long after the flowers have disappeared – and can smother smaller plants. Slugs are partial to the blooms of colchicums when they appear in September and October; plant the tubers 4 in. (10 cm) deep and top dress the soil with granite chippings or apply a slug bait.

Stake tall galdioli to prevent them from heeling over in strong winds or heavy rain. If the top bud is removed from spikes used for cutting, all the other flowers open uniformly. Gladioli need really copious waterings in dry weather so put on a gallon to the square yard twice a week.

A splendid bulbous plant not planted often enough is the summer hyacinth, *Galtonia candicans,* which begins to give us its spikes clad with pendent white bells at the end of July. Make a note to plant some in the autumn.

WEATHER

'An English summer; three fine days and a thunderstorm' is an unkind, but not entirely untrue, summary of many a July. Thunderstorms are most common over southern and eastern England, especially after a light southerly wind has brought a short spell of sunny, warm weather.

The average rainfall in July is quite high over most of Britain, due chiefly to the prevalence of unsettled weather, sometimes called the 'summer monsoon'. The Dog Days, 3 July to 11 August, seem to enjoy their own conditions. 'When the sun enters Leo in July, the greatest need will arise', 'As the Dog Days commence, so they end'.

St Swithin (15 July) is the most famous weather prophet in July, but there are several other saints who have been recruited into the ranks of meteorologists and who are thought to bring us indicator days foretelling thirty or forty day spells of wet or dry weather at this time of the year.

The reason behind such beliefs is that British weather does have a tendency towards persistence of type, behaving in much the same general way for some weeks: 'If the First of July be rainy weather, it will rain, More or less, for four weeks together.'

Most sayings emphasize the persistence of rainy or showery weather, but in Scotland they are more optimistic: 'St Swithin's Day, if you be fair, For forty days it will rain nae mair.'

Occasional rain or showers are more welcome in the garden than prolonged dry spells, but warm moist conditions can be favourable for the spread of many fungus diseases; in drier weather, pests are the greater problem.

Annuals, Biennials and Bedding Plants Stake weak-stemmed, tall annuals.

Line out wallflower seedlings, sown in May, in a nursery bed.

Sow biennials such as wallflowers, Canterbury bells, sweet williams and foxgloves.

Mulch dahlias, thin out the weaker stems, and tie others to thick stakes.

Prolong the lives of annuals by removing flower heads as they fade, to prevent seeding.

Everlastings like rhodanthe, helichrysum and honesty seedpods, for use in winter bouquets, should be cut when at their best and dried in small bunches hung in a cool airy position, *not* laid out on a hot greenhouse bench.

Rock Garden Plants Cut back straggly plants as they finish flowering.

Water rock gardens and raised beds in dry weather.

Collect seeds from plants you may wish to increase; store the dry seeds – or the ripening seed heads, so that the seeds fall out when ripe – in small, open-topped bags. Keep them in a cool place.

Sow primula and meconopsis seed as soon as it is ripe, in pans or pots of peaty compost. Place in a cold frame to germinate, but shade from direct sun.

Water Plants Cut down faded flower heads of marginal aquatics to prevent indiscriminate seeding.

Keep pools full of water, flooding them over occasionally to get rid of floating debris and to dampen the soil around nearby bog plants.

Watch for blackfly on water-lily leaves. Hose them off or, in bad outbreaks, place a weight – such as a wire hoop – over the foliage to sink it beneath the water. The blackfly will then be eaten by fish.

Patio Plants Plant and suspend more hanging baskets in suitable situations; use half baskets attached to walls or trellis where these could be improved with more colour.

Keep containers watered and old flowers removed.

Take cuttings from trailing perennials like *Calocephalus brownii*, *Helichrysum petiolatum* and *Campanula isophylla*.

Vegetables Plant leeks, Brussels sprouts and winter cabbages including savoys.

Sow swedes, red cabbage, and seakale beet.

Pinch out side shoots on outdoor tomatoes, except bush kinds; feed and water.

Pinch out growing tips on runner beans when they reach the top of their supports; spray in dry weather to encourage fruiting.

Continue to harvest salad crops while they are young and succulent.

Hoe regularly and water when necessary.

Start earthing up celery plants when they are 10-12 in. (25-30 cm) tall; repeat at three-week intervals.

Herbs Sow a second crop of parsley.

Take cuttings of bay, mint, sage and thyme.

Cut back sage lightly after flowering has finished.

Cut herbs ready for drying.

Fruit Summer prune trained apple and pear trees. (see also November, *Pruning Calendar*, p. 239).

Thin fruit on apple, pear and plum trees.

Prune blackcurrants (see November, *Pruning Calendar,* p. 239).

Pick loganberries. After harvesting, cut out old fruiting canes and tie in new ones.

Prepare new strawberry beds; at the end of the month start planting out rooted runners.

Cut out old raspberry canes after fruiting and tie in new ones. Remove suckers or canes coming up in paths and other unwanted places.

Cut off old leaves from strawberries which have finished fruiting; burn the foliage together with old straw and other debris.

Thin the fruit on the grapes in the greenhouse.

Plants under Glass Take cuttings of fuchsia and regal pelargoniums.

Rest hippeastrums by laying pots on their sides and withholding water.

Sow cyclamen seed. At end of month clean, repot and water old corms to start them growing again. Keep in a cold frame.

Late chrysanthemums should be staked, watered, fed and stopped as necessary.

Take soft cuttings of rock plants.

Root half-ripe heel cuttings of hebe, caryopteris, skimmia and ivies in a cold frame.

Pot on spring-rooted pelargoniums.

Prick off or pot up June-sown cinerarias, primulas and other ornamentals.

House Plants Continue feeding and watering house plants.

Stand hardier plants outside for a few weeks, plunging the pots up to their rims in moist soil or peat in light shade; top dress with moist peat. This is also a good idea if you go on holiday at this time. Cacti, however, can be placed in a sunny spot.

PLANTS IN THEIR PRIME

Trees and Shrubs Abelias; *Abutilon vitifolium; Aesculus* sp.; bupleurum; buddleias; callunas; *Calycanthus floridus; Carpenteria californica; Catalpa bignonioides;* ceanothus (various kinds); cistus; *Colutea arborescens; Cytisus* sp.; *Deutzia* sp.; escallonias; hebes; *Hypericum* sp.; *Fuchsia magellanica* 'Riccartonii'; *Genista* sp.; hydrangeas; *Jasminum revolutum; Kalmia latifolia;* lavenders; *Leycesteria formosa; Lupinus arboreus; Magnolia parviflora;* olearias; philadelphus; *Phlomis fruticosa; Potentilla fruticosa* and forms; rhus; roses; rubus; santolinas; senecios; *Spartium junceum;* spiraeas; tamarisks; vincas.

Climbers Clematis (many); *Jasminum officinale;* lathyrus (sweet peas); loniceras (honeysuckles);

Climbers in flower in July: (A) honeysuckle; (B) clematis; (C) sweet pea; (D) passion flower

Passiflora caerulea; Polygonum (now *Fallopia) aubertii, P. baldschuanicum (Fallopia baldschuanica)*; roses; *Schizophragma hydrangeoides; Solanum crispum, S. jasminoides;* wisterias.

Hardy Plants Acanthus; *Achillea* sp.; aconitums; althaeas (hollyhocks); alstroemerias; *Anaphalis margaritacea; Anthemis* sp.; anthericums; *Artemisia lactiflora;* astilbes; astrantias; *Baptisia australis; Campanula* sp. and forms; centaureas; *Centranthus ruber; Cephalaria gigantea; Chrysanthemum leucanthemum* and *C. maximum* vars.; delphiniums; dianthus; dicentras, *Dictamnus albus;* digitalis (foxglove); echinops; eremurus; erigerons; *Eryngium giganteum* and others, filipendulas; gaillardias; galegas; geraniums; geums; gypsophila; heleniums; heliopsis; hemerocallis; heucheras; hostas; inulas; kniphofias; *Lavatera olbia;* liatris; linarias; linums; *Lychnis chalcedonica and* others; *Lysimachia clethroides; L. thyrsiflora;* lythrums; macleaya; meconopsis; *Monarda didyma* and vars.; *Morina longifolia; Nepeta mussinii;* oenotheras; *Papaver nudicaule* and others; *Penstemon barbatus* and others; *Phlox peniculata* hybs.; *Phygelius capensis;* platycodons; polemoniums; *Polygonum bistorta* and others; romneyas; rudbeckias; *Salvia* sp.; thalictrums; *Tradescantia virginiana* vars.; trollius; *Tropaeolum polyphyllum;* verbascums; veronicas.

Bulbs *Allium* sp.; *Galtonia candicans;* gladioli; *Iris xiphoides* (English irises); *Lilium* sp. and vars.; tigridias.

Rock Garden Plants Acantholimons; achilleas; androsace; *Armeria maritima; Asperula suberosa; Astilbe simplicifolia;*

campanulas; convolvulus; *Dianthus* sp.; erodiums; gentians; geraniums; *Geum coccineum;* globularias; *Gypsophila repens* and vars.; *Helichrysum bellidioides; Hieracium aurantiacum;* hypericums (various); *Leontopodium alpinum;* lewisias; linarias; linums; oenotheras; onosmas; *Othonnopsis cheirifolia (Hertia cheirifolia)*; *Papaver alpinum (Papaver burseri)*; *Penstemon* sp. (shrubby kinds); primulas; sedums; sempervivums; silenes; *Thymus serpyllum* vars.; *Tunica saxifraga (Petrorhagia saxifraga)*; *Verbena chamaedryfolia (V. peruviana)*; veronicas; violas.

Water Plants *Acorus calamus;* alismas; *Aponogeton distachyus; Butomus umbellatus; Iris laevigata, I. kaempferi; Menyanthes trifoliata;* mimulus; *Myosotis palustris;* nuphars; nymphaeas; *Nymphoides peltata; Pontederia cordata;* primulas; *Ranunculus lingua,* sagittarias; typhas.

Annuals, Biennials and Bedding Plants Most kinds, including ageratums, antirrhinums, begonias, calceolarias, Canterbury bells, fuchsias, lobelias, marguerites, pelargoniums and other bedding plants.

CROPS TO ENJOY

Vegetables Globe artichokes; beet; broad beans: dwarf beans; carrots; cauliflowers; lettuce; peas; early potatoes; radishes; spinach; turnips;
Cucumbers, tomatoes under glass.

Fruits Most soft fruits, including red, black and white currants, gooseberries, loganberries, raspberries and strawberries; cherries and early apples and plums. Apricots, grapes, nectarines and peaches under glass.

PLANT ASSOCIATIONS

Golden-flowered *Hypericum* 'Hidcote' in front of purple-leaved *Prunus cerasifera* 'Pissardii' and silver-leaved *Pyrus salicifolia* 'Pendula'.

Red water-lilies with blue *Pontederia cordata* and deeper blue *Iris laevigata* in a pool.

Clematis x *jackmanii* with deep purple flowers wending its way through red- or pink-flowered climbing roses.

Lavender with *Lilium regale,* or any light-coloured lily, and a white rose like 'Iceberg'.

Double white *Philadelphus* 'Virginale'

fronted by blue delphiniums and pink pyrethrums.

GARDEN PROBLEMS

Algae in pools.
Aphids (on many plants)
Blackfly on water-lily leaves.
Black spot on roses.
Botrytis on strawberries.
Mildew.
Peach leaf curl.
Potato blight.
Slugs and snails in damp weather.
Suckers on roses.
Whitefly in greenhouses.
Woolly aphids on fruit trees.

Plants of the Month

FUCHSIA

There are about a hundred species of fuchsias, the majority native to South America, although a few are found in New Zealand. The small-flowered, red and purple *Fuchsia magellanica,* from Chile and Argentina, and its varieties have proved hardy in many parts of Britain, particularly in coastal areas; one well-known form called 'Riccartonii' reputedly originated on a hillside near Edinburgh. Visitors to Southern Ireland will find fuchsias naturalized in many areas, and miles of fuchsia hedges. According to Canon Ellacombe, writing in *In a Gloucestershire Garden* in 1895, fuchsias were at one time widespread in the Orkneys, for he declared, 'I have seen houses covered with them from the ground to the roof, with spaces cut out for the windows.'

The berries are edible and make good, if rather sweet, jam. Those of the tree fuchsia, *F. excortica,* are much esteemed in its native New Zealand, where its blue pollen is used as a face powder by Maori girls.

It seems that fuchsias first arrived in Britain around 1703, and one widely circulated story of their introduction links the plants with James Lee, an eminent botanist and nurseryman. Lee's Vineyard Nursery of Hammersmith was roughly where Olympia now stands. According to the legend Lee, while showing a visitor some of his new treasures, was told of a splendid new plant which the visitor had seen that day in a window at Wapping.

Fuchsia

Lee visited the house, and being much taken with the flower offered to buy it from the owner. In spite of being offered a good price, the lady refused to sell, saying that her husband/son – accounts differ – was a sailor and knowing her love of flowers had brought her the plant from Chile, Brazil or the West Indies. Again accounts differ, but since fuchsias are not native to the West Indies this source seems an unlikely one. Journeys by sailing ship were lengthy in those days, and as the plant had to be nursed for several weeks before it reached her and as the donor had gone back to sea, the lady felt obliged to keep it.

Lee was insistent, pointing out that the plant might die, but if he could buy it, the wife/mother could have three of its offspring in exchange, plus a large sum of money. Some accounts say that the sight of eight/eighty golden guineas was too much for the good lady; at any rate she parted with the plant from which Lee raised about three hundred cuttings, which he had no difficulty in disposing of at a guinea apiece.

In the 1880s fuchsias were exceedingly popular, with about 1500 named forms and species being grown. At suburban shows monster plants 8-10 ft (2.4-3 m) high and around 4 ft (1.2 m) across were not unusual; some were so large that they could not be transported in covered carts, but had to be brought to the show on canal barges.

Dictamnus albus

DICTAMNUS

Dictamnus albus (*D. fraxinella*), the bastard dittany or fraxinella of Eastern Europe and Asia, was introduced to England in Elizabethan days and is still treasured in hardy herbaceous borders for its handsome spikes of white or rosy-purple flowers on 1½-2 ft (45-60 cm) stems. It is a very permanent plant, yet never becomes invasive; I remember being shown a batch in the gardens of St John's College, Cambridge which had reputedly been growing in the same situation for over fifty years.

All parts of the plant – roots, ash-like leaves and flowers – have a strong smell when handled, due to a volatile oil which, on a sultry windless day, can be ignited with a taper or lighted match. The faded flower heads are extreme-ly rich in this secretion, and I have twice seen this inflammable exhalation set alight, without its harming the plant. This phenomenon, which was first discovered by Linnaeus and described in 1756 by Sir John Hill, has earned the plant the name 'burning bush' in England and 'gas plant' in America. It is esteemed as a sacred plant by Indian fire-worshippers on account of this strange happening. Could it, one wonders, be linked with the Bible plant mentioned in Exodus III 2-4 that 'burned with fire, and the bush was not consumed'?

Dictamnus needs well-drained soil, in full sun or light shade, and once established should not be disturbed.

New Plants from Old

Seed propagation is a natural means of increase and a method adopted by many plants, particularly vegetables and annuals. Natural species – plants which occur wild – produce seedlings which are near replicas of the parents, although there are usually very slight differences. Any marked distinction, perhaps flowers of a different colour, is not necessarily transmitted to its seedlings; it may happen, but the odds are against it. To perpetuate such a variety, it must be increased vegetatively from the original plant, by cuttings, division or layers. The resultant plants will then be exactly like their parent.

However, named types of annuals and vegetable varieties are purchased with every expectation of them coming true from seed. This is because the crop is constantly rogued by seedsmen, and every plant inferior or reverting to type is destroyed before it can set seed.

To grow plants from seed is a simple process. The hardy kinds are usually sown outside in well-prepared, well-raked soil. Drills (shallow, narrow trenches) are taken out with a hoe, about $\frac{1}{2}$ in. (12 mm) deep for small seeds like carrot and lettuce, up to 2 in. (5 cm) for the larger seeds of peas and beans. Later the seedlings will need thinning to give those remaining plenty of growing space.

Seeds of tender plants are usually started in a warm greenhouse or in a propagating case. They are sown thinly in pans, pots or boxes of seed compost, barely covered with soil and left to germinate. They should never be allowed to dry out and the soil must be kept damp and protected from hot, drying sun at this critical stage. After rooting, the seedlings can be potted separately, or pricked out 1-2 in. (2.5-5 cm) apart, according to size, in boxes of potting soil. Some will eventually be moved into larger pots, but half-hardy annuals and most frost-tender vegetables are usually planted outside after all risk of frost is past.

VEGETATIVE PROPAGATION

Division An easy method of increasing rhizomatous irises and plants with fibrous roots like asters and helianthus is by splitting them up into small segments. Division is normally carried out in early spring or early autumn (July in the case of the irises), either by cutting pieces from the side of the plant or more often by lifting a plant and dividing it into sections, each with one or two shoots and some roots. Divisions from the outer, younger edges of the clump are the easiest to establish; the old, worn centre is usually discarded.

Layering This is one of the oldest propagation methods and is still practised on woody plants as well as on strawberries and border carnations. For centuries gardeners have increased choice shrubs by a form of weaning: they pegged down a branch or two of the desired plant, made a wound in the area coming in contact with the soil, then left it to receive nourishment from the parent while at the same time making roots of its own.

It is a safe propagation method even if at times somewhat slow. It is not unusual for some shrub branches to take two years making sufficient roots to support the young plants: only with strawberries and garden pinks and border carnations is the method expeditious.

Shrubs can be layered in spring, summer or autumn, but preferably in spring when the sap is rising; strawberries and border carnations are layered in summer. Strawberries throw out long runners with several plantlets attached to each, but only those closest to the parent plant should be selected and then only three or four per plant. They can be pegged down directly into the soil or into small compost-filled pots sunk into the ground nearby.

Layering strawberries

With pinks and border carnations select an outer sturdy shoot of the current season's growth and remove the basal leaves. Using a sharp knife, make a cut halfway through each stem just below a joint; continue the cut along the centre of the stem for about $\frac{1}{2}$ in. (12 mm) to form a tongue. Peg the layer, holding the tongue open, into gritty soil and secure it with a layering pin, a piece of bent wire or a hairpin. The layers should root in four to six weeks and can then be separated from the parent and planted elsewhere in the garden.

The same principles apply to shrubs. Choose a young pliable branch as near the ground as possible and restrict the sap flow to the area to be buried by one of the following methods:

1 Cut a tongue in the stem, as with border carnations.
2 Remove a thin ring of bark or twist a piece of wire tightly round the stem.
3 Twist the branch in different directions so that the outer bark is ruptured. This is only possible with young and slender branches.

Obstinate shrubs may be encouraged to root by painting the wounds with a growth-promoting substance.

Air layering This is a specialized form of layering, variously referred to as air layering, marcottage or Chinese layering. It is useful with choice shrubs and trees difficult to propagate by other methods.

Choose a healthy young shoot and at a convenient place below the top growth girdle the stem with a sharp knife, removing about ½ in. (12 mm) of bark. Dust the wound with a growth-promoting substance, then pack damp sphagnum moss round it. Slip a tube of polythene film over the shoot and fasten it tightly with sticky tape below the cut and again at the top so that no opening is left and the bundle resembles a plump sausage. The film keeps the stem with its moss plaster moist, and in due course roots appear. At this stage the shoot can be severed and the layer carefully potted up.

Cuttings These can produce many young plants, all exactly like their parents, reasonably quickly. Various parts of a plant are used – leaves, shoots, stems or roots.

Soft cuttings The name given to soft young shoots of the current season's growth, with the lower leaves removed and severed immediately below a node or joint. The cuttings are inserted in a rooting medium, such as sharp sand, vermiculite, a mixture of sand (two parts) and peat (one part), in Jiffy 7s or in a proprietary rooting compost. Until rooting takes place the cuttings must be kept in a close atmosphere. This involves the use of a propagating case, a mist propagation unit (see p. 161) or a frame or greenhouse.

Bottom heat accelerates rooting, as does a hormone-rooting powder applied to the cut ends of the cuttings before they are inserted in the rooting medium. Except in a north-facing position or under a mist propagator, the cuttings must be shielded from bright sunshine while rooting takes place.

Many herbaceous perennials, house plants and alpines can be propagated from soft cuttings, as well as chrysanthemums, dahlias, shrubs and climbers.

Spring and early summer are favourite periods for the method and most cuttings are made at a length of 2-4 in. (5-10 cm).

Hardwood cuttings Hardwood cuttings are made from mature woody stems of shrubs, trees and fruit bushes. Young stems of the current season's growth are used (although tamarisk will root from pieces two to three years old). This form of propagation takes place in autumn.

Select straight sturdy shoots and remove the unripe tips to just above a joint. Cut the bases across just below another joint – the ultimate length of the cutting will be 4-10 in. (10-25 cm) long, according to the nature of the plant. Willows and poplars may be even longer, up to several feet (60 cm or more).

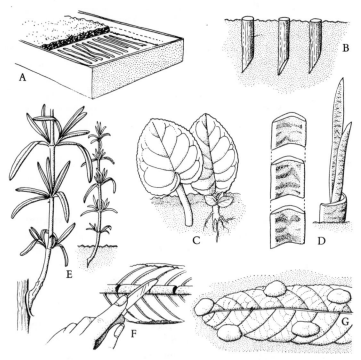

Different kinds of cuttings: (A) slender root cuttings; (B) root cuttings; (C) African violet leaf cuttings; (D) Sansevieria (mother-in-law's tongue) leaf cuttings; (E) rosemary heel cuttings; (F) cutting across veins; (G) pegging or weighting leaves on compost

Insert the cuttings vertically, to two-thirds of their length, in a trench, either in a sheltered spot outside or in a cold frame.

Heel cuttings Some cuttings root better if they have a piece of older wood attached, and this is the usual method for conifers, lavender, santolina and rosemary. Young side pieces are pulled from a mature stem with a sliver of the old stem attached. After trimming off the whisker of bark that comes away with the shoot, the cuttings are inserted in light soil in a cold frame or under cloches to root. Such cuttings, which are usually known as half-ripe or heel cuttings, are made in summer, usually July and August.

Root cuttings Certain plants root readily from root cuttings, a trait many gardeners associate with such pernicious weeds as couch grass, bindweed (*Convolvulus arvensis*) and ground elder, whose every segment makes another plant after being cut.

Among a number of plants which may be propagated by root cuttings are oriental poppies (*Papaver orientale*), anchusa, acanthus, echinops, bouvardias, Japanese anemones, eryngiums, rhus, tree poppies (*Romneya* sp.) and *Primula denticulata* as well as blackberries and loganberries. Herbaceous phlox and such rock garden plants as erodium, mertensia, pulsatilla and campanulas can be increased by root cuttings and the method is commonly used for propagating seakale and horseradish.

Root cuttings are usually made in winter, not from necessity but for convenience since the gardener probably has more time at that season. The whole plant is usually lifted, although pieces of root may be carefully taken from adult trees.

Long thick roots are cut up into 2-5-in. (5-12.5-cm) lengths, known as thongs. Because it is important that they are planted the right way up the cut made across the base of each cutting is at a slanting angle, to facilitate recognition. They are then inserted in an upright position in pots or deep boxes of gritty compost and left in a cold frame or greenhouse to root.

Slender root cuttings from plants like phlox and *Primula denticulata* are too delicate to be inserted in this manner. They are cut into 2-in. (5-cm) lengths and 'sown' (or laid) in boxes of sandy soil, then covered with $\frac{1}{2}$ in. (12 mm) of the same medium. Most root cuttings will produce shoots early in the spring.

Curiously, not all root cuttings produce perfect replicas of their parents. Variegated pelargoniums, for example, lose their variegation. Root cuttings from a juvenile acanthus differ markedly from those taken from an old plant, the offspring in each case producing the type of foliage and degree of maturity of their parents.

Leaf cuttings Certain plants produce adventitious buds on their leaves, which, when conditions are right, can develop to further plants. Sometimes this occurs naturally as with the blue-flowered water-lily *Nymphaea micrantha* which, at the end of the season, develops baby plants at the points where the leaf stalks join the blades. In shallow water these soon root down into the mud, the leaves rot and the young plants set up a separate existence.

The North American pick-a-back plant, *Tolmiea menziesii,* performs in a similar manner. Sometimes grown in a sheltered but shady border but more frequently as a pot plant, it has rough ivy-shaped leaves, each of them carrying a young plant in late summer. When detached, these root readily in sandy soil. Other examples of leaf reproduction which occur naturally can be found in some bryophyllums and the fern *Asplenium bulbiferum* which produces small plantlets at the frond margins.

The leaf stalks of African violets (saintpaulias), inserted like cuttings in peaty compost, will produce young plants in the leaf axils. Haberleas, ramondas and echeverias also root by this method. The leaves of *Begonia rex* and its cultivars, streptocarpus and lachenalias will root if the principal veins on the backs of the leaves are cut across and the leaves pinned down (cut side downwards) on a box of compost. Given bottom heat to stimulate rooting, new plants will form at the cuts. The same plants, as well as sansevierias, gesnerias and gloxinias, will also root from strips of leaves inserted vertically in compost.

Sometimes a leaf with a piece of half-ripe stem attached is removed and rooted with bottom heat. They are known as leaf-bud cuttings, and the method is commercially practised with ficus and camellias.

OTHER PROPAGATION METHODS

New plants can also be obtained by inserting a piece of the desired variety on to the rootstock of another, sometimes a more robust or sometimes a dwarfing plant. According to whether a bud or a shoot is inserted the process is variously known as budding and grafting.

Both grafting and budding are much used commercially in order to increase varieties of apples, pears, plums, cherries and peaches, as well as roses, lilacs, coloured hawthorns and walnuts. Sometimes the variety (called the scion) belongs to a different genus from the stock or root plant, but essentially there is a botanical relationship between the two. Thus coloured hawthorns may be grafted on to quickthorn, lilacs on to privet, *Clianthus formosus* on *Colutea arborescens* and pears on quince (*Cydonia oblonga*).

Grafting and budding is carried out a) to control the ultimate size of the resultant tree; b) because the variety is difficult or fails to grow on its own roots; and c) to hasten the production of flowers and fruit. Disadvantages of the methods are a tendency to suckering from the rootstocks, particularly noticeable in roses, lilacs and plums, and occasionally brittleness at the joins so that the tree or branch snaps in strong gales.

MIST PROPAGATION

For several decades mist propagation systems have been standard equipment in thousands of nurseries and parks departments. Private gardeners have been slow to adopt mist although it has proved to be a great aid in propagation by cuttings – and in many cases by seed.

In the past cuttings were rooted under belljars, which were the original cloches, *cloche* being French for bell, but these are now collector's pieces. Their place has to some extent been taken by glass or plastic cloches in a wide choice of shapes and sizes.

Alternatively, cuttings can be rooted in a cold frame heated by an electrical soil-warming cable, covered with sand or a sand/peat mixture. The cable, which is controlled by a rod-type thermostat inserted in the sand bed, keeps the temperature at around 13-16°C (55-60°F). Cuttings of many plants – shrubs, climbers and perennials – can be rooted in a soil-warmed frame.

There are also various types of electrically-heated propagating cases which can be used on a sunny window-sill or on a greenhouse bench. They have their drawbacks because they must be shaded from strong sun during the day with newspaper or other material. Propagation cases and frames must also be ventilated and watered as required.

With a mist propagation bench all chores are eliminated, yet consistently good results are obtained. The cuttings are simply inserted into the rooting medium on the bench, the mist is switched on, and the cuttings root.

When a cutting is inserted in a pot or box of sand or compost, it becomes a slowly dying piece of vegetation; it is transpiring moisture from its leaves faster than it can be replaced from the base since there are no roots. That is why we shade it, to lessen the rate of transpiration, although depriving it of light hastens its demise. On a mist bench, where the leaf surfaces are constantly covered with a thin layer of moisture, transpiration or water loss is almost eliminated; the cuttings can be kept in full sunlight, they do not wilt and are therefore healthy vigorous pieces of vegetation which normally root quickly. By other methods, it is a race between wilting and dying or rooting.

In a mist unit, most cuttings root much more quickly than they would by any other method and it is also possible to root plants which are notoriously difficult. The great point about a mist unit is that it is entirely automatic. Once the cuttings are inserted in the bed or bench, or in pots or trays, you can forget them until they are ready for potting.

Setting up a mist unit A greenhouse, with electricity and water, is essential. A rooting temperature of 21-24°C (70-75°F) must be maintained and this is achieved with an electrical mains voltage soil-warming cable. The base of the bench must be strong enough to support a considerable weight of sand and water. I use corrugated asbestos sheets laid over several lengths of old water piping, or something similar placed lengthwise to reinforce the sheets. Drill two or three holes per square foot (30 square cm) in the sheets to give adequate drainage. The bench should be surrounded by wooden boards 8 in (20 cm) high. Over the base spread a 2-in. (5-cm) layer of small pebbles or coarse gravel; or Hortag, the proprietary horticultural material made from fired clay, is very popular for covering greenhouse benches because green algae does not grow on it. Never use boiler ash or clinkers near soil-warming cables as they have a corrosive effect.

On top of the drainage layer spread a 2-in. (5-cm) layer of sharp washed sand or grit – not builder's yellow sand – and on this lay the soil-warming cable. On top of this place a 2-in. (5-cm) layer of rooting medium, which may consist of pure *coarse* sand, or a mixture of 80 per cent coarse washed sand and 20 per cent fine peat. By trial and error you will find the rooting mixture most suitable for different types of plants. Sand or grit *must* be really coarse, up to what is known in the trade as $\frac{1}{4}$-in. (6-mm) crushed grit. If you wish to root cuttings in pots or seed trays, omit the layer of rooting medium, but be sure to pack peat around and between pots and boxes to conserve bottom heat.

Provided the root temperature of 21-24°C (70-75°F) is maintained, the air temperature in the greenhouse may be allowed to fall as low as 1.5-4°C (35-40°F).

The simplest and most efficient mist propagation kit for an amateur's greenhouse consists of two mist jets, a filter, a solenoid valve which turns the water on and off, and a solar controller which activates the solenoid valve.

The solar controller obviously turns on the mist more frequently in bright sunny spells than when the sky is overcast. It may produce short four-second bursts of spray every few minutes during sunny spells, or much more infrequently in dull periods and not at all at night.

One rather extraordinary thing about mist propagation is that while we may think that with efficient mist controllers the leaf surfaces of cuttings never dry out, this is apparently not so. There can be short periods when they are dry. Some growers switch off the mist a day or two after the cuttings have been inserted, allow the leaves to dry, then spray them with a water-borne anti-desiccant such as is sprayed over Christmas trees and other greenery to prevent needle drop or leaf shrivelling. This is allowed to dry on the leaves and, after an hour or so, the mist is switched on again. The use of an anti-desiccant combined with mist hastens rooting and increases the success rate considerably.

As regards costs, a mist unit, complete with plastic piping, retails at the present time (1982) around £130, the soil-warming cable being an extra. This unit, with two nozzles, would cover a bench area around 6 by 3½ ft (1.8 x 1m) and should be capable of producing many hundred rooted cuttings every year. Given the cost of shrubs, pot, bedding and herbaceous plants, a mist unit can pay for itself handsomely in a year or two. For me, though, its greatest merit is that once the cuttings are inserted and the mist turned on, we can forget about them.

Hormone-rooting compounds There are various hormone-type rooting compounds on the market which hasten rooting. The moistened base of the cutting is dipped in this powder before it is inserted in the rooting medium. Some rooting compounds contain a fungicide, such as captan, which helps to prevent rotting. I do not use rooting compounds for all cuttings; for example, they are not necessary for dahlias, chrysanthemums, geraniums or fuchsias, although they do accelerate the rooting of semi-hardwood shrub cuttings.

 # AUGUST

The Month in the Garden

When I was a child I thought August the most wonderful month of the year, associating it, I suppose, with holidays, the harvesting of corn and various fruits, and long, hot summer days. Nowadays I am not so sure that it is an ideal month for the gardener. There are weeds everywhere, but the ground can be hard and dry, making watering imperative, and much of the early colour will have disappeared.

General Tasks To maintain a tidy appearance and continuity of flowering with plants like sweet peas, roses, violas and pansies (except the F_1 hybrids which are usually sterile), calendulas and nasturtiums, it is essential to stop them from setting seed. A few minutes spent removing dead blooms pays dividends, and if petunias and white alyssums have become tired-looking and lanky, cut them back by two-thirds to encourage new growth and further flowers. I do this with petunias twice in a good growing year, feeding the plants afterwards and invariably obtain worthwhile results.

Apart from annuals and tender bedding plants like pelargoniums (geraniums), heliotropes, gazanias and fuchsias – all of which should be at their brightest and best this month –

one of the most reliable stand-bys for mixed and perennial flower borders is the herbaceous phlox. New varieties are brilliantly coloured with heavy flower trusses of pink, red, purple and white, often with contrasting eyes or centres. They are, however, one of the first plants to show the effects of drought: leaves flag, and growth is stunted so that only poor heads of bloom are produced. Dryness at the roots, which are very near the surface, also encourages mildew.

Apart from watering when necessary (we find that our well-drained soil needs the equivalent of 1 in. (2.5 cm) of rain ($4\frac{1}{2}$ gallons per square yard or 20 litres per square metre) every week or ten days in August, either naturally from rain or by watering with a hose), it is a good plan to keep the ground cool and damp with a compost mulch. For more information on mulching and watering, see May, p. 119 and April, p. 95.

see May, p. 119 and April, p. 95.

WEATHER

'August ripens, September gathers in; August bears the burden, September the fruit' is a saying from Portugal, but is equally true in the British Isles.

Although August weather often follows the pattern set by July, there is always the hope that a dry spell of warm sunshine will set in. In Germany they pin their faith on 10 August:

'If on St Lawrence's Day, the weather be fine, A fair autumn and good wine may be hoped for', but on the other hand 'Thunderstorms at the beginning of August, will generally be followed by showers throughout the month.'

August is a wise time to launch a major onslaught on garden weeds to prevent the threat of 'one year's seeding, seven years' weeding'. The rule informing is: 'Cut thistles in June, they'll come again soon; Cut in July, then they may die; Cut them in August, die they must.'

With the nights rapidly growing longer, surface cooling in calm clear conditions can lead to heavy dewfalls, for example on 24 August: 'St Bartholomew, comes the cold dew', although the same is said of St Matthew on 21 September.

24 August may also give some useful indication of subsequent weather: 'As St Bartholomew's Day, so the whole autumn', and a cold misty start to this day is said to presage a hard winter.

Propagation August is a good time for propagating bedding plants of all kinds by cuttings. At this season, while there is still plenty of sunshine and natural warmth, cuttings root readily in a cold frame, greenhouse or under cloches. Bedding plants – geraniums, calceolarias, penstemons and heliotropes – should show plenty of sturdy young shoots in August. Gardeners frequently delay taking cuttings until frosty nights are imminent; then they fail to root properly, or rot off during the winter months. The earlier cuttings are taken, the sooner they will root, and the best cuttings come from non-flowering shoots. This is vital with calceolarias as they will not root from flowering stems.

Geranium Cuttings For these I use fat sturdy stems with three or four joints. The lower leaves are removed, together with any buds or flowers, and a straight cut is made with a razor blade or sharp knife immediately below the bottom joint. Opinions differ as to whether the cuttings should be inserted immediately or left on a shady bench for a couple of hours for the wound to dry. Some say drying assists callusing at the cut, others that partial drying can cause cracks in the callus, allowing disease spores easy entry. I have used both methods and found little difference in the final analysis. It is advantageous to root geraniums in small pots of light, friable compost (because they are intolerant of heavy, badly drained soil) where they can remain throughout the winter.

Root Cuttings Although plants propagated from root cuttings are usually dealt with in winter, I find herbaceous phloxes give better results when root cuttings are taken in summer (see also July, *New Plants from Old,* p. 154). The plant is lifted, the roots washed and cut into 1½-in. (3-cm) pieces. It is important to keep them the same way up, so that the tops can be recognized when it comes to planting. Gather the cuttings together in small bundles of ten or a dozen, tie them loosely together with wool and plant the bundles (right way up) in 5-in. (12.5-cm) pots of sandy soil. Stand the pots in a cold frame, shaded from sun, and keep them watered. Directly signs of growth appear, lift the bundles carefully, separate and pot up each cutting – if this operation is delayed too long the roots become hopelessly entangled.

Budding is another propagation method which can be carried out this month and until early September. It is the recognized way of increasing many rose varieties, ornamental cherries, peaches and almonds.

Trees and Shrubs Continue taking cuttings of hydrangeas, cistus, escallonia and choisya and half-ripe (heel) cuttings of ceanothus, cytisus, lavender, rosemary, syringa, *Skimmia japonica,* olearias, fuchsias, jasmines, hebes, buddleias, caryopteris, pernettya, *Laurus nobilis* (bay), ivies and hollies. Root the cuttings in a cold frame or cool greenhouse.

Most early summer-flowering shrubs will have finished flowering now and can have old and weak stems thinned out and the remaining growths shortened. They include ceanothus, *Buddleia alternifolia,* escallonia, lavender and senecio.

Rhododendrons and azaleas can be layered now. Pack plenty of moist peat round the wounded areas (see July, *New Plants from Old,* p. 154) to encourage rooting, but leave the shoot itself exposed.

Ericas and other heathers with short side shoots bearing new season's growth at their tips can now be rooted. Insert them in pans or pots of two

parts sand and one part finely sifted peat. Larger cuttings will root under a mist propagator (see July, p. 161).

Climbers Mulch, feed and water sweet peas. Pick the flowers regularly.

Prune wisterias to prevent them from damaging tiles, roofs and gutters. Remove tips of young shoots to within three leaves of the base to control excessive growth and stimulate flower buds.

Roses Remove suckers and deadhead as necessary.

Cease applying fertilizers.

Bud new roses.

Lawns Keep the grass cut and edges trimmed. Continue to apply selective weedkillers except in dry weather.

Hardy Plants Propagate phlox from root cuttings (see p. 165).

Cut back old and untidy flowering stems from delphiniums, poppies and others; remove supports.

Look for weak spots and gaps in herbaceous borders and plan new groupings.

Bulbs Daffodils which were lifted and stored earlier can be replanted towards the latter half of the month. New bulbs should be ordered for containers, for beds and for forcing.

Dividing daffodil bulbs before replanting

Lilium candidum bulbs can be planted now. Cover them with only 1-2 in. (2.5-5 cm) of soil. On heavy soil pack a little sand round the bulbs.

Save a few ripening pods on *Lilium regale*. The seeds can be sown later to produce flowers in about three years.

Annuals, Biennials and Bedding Plants Cut back violas and pansies to encourage basal shoots for cuttings.

Watch for earwigs attacking dahlias and chrysanthemums. They may be trapped in small pots or half-open matchboxes, stuffed with hay and inverted on canes and stakes. The earwigs dislike light and crawl into these during the day. Remove and destroy them daily.

Disbud chrysanthemums by removing side shoots for large flowers, completing this on outdoor varieties by the third week in August.

Remove dead flower heads from annuals in beds, containers and hanging baskets.

Rock Garden Plants Take cuttings of helianthemums, dianthus, saxifrages, alyssum, saponaria and others which are producing new shoots after being cut back earlier. They can be rooted under mist in a greenhouse, in a shaded frame or under cloches in sandy soil. Spread 1 in. (2.5 cm) of sharp sand on top of the soil before inserting the cuttings.

Water Plants Cut down old flowering stems of rushes, alismas, typhas and the like, to prevent seeding.

Keep pools full of water.

Watch for blackfly on lilies and take appropriate measures (see July, *Water Plants*, p. 148).

Patio Plants Replace tired container plants; remove dead flowers and water regularly in order to maintain an attractive display.

Before going on holiday, arrange with a neighbour to water all pots and containers; or move them into shade.

Vegetables Harvest runner beans regularly or the crop will cease.

Gather sweet corn when the seeds exude a milky juice if pressed with the thumbnail.

Remove side shoots from outdoor tomato plants; stop them when four to five trusses have set.

Bend down tops of onions to ripen them. Dig them up when dry.

Harvest second early potatoes and garlic.

Sow onions, salad onions, corn salad and winter spinach for overwintering.

Herbs Sow angelica.

Continue harvesting herbs for drying.

Fruit Plant new strawberry bed.

Protect ripening fruit from birds and wasps.

Remove and burn apples, pears or plums with brown rot infection.

Plants under Glass Clean and paint greenhouses ready for the winter.

Continue potting and starting cyclamen corms.

Rest hippeastrums by laying the pots on their sides and withholding water until spring.

Take cuttings of fuchsias, crassula, coleus, begonias and tradescantias.

Sow schizanthus, cinerarias, stocks and cyclamen in a cool house for spring displays.

Pot up lachenalias, freesias and bulbs for Christmas flowering.

Pot on calceolarias sown earlier; keep them cool.

House Plants Feed and water as necessary.

During holiday absences put hardier plants outside (see June and July, *House Plants*, pp. 129 and 149) and stand the rest in the sink with a bucket of water oh the draining board. Take short lengths of thick knitting wool, putting one end in each plant pot and the other in the water. Large pots may require more than one wick. Water will be syphoned by capillary action along the wool and down to the plants. Alternatively, place each pot in a plastic bag with a tablespoonful of water in the base. Blow in the bag to keep it expanded and seal the top with a rubber band or clothes peg.

PLANTS IN THEIR PRIME

Shrubs in flower in August: (A) *Potentilla fruiticosa;* (B) *Hibiscus syriacus;* (C) *Hypericum patulum,*St John's wort

Trees and Shrubs Abelias; *Abutilon vitifolium; Aesculus parviflora; Buddleia variabilis* varieties;

Bupleurum fruticosum; callunas; *Calycanthus floridus; Ceanothus caeruleus* hybrids; clerodendrons; *Clethra alnifolia; Colutea arborescens; Desfontainea spinosa;* ericas; escallonias; eucryphias; hardy fuchsias; *Hibiscus syriacus;* hypericums; indigoferas; *Koelreuteria paniculata;* lavenders; *Magnolia grandiflora;* olearias; *Potentilla fruticosa* and varieties; roses; *Spartium junceum;* spiraeas; *Tamarix gallica, T. pentandra;* yuccas.

Climbers Clematis (many including C. x *jackmanii,* C. *orientalis,* and C. *tangutica*); *Jasminum officinale; Lathyrus latifolius* (everlasting pea); loniceras (honeysuckles); *Polygonum (Fallopia) baldschuanicum* (Russian vine); roses; *Solanum crispum, S. jasminoides;* tecomas; *Tropaeolum speciosum.*

Hardy Plants Acanthus; achilleas; aconitums; adenophoras; *Althaea rosea* (hollyhocks); alstroemerias; *Anaphalis margaritacea; Anemone japonica* hybrids; anthemis; *Artemisia lactiflora; Asclepias incarnata, A. tuberosa; Aster amellus* varieties; *Astilbe* x *arendsii* hybrids; *Boltonia asteroides;* campanulas; catananches; *Centaurea montana* and varieties; chelones; *Chrysanthemum maximum* and varieties, also early-flowering kinds; cimicifugas; clematis (herbaceous types); *Coreopsis grandiflora* and varieties, C. *verticillata;* dianthus (border carnations and pinks); *Dierama pulcherrimum;* dracocephalums; *Echinacea purpurea;* echinops; *Erigeron speciosus* and varieties; eryngiums; filipendulas; *Galega officinalis; Gentiana asclepiadea;* geums; gypsophilas; heleniums; helianthus (sunflowers); heliopsis;

hemerocallis (day-lilies); heucheras; hostas; inulas; kniphofias; *Lavatera olbia*; *Liatris pycnostachya*, *L. spicata*; *Linum narbonense*, *L. perenne*; *Lobelia cardinalis*, *L. fulgens* and varieties, *L. siphilitica*; *Lychnis chalcedonica*, *L. coronaria*; *Lysimachia thyrsiflora*; *Lythrum virgatum* varieties; *Malva alcea* hybrids; *Monarda didyma* varieties; nepetas; oenotheras; *Papaver nudicaule* varieties (Iceland poppies); *Penstemon barbatus*; *Phlox paniculata* hybrids; *Phygelius capensis*; *Physostegia virginiana*; platycodons; polygonums; potentillas; *Romneya coulteri*, *R. trichocalyx*; *Rudbeckia laciniata* and varieties, various other rudbeckias; *Salvia nemorosa*, *S. sclarea*, *S. uliginosa*; *Saponaria officinalis* 'Plena' (soapwort); *Scabiosa caucasica* and varieties; sidalceas; solidagos (golden rod); stokesias; *Thalictrum dipterocarpum* and varieties; *Tradescantia virginiana*; verbenas; veronicas.

Bulbs *Acidanthera bicolor* 'Murielae'; *Allium beesianum*; crinums; crocosmias; *Cyclamen europaeum*; *Galtonia candicans*, summer hyacinth; gladioli; lilies; tigridias.

Annuals, Biennials and Bedding Plants Ageratums; antirrhinums; asters (callistephus); begonias, tuberous and *B. semperflorens*; calceolarias; Canterbury bells; chrysanthemums; dahlias; fuchsias; geraniums (pelargoniums); impatiens; lobelias; marguerites; marigolds (African and French tagetes); nemesias; nicotianas; *Phlox drummondii*; petunias; salpiglossis; salvias; stocks; verbena.

Rock Garden Plants *Achillea argentea*, *A. tomentosa* and varieties;

campanulas; *Ceratostigma plumbaginoides*; *Convolvulus althaeoides*, *C. cneorum*; *Corydalis lutea*; gentians; geranium species and varieties; *Geum montanum*; *Gypsophila repens* and varieties; linums; lithospermums; oenotheras; *Onosma albo-rosea*; *Penstemon heterophyllus*; *Polygonum affine*, *P. vaccinifolium*; potentillas; *Rhodohypoxis baurei*; *Rosa chinensis* 'Minima' (*R. roulettii*) and other dwarf roses; sedums; *Verbena peruviana* (*V. chamaedryfolia*); violas; *Zauschneria californica*, *Z. cana*.

Water Plants *Alisma plantago*; *Aponogeton distachyus*; eriophorum (cotton grass); mimulus; nymphaeas (water-lilies); *Orontium aquaticum* (golden club); sagittarias (arrowheads); typhas (reed mace).

CROPS TO ENJOY

Vegetables Globe artichokes; broad beans; French beans; runner beans; beetroot (round); cabbage (spring-sown); carrots; cauliflower; cucumbers; kohl-rabi; lettuce; marrows; onions; peas; potatoes; radishes; spinach; sweet corn; tomatoes; turnips.

Fruit Apples; apricots; blackberries; cherries; late currants; figs; gooseberries; grapes; melons; nectarines; mulberries; peaches; pears; plums; raspberries.

PLANT ASSOCIATIONS

Any shrub, tree or herbaceous perennial with purple foliage, such as *Sedum maximum* 'Atropurpureum', *Corylus maxima* 'Purpurea', *Prunus persica* 'Foliis Rubis', *Cotinus coggygria* 'Rubrifolius' or *Phormium tenax* 'Purpureum', with blue-flowered agapanthus or *Lilium auratum*.

Blue hydrangeas and dwarf pink roses or pink lavateras.

Fuchsias with low-growing, silver-leaved plants like *Senecio bicolor* (*S. cineraria*), *Stachys olympica* 'Silver Carpet' (non-flowering and very compact) or *Centaurea gymnocarpa*.

Blue and pink cup-and-saucer Canterbury bells with stocks.

GARDEN PROBLEMS

Pests and diseases, particularly aphids; thrip damage, brown rot on fruits, earwigs on dahlias.

Virus on dahlias shown by mottled foliage, dwarfing and general discoloration.

Storm damage; stake early.

Plants of the Month

CISTUS

Cistus are small evergreen shrubs native to the Mediterranean region, where the white, pink or purplish-red flowers, which bear some resemblance to wild roses, are much visited by pollen-gathering insects. Commonly called sun roses, they are closely related to helianthemums, the rock roses of gardens.

In Britain, cistus need frequent renewal, for although young plants normally survive, older specimens can be killed off in a bad winter. However, since cuttings root readily this is not too difficult. Although the flowers open very early in the day, they only last a few hours before shedding their petals, littering the ground like confetti. The following day hundreds of new flowers appear, and this goes on for five or six weeks. We once planted a hedge of the gum cistus, *C. ladanifer,* either side of an entrance drive, where the scent from the fragrant leaves and the large purple-blotched, white flowers spreading their petals like miniature handkerchiefs were a joy each summer.

Cistus ladanifer and the pink *C. creticus* (*C. villosus* var. *creticus*) both have sticky leaves, due to a secretion of aromatic gum or resin. This is known as ladanum or labdanum and after distillation is used in perfumes (particularly as a substitute for ambergris since its scent is similar), soaps and many cosmetics. Apparently the gathering and selling of labdanum is a trade of great antiquity, and Herodotus, Pliny and Dioscorides all describe methods of collection. Sometimes the leaves were gently brushed with a comb-like instrument, which had strips of untanned leather instead of teeth. This was

Cistus ladanifer

later scraped off with knives, but the great natural collectors were goats, who picked up a lot of labdanum on their beards while browsing on and between the shrubs. This could be combed off or, according to Dioscorides, the beards were severed. The eminent Egyptologist, Percy Newberry, suggests that these beards were used by some Pharaohs on certain occasions as attachments worn beneath their chins – the original goatees? Certainly they are plainly visible on effigies of the god Osiris and such kings as the young Tutankhamun. If these were indeed goat beards the traffic in labdanum must, according to Alice Coats in *Garden Shrubs and their Histories,* date back to the First Dynasty – to 3188 BC.

PINKS AND CARNATIONS

Pinks and carnations are loved by most people, but how many know that the colour pink derives from the flower – and not the other way round? The predominant parent of garden pinks was probably *Dianthus plumarius,* a native of the calcareous mountains of southern Europe, with sweetly-scented, single white or deep pink flowers, often with a darker central blotch. The deeply cut petals are said to have suggested to botanists the 'pinks' or ornamental openings made by pinking shears or scissors in Elizabethan clothing. The outer garment was slashed to reveal another colour underneath which was often pale red, rose, light red, blush or flesh-coloured, but never pink. Pink as a colour did not appear until 1720.

Carnation

Between 1828 and 1850 pinks were widely cultivated by the muslin weavers of Paisley in Renfrewshire. They raised over three hundred varieties, but perhaps the best known pink is the large, floppy-petalled, fragrant white called 'Mrs Sinkins'. This was bred and named for her by her husband, the

Master of Slough Poor Law Institution. In 1938 when Slough became a borough, this pink was incorporated in its coat of arms.

Border carnations are derived from *Dianthus caryophyllus,* described by Theophrastus before 300 B C. They were introduced to Britain in the fifteenth century and widely grown in the sixteenth century, under the name gillyflower. A favourite variety at that time and one still grown today – although Montague Allwood said that the original stock was lost many years ago and another substituted – was the richly fragrant 'Old Clove' carnation which originally came from Holland. The similarity of its scent to that of the unopened buds of *Caryophyllus aromaticus* (now *Syzygium*), the cloves of commerce, gave the plant both its English and Latin names. At one time the custom of throwing carnation petals into flagons of wine or beer for flavouring caused it to be known as 'sops in wine'.

Montague Allwood said that the showing of florists' flowers, and carnations in particular, was highly popular in the eighteenth century. Prizes were lavish by today's standards, including silver cups and spoons, sets of china, punch ladles and copper kettles, so competition was keen. A barber called Kit Nunn, in my home town of Enfield, was adept at preparing carnations for the show bench, excelling 'in ability to dress artificially or change the appearance of the flowers'. Without his help no one in Enfield could hope to succeed in winning the major prizes.

William Cobbett went still further. 'For my part', he wrote, 'as a thing to keep and not to sell; as a thing, the *possession* of which is to give me pleasure, I hesitate not a moment to prefer the plant of a fine carnation, to a gold watch set with diamonds.'

Young Plants in Old Bottles

When I was a child, my father told me that if I pushed an empty bottle, neck downwards, into the soil in a moist, shady spot, a fern would grow inside. I tried it, but the weeks went by and nothing happened. Two years later, coming across the bottle by chance, I prised it out of the ground and there, sure enough, were several baby ferns.

My father knew of Nathaniel Ward's experiments a century and a half earlier. Ward, a London physician and naturalist, found that his specimens – particularly ferns and mosses – quickly died in the smog of the city, and so he constructed a closed glass case. Inside its clean moist atmosphere his plants thrived; the idea caught on and soon 'Wardian Cases', often built on to north-facing windows, became highly fashionable.

The present generation is content with smaller containers, and attractive little gardens can be built inside carboys, goldfish bowls and aquaria, sweet jars and even champagne jeroboams.

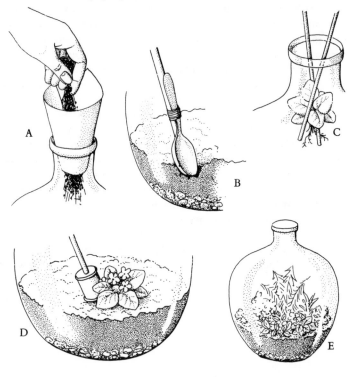

Planting a bottle garden: (A) introducing the soil compost; (B) digging a hole for a plant; (C) dropping the plants carefully; (D) firming the soil with a cotton reel on a cane; (E) the finished garden

The beauty of closed container gardens is that when they are properly constructed and lighted they need little attention. My hall carboy has been sealed for nearly three years and is never tended or watered. A lamp head in the stopper augments natural light when required, enabling the plants to grow and maintain greenness.

In the early mornings and evenings (when the temperature changes) there is a slight mistiness, but this soon clears. Bottle plants are self-supporting; moisture given off by the leaves condenses on the glass and drops down again to the plant roots. Carbon dioxide, used during daylight to make food, results in enough oxygen being returned to the atmosphere for normal respiration. A perfect cycle!

Bottle-gardening is not difficult, but all the ingredients have to be right. I use a compost containing a good deal of peat – generally three parts of peat to one each of coarse sand and sifted loam. A proprietary loamless compost obtainable from garden centres also gives good results.

A carboy, with its very narrow neck, is the most difficult to plant. For this you will need planting tools; I use a dessert fork, a dessert spoon and an empty cotton reel, each lashed to the end of a cane. They *must* be securely fixed, for if they slip off inside the bottle they cannot be recovered without emptying everything out.

Start with a clean dry container and pour in enough moist compost (not wet or it will stick to the sides) to reach approximately one-third up the sides. Now use the cotton reel to tamp this down and then drop the plants – which must be small – through the opening. Deal with each one separately and, using the fork and spoon, take out a planting hole and return the soil. The cotton reel can be used for firming if necessary.

Vary the plants and look for different shapes, shades and foliage textures – few flowering plants survive unless the lighting is very good, so it is best to avoid them. If the compost is on the dry side, add a *little* water carefully from a small can, pouring it round the sides, so that it will run down to the soil.

The cork can be left in or out. I prefer the former, but since a new bottle is inclined to mist, you might leave it open for the first few days. If you don't use a cork, some watering will be necessary as time goes on and evaporation takes place. The main troubles of bottle gardens – leaf-drop, yellow foliage and constant misting – are due to over-wet compost, cold, and poor light. A 60-watt light bulb, fixed above the stopper, with a shade throwing the light downwards, takes care of most problems.

As regards the plants, I find most of the peperomias satisfactory; the species have varied leaf shapes and patterns. Small-leaved ivies are attractive for a time, and so are the gold-spotted *Dracaena godseffiana* (*D. surculosa*), small ferns, fittonias, *Ficus pumila* (creeping fig), mosses, pileas, marantas, philodendrons and even a small *Begonia rex*. Avoid anything too rampant, such as tradescantia, or it will soon take over the whole bottle.

Selaginella, with its delicate feathery growth, is perfect for the background. The closed container provides ideal conditions for this plant, since it only thrives in a moist atmosphere. Selaginella is not often offered for sale, but once obtained it will set the seal on a bottle garden.

Plant Disorders

Plant growth can be reduced, deformed or otherwise affected by a variety of factors. Shortages of one or more of the basic plant foods, for instance, can lead to abnormal growth. Then there are physiological disturbances which are more difficult to understand and to correct, and finally there is the constant risk of attack by pests and diseases.

NUTRITIONAL PROBLEMS

These problems can normally be solved quite easily by the application of a general fertilizer containing a fairly even balance of nitrogen, phosphate and potash. Excessive application of a single plant food such as potash should, however, be avoided since this can cause the other plant foods to become unavailable to plants. It must also be appreciated that nitrogen and phosphate supplies in the soil are not readily available to plants growing in highly acid soils, and it is therefore desirable to reduce the soil acidity with lime. High alkalinity has similar effects and should be corrected by incorporating acid peat into the soil or by working in flowers of sulphur.

Trace element deficiencies can seriously affect plant growth. A classic example of this is the yellowing (chlorosis) of the foliage on acid-loving plants such as rhododendrons, azaleas, camellias and magnolias when these are grown in alkaline soil. The condition is due to iron deficiency and can be corrected by the use of a proprietary sequestrene compound. Other minor element deficiencies are best dealt with by applying foliar feeds containing a mixture of trace elements.

PHYSIOLOGICAL DISORDERS

Various rather complex and not fully understood factors can induce dramatic effects on plant growth as is shown by the following examples:

Blindness Pot-grown bulbs, such as narcissi and tulips, sometimes fail to produce flowers if growing conditions are not suitable. Usually waterlogging or excessive dryness is to blame, or perhaps too high temperatures.

Blossom end rot This disease of tomatoes shows as circular brown patches on the skin of the fruit at the blossom end. It is caused by a shortage of water at an early stage in the development of the fruit, and can be prevented by regular and careful watering.

Bud-drop The dropping of flower buds is usually due to unsuitable cultural conditions. Dryness of the soil during flower-bud development, for instance, can cause this disorder in camellias, sweet peas and wisteria. Extreme differences in night and day temperatures can also affect some plants.

Cox spot Tan-coloured, irregularly shaped spots are frequently found on the leaves of Cox's Orange Pippin apple trees. The causes of this disorder are not fully understood, but fortunately it does not seem to have any major effect on cropping.

Fasciation This is a condition where several shoots fuse together to form a flat, strap-shaped organ. Although uncommon, it can occur on a wide range of different plants, including forsythia, cotoneaster, delphinium and some primulas. The abnormality clearly originates from a malfunction of the growing point but the reasons for this growth upset are not understood. Since the condition cannot be corrected, the only remedy is to prune off the malformed shoots.

Greenback This physiological disorder shows up in failure of the stalk end of tomato fruits to ripen. It can be avoided by growing greenback-resistant varieties.

Oedema (dropsy) The first sign of this trouble is the appearance of small swellings on leaves and stems. Later these swellings may burst and turn brown. Oedema can occur on many types of greenhouse plants, but is most common on pelargoniums and succulents. It develops due to a combination of excessively moist soil, high humidity and high temperatures and can be corrected by reducing watering and increasing ventilation.

GENERAL PESTS

Aphids Greenfly and blackfly are major pests of a wide range of greenhouse and garden plants. They feed on the sap, weakening and distorting plant growth. In addition, they produce quantities of sticky honeydew which becomes covered with sooty moulds. Aphids also transmit damaging virus diseases. Some control is given by natural predators, such as ladybirds, lacewings and hover flies, but it is usually necessary to use an insecticide. Chemicals based on pirimicarb are of special interest since they have no ill effects on predators and yet kill the aphids very effectively.

Birds Sparrows can cause serious damage to the flowers of polyanthus, crocus, wisteria and runner beans. Bullfinches, on the other hand, attack the buds of fruit trees, ornamental cherries, forsythias and other flowering shrubs, while wood pigeons can cause havoc among brassicas. Ripening fruits of apple and pear are often pecked by blackbirds.

Spraying buds and ornamental fruits with a bird repellent, such as one based on aluminium ammonium sulphate, is often effective provided that there is alternative food for the birds. It is usually necessary to repeat the spray after three or four weeks. It may also be used to protect crocuses, polyanthuses and primroses.

Bird scarers give some measure of temporary control while black thread strung between branches and over flowers is also reasonably effective. Complete protection can only be obtained by the use of netting or fruit cages.

Capsid bugs These insects feed on young leaves, shoots and flower buds, producing small, brown, callused spots. Later the attacked leaves may become puckered and torn. Affected growing points produce distorted growth and may become 'blind'. The pests can be controlled by repeat applications of a general insecticide.

Caterpillars These readily recognized pests are generally foliage feeders, but some are stem borers and are not noticed until the affected shoot suddenly dies. Most species feed openly on the surface tissues of plants, but some shelter in clusters of leaves which they tie together with silk threads, while others protect themselves with webbing tents.

Exposed caterpillars can be controlled either by hand picking or with a general insecticide. Where the caterpillar is protected within leaves or in a 'tent', only hand picking or pruning off of the affected part is effective.

Cutworms These soil-dwelling caterpillars gnaw the bases of stems, causing plants to collapse. They can be hand picked by searching the surface soil near the affected plants but they are rather difficult to spot because of their drab colour. A better approach is to water on a soil drench of spray-strength general insecticide.

Froghoppers The pests are easily spotted because of the white frothy 'cuckoo spit' which covers the larvae feeding in the leaf axils. Control by hand picking or by applying a forceful spray of general insecticide.

Leafhoppers Small, pale-coloured jumping insects feed on the underside of leaves, causing pale mottling of the upper surface. A special feature of these pests is their moulted skins which remain attached to the leaves, and they are sometimes called ghost flies. Control with general insecticides, provided that the spray is directed towards the underside of the leaves.

Leaf miners The small grubs of this pest tunnel into plant tissue, producing distinctive pale-coloured linear 'mines' in the leaves. Some species, however, cause pale or brownish blisters which can be found on carnations, chrysanthemums and holly. Generally these pests cause little real damage although they disfigure the foliage. The carnation leaf-miner grub, however, may migrate into the stem tissues causing the death of the affected shoot. Some control can be achieved with a general insecticide provided that the treatment is begun in the early stages of attack.

Red spider mites These tiny pests, which are only just visible to the naked eye, feed on the undersides of leaves, causing the foliage to become bronzed or otherwise discoloured. Control by repeat sprays of derris, fenitrothion, formothion or pirimiphos-methyl.

Scale insects Scale insects, unlike other pests, spend most of their lives fixed firmly to the surface of a plant. They are readily recognized because of their shell-like covering. Like all sap-sucking pests, they excrete quantities of sticky honeydew which becomes covered with sooty moulds. They not only weaken the plants but also disfigure the foliage.

Outdoors scale insects attack a wide range of shrubs and trees, and in the greenhouse they feed on both shrubby and herbaceous plants. Scale insects on woody plants can be removed by scraping the bark. Foliar infestations are more difficult to deal with. Some adults can be removed by gentle scraping but it is generally necessary to supplement this treatment with repeat sprays of malathion or pirimiphos-methyl.

Slugs and snails These are common and very damaging pests of herbaceous plants and vegetables. Most types are readily controlled by scattering slug pellets or watering on a soluble slug bait round endangered plants. The small, black-keeled slugs are exceptions to this rule since they spend most of their time under the soil, even though they may sometimes feed on the surface. Keeled slugs feed on plant roots, tunnel into bulbs, corms, tubers and rhizomes and are particularly damaging to maincrop potatoes. Early varieties are less susceptible and these should be preferred where these pests are a common problem.

Thrips These minute insects feed by scraping the surface tissues of plants and sucking up the juice. Damaged leaves develop a characteristic pale or silvering mottling while the feeding areas on petals show up as white flecks. Small blobs of liquid excreted by the insects become covered with a brown mould growth which further disfigures the plants. Thrips, like aphids, also transmit virus diseases. The normal method of control is repeat sprays of a general insecticide. As an added precaution, gladiolus corms and lily bulbs should be sprinkled with an HCH or pirimiphos-methyl dust prior to storage as the pests can overwinter on corms and bulbs.

Weevils These small wingless beetles spend the day in the soil and only ascend the plants at night in order to feed on the foliage. They eat holes in the leaves and cut deep notches in the leaf margins. Some species also gnaw the bark of shoots, often girdling them. Leaf and flower stalks may also be bitten through. The fleshy white grubs live in the soil and can be extremely damaging not only to plant roots, but also to bulbs, corms and rhizomes.

Some protection against the grubs can be obtained by working a soil insecticide into the soil before planting. Attacks by adult weevils on the foliage can be repelled by repeat sprays of a general insecticide or by dusting the surrounding soil with an insecticidal powder.

Whitefly Small white moth-like insects which weaken plants by sucking the sap. They also disfigure the foliage by excreting honeydew which becomes covered with sooty moulds. They are particularly difficult to control because their larval stages, which are also sap feeders, are resistant to most insecticides. Some pyrethrin derivatives are active against this pest, and the latest of these, called permethrin, is particularly effective. So, too, is pirimiphos-methyl. Even so, it is necessary to apply at least three sprays at intervals of four to seven days in order to obtain effective control. Care should be taken to spray thoroughly the underside of the leaves.

GENERAL DISEASES

Grey mould (botrytis) A disease, favoured by damp, humid conditions, which is particularly damaging to flowers, but also attacks foliage and can enter stem wounds, causing internal rot. On foliage the disease first shows as brown areas but it quickly spreads to a general rot. Affected areas may become covered with a grey mould. Indoors and in the greenhouse, the disease can be guarded against by avoiding wetting the foliage and by preventing the build up of high humidity by sensible ventilation. Infected plant parts should be removed and a spray of general fungicide applied. An easier approach in the greenhouse is to use tecnalin-based smokes.

Powdery mildews These diseases show up as a white or greyish powdery fungal covering of stems, leaves and flowers. Fungicides which are effective against powdery mildews include benomyl, bupirimate, carbendazim, dinocap and thiophanate-methyl.

Rusts Various types of rust fungi attack a wide range of garden plants. In most cases the disease first shows as powdery brown or black spore pustules on the lower surface of the leaves. Later, corresponding yellow areas develop on the upper leaf surface.

White rust of chrysanthemums produces different symptoms. The spore pustules are whitish-yellow at first and only later turn brown while light green depressions appear on the upper surface. White rust is a notifiable disease and suspected cases should be reported to the Ministry of Agriculture.

Repeat sprays of maneb, mancozeb, thiram or triforine are normally recommended for the control of rusts. Rust-resistant antirrhinums are available and should be grown in preference to other varieties.

Stem and foot rots This type of disease shows up as a blackening of the base of the stem or as a rotting of the roots. The fungi are soil-borne and favoured by waterlogging of the soil. Unfortunately there is no effective method of curing these diseases, and infected plants should be dug up and destroyed. In the greenhouse, the use of sterile growing compost coupled with sensible watering gives excellent insurance against attack. Outdoors, the best approach is to improve the soil by the addition of large quantities of bulky organic matter.

In addition to the general troubles already described, most areas of the garden are subject to more specialized pest and disease problems:

HERBACEOUS PLANTS

Root aphids These feed on the roots of a wide range of herbaceous plants causing them to make poor growth and to wilt in hot weather. Should such an infestation be suspected, the plant should be dug up and its roots examined for the presence of aphids; some types are particularly easy to spot because they are covered with a powdery white wax. Infested roots should be thoroughly washed, then dipped in spray-strength insecticide before being replanted. If this procedure is not possible the pests can be controlled by applying a heavy soil-drench of spray-strength general insecticide.

WATER PLANTS

Controlling pests in ornamental pools presents special problems because pools usually contain fish which are affected by insecticides, even such non-toxic products as derris.

Aphids The water-lily aphid can infest a range of water plants but is particularly damaging to water-lilies. The best method of controlling this pest is to submerge the leaves for several days to allow the fish to feed on the aphids.

Caddis fly The larvae, sometimes known as caddis worms, build themselves protective tubes of sand, grit and vegetable debris and feed on the underwater parts of plants. Annual cleaning of the pool reduces the risk of a build up of this pest, but the best method of control is to stock the pool with plenty of fish which will feed on the larvae.

Caterpillars The caterpillars of the brown china mark moth can cause serious damage to water-lily leaves. This caterpillar is unusual since it can live under water by constructing a case of two oval leaf pieces tied together. The only way to control this pest is by hand picking them from the leaves.

Water-lily beetle Both the adult and larval forms of this beetle feed on water-lily foliage and flowers, making irregular holes. They can be controlled either by washing them off with a spray of water or by submerging the leaves to allow the fish to feed on the beetles.

GREENHOUSE AND INDOOR PLANTS

Fungus gnats (*Sciarid flies*) The first danger sign is the presence of dark gnats around the plants. They lay eggs in the growing compost which hatch out to small, white, root-feeding grubs. Infested plants make poor growth and show a tendency to wilt. Control with a heavy soil-drench of spray-strength general insecticide, such as HCH, malathion or pirimiphos-methyl.

Mealy bugs These sap-sucking insects can be recognized by their white, powdery, waxy covering. Most mealy bugs feed on the foliage, but some species are root feeders. The latter produce similar symptoms to those given by root aphids, and the method of control is the same. Foliage feeders can be gently wiped off, but this treatment needs to be supplemented with repeat sprays of malathion or pirimiphos-methyl.

TREES AND SHRUBS

Honey fungus (Armillaria mellea) This is by far the most damaging soil-borne disease of woody plants, privet and rhododendrons being particularly susceptible. Normally the first sign of attack is an out-of-season yellowing and die-back of the foliage, but in some cases the first indication of trouble is that the tree or shrub fails to come into leaf in spring. The presence of white fan-like fungal growths under the bark at the base of the stem confirms that honey fungus is the cause. Later, honey-coloured toadstools may appear round the dead trunks. Dead trees and shrubs should be dug up and burnt, together with as much root as possible. The soil should be changed before replanting. Nearby trees and shrubs can be protected from attack by drenching the soil round them with phenolic emulsions.

Cankers These show up in the form of sunken patches on the bark, with areas of rotting wood below. Branches which become completely girdled with cankers are killed. Small branches affected by cankers can be pruned off; on larger branches, the brown, diseased areas should be cut out with a sharp knife down to clean wood, and the wound painted with a proprietary canker paint.

ROSES

Black spot This common and damaging disease shows up as large, circular, dark spots on the leaves, and sometimes on young stems. Later, affected leaves turn yellow and fall prematurely. Control with regular sprays of a general fungicide at intervals of ten to fourteen days. To avoid the build up of chemical resistance by the fungus, the fungicide should be changed at least every season.

Chafer beetle The adult beetles feed on the foliage and also tunnel into flower buds. They can be controlled with a general insecticide.

Leaf-rolling sawfly Infestation by this pest is shown by the presence of leaflets rolled into tight tubes. Chemical control is difficult because the grubs are protected within the rolled-up leaflets. Remove and burn affected leaves and apply a general insecticide as insurance against further attacks.

FRUIT

Apple and pear scab Infected leaves show patches of olive-green fungal growth and dark-coloured scabs develop on the fruits. The disease can be controlled by applying four fungicidal sprays at intervals of about a fortnight, starting when the young green flower buds are first seen; do not spray when the trees are in flower.

Codling moth This is principally a pest of apple trees. Caterpillars of the moth hatch in late June and quickly move on to the fruit where they tunnel into the core. Control with a general insecticide in late June and again in early July. The non-toxic pyrethrin derivative, permethrin, is excellent for this job since it is particularly active against caterpillars and also has long-lasting effects.

Raspberry beetle This pest not only attacks raspberries, but can also infest blackberries and loganberries. The small white, maggot-like grubs feed on the ripening fruit and are often not noticed until the fruit is picked. Control with derris, malathion or permethrin in the late blossoming stage when the first fruit begins to colour.

Silver leaf This disease of plums first shows as a silvering of the foliage on infected branches. Later the branches show progressive die-back, and small bracket-shaped fruiting bodies may develop on the dead wood. Control by cutting back infected branches to about 6 in. (15 cm) below the level of the purple-stained infected wood. Finally, paint the cut surfaces with a canker paint.

VEGETABLES

Clubroot This soil-borne disease of brassicas causes plant roots to thicken and become distorted. Growth is stunted, and diseased plants tend to wilt in warm weather. The disease is favoured by poor drainage and by acid soil. Ground on which brassicas are to be grown should be improved with the addition of bulky organic matter, and acidity lowered with application of lime. Crop rotation, coupled with good weed control, also helps to reduce the incidence of the disease. Such measures should be supplemented by the application of a clubroot fungicide, such as benomyl, calomel or thiophanate-methyl, to the open seed drills, seedling roots and planting holes.

Rootfly The tiny grubs of these flies can be very damaging to brassicas, carrots and onions. The foliage of infested plants loses its usual green colour, and the plants tend to wilt in warm weather. Early attacks can be prevented by the application of a soil insecticide after sowing. Repeat treatments may be needed some weeks later to deal with later attacks. Carrots sown at the end of May and harvested before the end of August are usually free from this trouble.

 SEPTEMBER

The Month in the Garden

This is Keats's 'season of mists and mellow fruitfulness', and a rewarding month for gardeners since much produce can now be harvested, yet there are still interesting flowers coming along to bridge the gap between summer and autumn.

General Tasks Apart from gathering crops for storage, September tasks include removing summer bedding plants and getting the ground ready for spring replacements; lawns need a deal of attention; the bulb planting season is here; and there is a general need to cut down, dig out, replant and tidy up.

Nevertheless six weeks or so of colourful flowering remain, and we should do everything possible to retain and extend the interest.

Dahlias are at their best, with flowers of fiery red and deep glowing purple, bright pinks and oranges and sunshine-yellow. Michaelmas daisies unfold in every variety of shades of blue; early-flowering chrysanthemums are at their best, and such bedding plants as cal-ceolarias, pelargoniums and penste-mons show no sign of summer's passing. And yet, in the Indian summer of one year, and while the garden is still rich with colour, we must look

ahead and plan for another year's display.

At the beginning of the month the emphasis should be on propagation, particularly if this was not possible in July and August. As the days get shorter and cooler, cuttings take longer to root and newly potted plants make little fresh growth. Haste is all import-ant, particularly to make cuttings of pelargoniums, calceolarias, heliotropes and a variety of silver-foliaged plants which are used for hanging baskets and containers. Buying summer bedding plants becomes more expensive every year, and a few hours spent making and inserting cuttings will be well worth-while (see also July, *New Plants from Old,* p. 154). In the process of clearing borders, certain plants can be discarded, especially those which produce better results from young cuttings or from seed – like antirrhinums, stocks, agera-tum, tagetes and even heliotropes and pelargoniums. Young plants of the last two winter well in a frost-free greenhouse, but if you want to retain a few of the older specimens lift the plants carefully, cut them back by about half, always to strong shoots lower down on the stems, then pot them, separately or several boxed together, in light sandy compost. Some people lift and tie several pelargoniums together, and hang them up in a frost-free attic or garage, but this is a method I would not advocate – except as a measure of desperation. If you don't have a greenhouse, it is better to pot the plants and stand them in a sunny window. Take cuttings from them the following spring.

The work of dismantling and re-planting display beds should not be rushed. Summer bedding takes more out of the soil than spring bedding, so for good results the beds should be deeply dug and manured in early autumn. Use manure of a bulky nature, such as decayed farmyard manure or garden compost; otherwise dig in leaf-soil, moist peat or spent hops if these can be bought at a reasonable price. Early October is time enough to plant out spring bedding.

Bulbs If desired, bulbs to be forced for Christmas flowering should be planted in September. Late-blooming kinds to provide continuity can be dealt with at weekly or fortnightly intervals until late October. For details of planting see *Bulbs for Forcing and Garden Decoration,* p. 196. Other bulbs to plant this month are the smaller types, like winter aconites, crocuses, bluebells and scillas, none of which should be left lying around for long or they will shrivel. This is a common cause of failure, particularly with winter aconites.

This month and next are ideal times for renovating existing lawns or seeding new ones in the South. Sweep and vigorously rake old lawns, dragging at the grass to pull out the matted thatch of compacted grass cuttings, stems of couch grass and other unwanted debris. Then spike the lawn all over, using a mechanical spiker if possible (see *Making Lawns,* p. 204), otherwise the task is wearisome and time-consuming. If the spiker is of the type which removes cores of soil, discard these, top dress the lawn with a proprietary autumn feed and brush it into the holes.

Trees and Shrubs Many hardy evergreen shrubs can be rooted from cuttings outdoors in September, in a cold frame or under cloches in a sheltered border. Some will even root without the protection of glass. Use slips of the current season's growth, pulled off the plant with a heel of older wood attached, or cut across immediately below a joint. Such cuttings are called ripe or hardwood cuttings and are made longer than the soft cuttings taken in spring and early summer – 6-10 in. (15-25 cm), according to the habit of the shrub. Insert in well raked, light soil, with a dusting of sand on top, setting each cutting in the ground for a third of its length. It will probably not produce much shoot growth until spring, but roots will form. Keep the soil moist and protect the cuttings from direct sun. Privet, aucuba, rosemary, potentilla, berberis and phlomis will all root in this manner, and yew and juniper will also do so in a cold frame.

Plant evergreens at the end of the month, retaining a good ball of soil round the roots. Spraying the foliage with an antidesiccant spray, such as is used on Christmas trees, is a good idea as it stops the shrubs from dropping their leaves while settling in. Another good idea is spraying over the foliage with soft water when the weather is dry.

Transplant any large plants which need moving, but keep small rooted cuttings in a frame until spring. Evergreen hedges can be planted from the middle of the month in clean, well manured ground.

This is a good time to plant a heather bed, adding plenty of moist, never dry peat, in the soil and as a mulch after planting.

Climbers Plant new climbers from pots in good soil. Put up trellis or wires on which to train the climbers in due course.

Roses Prune ramblers by cutting out old flowered stems to ground level; tie in new stems. If these are few, cut the old stems back to a mature new side shoot lower down.

Ripe side shoots from ramblers and climbers make good cuttings. Make these 10-12 in. (25-30 cm) long, cutting them just below a leaf joint at the base and just above the top leaf. Remove any thorns and all leaves which will be below ground, but retain the top two and plant the cuttings 4-6 in. (10-15 cm) deep in shade. A little sand at the base and treating the ends with hormone-rooting compound helps rooting.

Remove faded flowers from garden roses to encourage blooms for as long as possible.

Lawns Spike and rake lawns, then apply an autumn dressing. Water this in if there is no sign of rain for forty-eight hours.

Control weeds.

Sow new lawns during showery weather at the end of the month, using approximately 1½ oz. of grass seed per square yard (40g per square metre) of lawn.

Hardy Plants Prepare herbaceous borders ready for winter by the middle of this month. Cut back the old growth of perennials nearly to ground level unless the garden is in a very exposed part of the country, when the old growth can be left until spring to provide winter protection. Plants like red-hot pokers (kniphofias) should not have their foliage removed; instead gather it together over the crowns and tie it round with raffia. This prevents water from getting in and freezing the crowns in winter.

Divide perennials if the clumps are too large or exhausted. Retain and replant the outer pieces of Michaelmas daisies (asters), helianthus and other fibrous-rooted plants because these will be younger and more vigorous than the centre area.

After weeding established borders, fork between the plants to remove footprints. New perennials can be planted at the end of the month.

Bulbs Plant small bulbs in rock gardens and under trees.

European and most American lilies, which produce their roots from the bases of the bulbs, can be planted at the end of September and into October. *Do not plant* stem-rooting oriental lilies, which have roots above the bulb as well as below, until spring.

Plant bulbous irises (Dutch, English and Spanish), 3 in. (7.5 cm) deep in good soil and 5-6 in. (12.5-15 cm) apart. Put cloches over a few planted in rows in a sunny position, to produce early flowers for cutting.

Algerian irises (*Iris unguicularis*) can

WEATHER

'What July and August do not boil, September cannot fry' and indeed by this time of the year high summer temperatures are a thing of the past. In Scotland and the North, September is beyond question an autumn month, but southern England may still retain the milder habits of summer. It can also be a comparatively dry month, but on occasion it can rain heavily, as happened in 1976 following a very dry summer: 'September dries up ditches or breaks down bridges'. By now top fruit is maturing in the garden, and growers face an anxious time. The period of greatest threat from summer hail-storms is almost over, but strong winds and gales are always a danger, hence the plea: 'September blow soft, Till the fruit's in the loft'.

September gales are never the strongest of the autumn, but they often do the most damage, because the wind finds out the weak spots and can cause havoc to apples and pears when they are almost due for picking.

Many weather sayings favour the idea of persistence in early autumn, and quiet weeks before the equinox and after are said to foretell that the temperature will continue higher than usual into winter. In the same way a south wind on 21 September (St Matthew's Day) indicates that the rest of autumn will be warm.

Warm it may be, but the nights are drawing in and on 21 September 'St Matthew, get candlesticks new', or in another version 'St Mary (25 March) blows out the candle; St Michael (25 September) lights it again'.

There is no longer the opportunity to spend long evenings in the garden.

window against the wall in early November to keep the roots dry and encourage early flowering.

Plant crown imperials (*Fritillaria imperialis*), 6 in. (15 cm), deep, if this was not done last month.

Annuals, Biennials and Bedding Plants At the end of the month, clear summer bedding as outlined in *General Tasks*.

Plant wallflowers in their flowering positions.

At the same time remove poly-anthus from their summer quarters (see May, *General Tasks*, p. 103) and plant in their flowering positions.

Rock Garden Plants Plant small bulbs, such as *Iris reticulata, I. histrioides, Narcissus asturiensis,* anemones, leuco-jums, scillas, snowdrops and crocuses.

This is a good time to build a new rock garden or construct and furnish a dry wall. Use small plants from pots, placing them on their sides in the spaces left between the bricks or stones. See also June, *Rock Gardens*, p. 138.

Water Plants Cut down plants going to seed, and remove dying water-lily leaves. Feed fish this month and in October with a high protein diet to prepare them for a long winter fast.

Patio Plants Remove and discard plants which are past their best; as the containers are emptied fill them with fresh compost. They can be planted for winter and spring displays at the end of the month or early in October.

Clean and store containers and hang-ing baskets not required for spring bedding.

Tidy the area and scrub the paving if necessary.

be planted at the foot of a south wall. Lean an old frame light or discarded

Vegetables Plant out spring cabbages from summer sowings, 12 in. (30 cm) apart, in rows 1½ ft. (45 cm) apart.

Harvest potatoes and root crops for storage, as well as marrows, squashes and onions.

Sow turnips for turnip tops.

Tidy the ground and start digging and manuring vacant ground, leaving the soil rough, particularly if it is heavy soil.

Pick tomatoes unlikely to ripen and store with red ones indoors. The ethylene gas from ripe fruits helps to ripen green fruits.

Herbs Continue drying leaves of mint, fennel, basil, marjoram and parsley.

Dig up and plant a few mint roots in a seed tray with garden soil; cut back the old stems and keep indoors or in a greenhouse. The sprouting shoots will be useful in winter. The same procedure can be carried out with chives.

Fruit Continue harvesting tree fruits, perpetual strawberries, autumn-fruiting raspberries, figs, grapes and mulberries.

Plant out strawberries. Cut off and burn leaves of older plants as disease control if omitted last month.

Greaseband apple and cherry trees to trap winter moths before they can crawl up and lay their eggs.

Plants under Glass Pot on primulas and calceolarias raised from seed, cyclamen seedlings and any other plants needing attention.

Shelter any frost-prone plants brought in from the garden and take cuttings of tender bedding plants.

Plant bulbs for Christmas flowering.

House pot-grown late-flowering chrysanthemums.

Sow lettuce in a cold frame or under cloches.

Give less water and do not dampen down greenhouse floors after midday.

To prevent mildew in the greenhouse install a small electric fan near the roof and keep this going at all times. It creates a buoyant atmosphere and circulates warm air. See January, *Greenhouse Gardening*, p. 18.

House Plants Reduce watering and feeding slightly, especially of cacti and succulents.

GARDEN PROBLEMS

Mildew on a wide range of plants; spray with a suitable fungicide containing dinocap.

Overwatered house plants indicated by yellowing or drooping leaves and over-heavy pots.

Earwigs on dahlias; trap as recommended in August, Annuals, Biennials and Bedding Plants, p. 167.

Wormcasts on lawns; apply a chlordane wormkiller. Sweep the casts off with a brush to disperse the soil.

Wasps on fruit; locate the nests and destroy them with a carbaryl preparation.

Bird pecks on fruit; cover fruits with nylon netting or stockings if trees are small.

Honey fungus on trees and bushes evidenced by sudden wilting of leaves, followed by a ring of yellow toadstools round the base in September and loose bark with whitish mould beneath. Remove the trees with as many roots as possible and pour a creosote preparation into the hole. See also August, Plant Disorders, p. 176.

Remove dead leaves and blooms regularly.

Finish any necessary repotting.

PLANTS IN THEIR PRIME

Trees and Shrubs Abelias; berberis (berries); *Bupleurum fruticosum; Caryopteris* species and varieties; *Ceanothus coeruleus, C. azureus* and varieties; *Ceratostigma willmottianum; Clerodendrum trichotomum, C.t fargesii; Colletia armata; Colutea arborescens;* cotoneasters (berries); *Desfontainea spinosa* (as a warm-wall shrub); ericas; *Fuchsia* 'Riccartonii'; hebes; *Hibiscus syriacus* and varieties; *Hydrangea arborescens* 'Grandiflora', *H. hortensia* varieties, *H. paniculata* 'Grandiflora'; *Hypericum calycinum* and others; indigoferas; *Itea virginica; Leycesteria formosa; Perovskia atriplicifolia; Potentilla fruticosa* and varieties; roses; *Rubus ulmifolius* 'Bellidiflorus'; *Spartium junceum;* spiraeas; *Tamarix pentandra; Teucrium fruticans;* vincas; yuccas.

Hardy Plants *Achillea filipendulina, A. ptarmica;* aconitums; *Actaea spicata* (berries); *Anemone hupehensis* (*A. japonica*) varieties; *Anthemis tinctoria* and others; asters (Michaelmas daisies); *Catananche caerulea; Centaurea montana* and varieties; chrysanthemums; cimicifugas (bugbanes); *Coreopsis grandiflora* and varieties; *Dierama pulcherrimum;* echinaceas; *Eupatorium purpureum;* gaillardias; *Galega officinalis; Gentiana asclepiadea; Geum coccineum* varieties; *Gypsophila paniculata* and varieties; heleniums; helianthus (perennial sunflowers); heliopsis; hemerocallis (day-lilies); hostas; inulas; *Kirengeshoma palmata;* kniphofias; *Lavatera olbia;* liatris; ligularias;

Lobelia cardinalis, L. fulgens and hybrids; lysimachias; *Lythrum salicaria, L. virgatum* and varieties; *Monarda didyma* and varieties; nepetas; oenotheras (evening primroses); penstemons; phlox; *Phygelius capensis;* physalis (fruits); *Physostegia virginiana;* polygonums; potentillas; romneyas (tree poppies); rudbeckias; salvias; *Saponaria officinalis* 'Plena' (soapwort); *Scabiosa caucasica* and varieties; *Sedum spectabile* and varieties; solidagos (golden rod); *Stokesia laevis;* thalictrums; tradescantias; verbenas; veronicas.

Bulbs *Amaryllis belladonna;* colchicums in variety; *Crinum* x *powellii; Crocosmia masonorum* and others; *Crocus speciosus, C. sativus; Cyclamen purpurascens, C. europaeum, C. hederifolium* (*C. neapolitanum*); lilies, wide range especially oriental varieties; *Schizostylis coccinea* and varieties; *Sternbergia lutea;* tigridias.

Autumn-flowering bulbs: *Nerine bowdenii* (left); *Colchicum* (centre); *Schizostylis coccinea* (right)

Rock Garden Plants *Achillea tomentosa; Astilbe chinensis pumila;* campanulas; gentians; *Geum borisii; Lithospermum prostratum (Lithodora diffusa)* and varieties; oenotheras; polygonums; potentillas; sedums; *Tunica saxifraga (Petrorhagia); Verbena peruviana (V. chamaedryfolia);* violas; *Zauschneria californica.*

CROPS TO ENJOY

Vegetables Runner beans; beetroot; broccoli; cabbage (spring-sown); carrots; cauliflower; celery; cucumbers (ridge and greenhouse); lettuce; marrows; parsnips; peas; potatoes; radishes; spinach; tomatoes; turnips.

Fruit Apples; apricots; blackberries; cherries (morello); blackcurrants; figs; melons; nectarines; peaches; plums; raspberries (autumn fruiting).

PLANT ASSOCIATIONS

Caryopteris x *clandonensis* 'Arthur Simmonds' with a bold planting of *Monarda didyma* 'Cambridge Scarlet' in front.

Phygelius capensis against a warm wall with *Amaryllis belladonna* and *Verbena peruviana* in foreground.

Kirengeshoma palmata in a shady moist border, with ferns and blue *Gentiana asclepiadea.*

Cyclamen hederifolium growing round the bole of a large deciduous tree. A few mauvy-blue *Crocus sativus* can be interplanted.

Lobelia fulgens with white *Anemone japonica.*

A bold grouping of *Lilium speciosum* and violas.

Spartium junceum, heliopsis, dwarf golden rod and yellow violas in a symphony of yellows and golds.

Plants of the Month

LILIUM REGALE

The splendid summer-flowering regal lily (*Lilium regale*) was discovered in 1904 by E. H. Wilson, commonly known as Chinese Wilson, in the practically inaccessible River Min Valley on the borders of China and Tibet. There it was growing in tens of thousands and must have presented a remarkable sight. It has never been found growing in the wild anywhere else.

This find was probably the most important of Wilson's many plant introductions, for *Lilium regale* flourishes in British gardens, is long-lasting when well grown, flowers from seed in three years, and the large, elegant, glistening, white trumpet flowers are richly fragrant.

In the summer of 1910 Wilson went back to collect more bulbs, arranging for some seven thousand to be collected in the autumn and shipped to America. He then set back down some two hundred miles of rough road and interminable gorges, travelling in a sedan chair – a necessary form of transport to preserve face. Suddenly the party was hit by a rock avalanche and Wilson's leg was broken twice below the knee. Fortunately he was not knocked unconscious, for his bearers would probably have deserted. Following his instructions, the bearers made a rough splint from the legs of his camera tripod. But while this was being fitted, a heavily-laden mule train came along. The road was too narrow for it to pass, and the site was extremely dangerous as there could be another rockfall. There was nothing for it but to lay Wilson on his back and allow the fifty-odd mules to step over his body. It must have been a nerve-racking experience, yet not a single hoof touched him, and three days later he was carried to a missionary station at Cheng-tu and received medical attention. By that time infection had set in and amputation was advised, but this Wilson would not allow. Many months later he reached Boston, Massachusetts, where the twisted leg was broken and reset, although he limped slightly for the rest of his life.

Lilium regale

Soon afterwards the bulbs arrived and became the progenitors of all the regal lilies grown in the world today.

Wilson was an Englishman, born in 1876 at Chipping Campden in Gloucestershire. After working and plant collecting for the firm of Veitch at Coombe Wood, he emigrated in 1909 to America, joining the staff of the Arnold Arboretum, of which he ultimately became keeper. He died in 1930, yet for all his years in America and China never learnt Chinese and never took out American citizenship.

DAHLIAS

Few flowers can compare with the dahlia for diversity of form and brightness of colour, so no wonder it is sometimes called the queen of the autumn garden. Dahlias are native to the New World, particularly Mexico, Colombia and Guatemala, and were cultivated long before Europeans reached that continent. Botanists accompanying the Spanish conquistadores in the early sixteenth century found the Aztecs growing garden forms not found in the wild. According to Philip Damp, in *Growing Dahlias,* they used the split hollow stems of the tallest species – probably the tree-like *Dahlia maxonii,* which grows to 18 ft (5.4 m) or more – for conveying water over distances in a viaduct-like system. This is probably why the Aztecs called them *acocotli* or *cocoxochite,* meaning hollow pipes or water tubes.

The first seeds to arrive in Europe in 1789 were sent by Vincent Cervantes of the Botanic Gardens in Mexico City to the Abbé Cavanilles of the Royal Garden at Madrid. Cavanilles called the genus *Dahlia* after the Swedish botanist Dr Andreas Dahl, who was a pupil of Linnaeus, but through a botanical misunderstanding Professor Wildenow of Berlin changed the name to *Georgina* in honour of the Russian Professor Georgi, a botany teacher at St Petersburg. It is still called Georgina in parts of Russia, Germany and Scandinavia.

The earliest forms to be named and the parents of so many garden varieties were *D. pinnata,* a double purple, *D. rosea,* a single rose, and *D. coccinea,* a single red.

The tuberous roots were originally treated as a vegetable, but their bland taste did not suit Europeans or their cattle, and they were soon rejected as unpalatable. However, they still constitute a food crop for some tribes of American Indians.

As dahlias became better known and more varieties were grown, their cultivation spread to France, Britain, Germany and other countries. In France, the Empress Josephine is reported to have been greatly taken with the flowers and planted the first tubers in her garden at Malmaison 'with her own hands'. Later, when the blooms were at their best, she reputedly invited Marie Louise, the Austrian princess who had supplanted her as Empress, and her entourage to a garden party, where she soon made it clear that the flowers could be admired but not acquired.

Varieties of dahlia

As the collection grew one lady-in-waiting – the Countess de Bougain-ville according to one account – piqued at being denied a bloom, determined to obtain some roots and prevailed upon a Polish prince to obtain a few tubers. Knowing the futility of approaching Josephine, the Prince bribed her gardener, Pierre, to part with a hundred plants for as many golden louis. Foolishly the lady-in-waiting boasted of her acquisition, which, when the story reached the ears of Josephine, so incensed the Empress that she sacked her gardener, banished the prince and his lady from her presence and ceased growing dahlias.

Interest in the flowers appears to have waned for some years until a new type arrived from Mexico in 1872. There seems to be some mystery about this plant for it was the only survivor of a large consignment sent to a Dutch nurseryman, J. T. van der Berg, and its counterpart has never again been found in the wild. However, it received instant acclaim and was widely propagated. It was named *D. juarezii* after the President of Mexico, but because of the similarity of the flower colour to that of *Cereus speciosissimus* (*now Heliocereus speciosus*) soon became known as the cactus dahlia. Its offspring are well-known garden flowers, now vastly improved and variously coloured.

Bulbs for Forcing and Garden Decoration

According to most bulb growers' catalogues bulbs mean corms and tubers as well as the true bulbs like lilies and hyacinths. But whatever their botanical distinctions, one can never have enough of them.

There are bulbs for forcing to give early blooms indoors, bulbs for rock gardens, for greenhouses and homes, for window boxes and other containers, as well as bulbs for naturalizing, seasonal bedding and permanent borders. September/October is the right time to plant many of them, although others may be put in the ground in spring, for summer flowering, and a few planted in July and August to bloom in early autumn.

FORCING

Bulbs for forcing can be grown in a variety of ways. Narcissi of the Tazetta group, for example, like 'Cragford' or 'Paperwhite Grandiflora', can be brought to flower by wedging the bulbs on heaped pebbles in a saucer with a little water at the bottom. Crocuses and hyacinths will also grow satisfactorily without soil, usually by lodging the bulbs in special bulb glasses, with water just below their bases.

Perhaps the greatest interest for many people lies in forcing bulbs in the home. For Christmas bloom, the multiflora and Roman hyacinths never fail, and many people prefer their delicate spikes, several to a bulb, to the more robust, larger-flowered Dutch hyacinths. Grow them in bowls of bulb fibre. Apart from white Roman hyacinths there is a pink form, known as 'Rosalie', and a lavender-blue form. These small-flowered hyacinths are frequently referred to as *Bellevalia romana* by botanists.

The true large-flowered hyacinths must be of top quality for Christmas forcing, although somewhat smaller bulbs are fine if you are prepared to wait until January or February for their blooms. Whatever the type, they should be heavy solid bulbs, free from disease, bruises and blemishes.

Hyacinths can be grown in a variety of media – I have successfully used moist pellets of newspaper, brick rubble, Hortag (expanded clay and fuel-ash pellets) and sphagnum moss mixed with sand and lumps of charcoal. The easiest and cleanest method is to use prepared bulb fibre made from sphagnum peat moss with added oyster shell, charcoal and fertilizers. It should be dampened to the stage where only a few drops of water can be expressed when it is squeezed in the hand.

Pack the bulbs closely, without touching, on a bed of fibre in a bowl, then add more fibre between and around them until only the noses of the hyacinths remain uncovered. Wrap the bowls in several sheets of newspaper and stand them on a flat surface outdoors with about 6 in. (15 cm) of leaves, light soil, moist peat or ashes over the top. Those without a garden can keep them in a dark, but cold, room or cupboard. Aim for a temperature of 4·5°C (40°F) at this stage and maintain this for eight to nine weeks.

At the end of that period the bowls should be full of roots with white shoots about 1 in. (2.5 cm) long showing at the top of the bulbs. When this occurs bring them into a light but cool place, 10°C (50°F), until the leaves are well developed and the flower buds show. They can then be taken into the living rooms and brought to flower.

Forced narcissi do well in soil compost, but must be kept cool; 10°C (50°F) is ideal. The bunch-flowered kinds like 'Cragford', 'Soleil d'Or', and the paperwhites can be wedged on pebbles in bowls, with rainwater for preference at the bottom, but just below the level of the bulbs. Kept in a temperature around 7°C (45°F) for a few weeks before being brought into the living rooms, they flower perfectly and persist for a long time. Keep them in a light place and turn the bowls a little each day so that the growth is uniform.

EARLY DAFFODILS

Spring can be anticipated outdoors as well as in, with cool-treated daffodils. They flower several weeks ahead of time, and in a mild winter I once had flowering plants in sheltered corners outdoors at the end of January, though normally they start to bloom in February and March. They are the early daffodils seen each spring in many London parks.

These daffodils are extremely resilient. After a heavy frost the stems fall flat on the ground, but recover miraculously and stand upright again after a few hours of thaw. Cool-treated daffodils must be planted immediately they arrive and only set 1 in. (2.5 cm) deep in the soil, unlike normal bulbs which need 5-6 in. (12.5-15 cm).

Planting bulbs in a double layer produces a spectacular effect

INDOOR BULBS

Amaryllis bulbs are expensive, but last for years if properly rested after flowering. When they arrive, stand them in 1 in. (2.5 cm) of tepid water and place them in a warm airing cupboard for about five days. Thereafter pot them up in a compost composed of equal parts of loam and leaf-mould with enough sharp sand to ensure good drainage. The neck of the bulbs should be left half exposed and the pots should be just large enough to support them comfortably. Keep them warm, in a box of peat resting on a radiator, or on the mantlepiece. When the buds appear place the pots in a light but warm window and water as necessary with tepid water.

The leaves appear after flowering, and they should be fed and watered until the foliage begins to die down. Gradually withhold water, dry off and rest the bulbs.

OUTDOOR BULBS

There is a wide range of outdoors bulbs besides the ubiquitous narcissi, hyacinths and tulips.

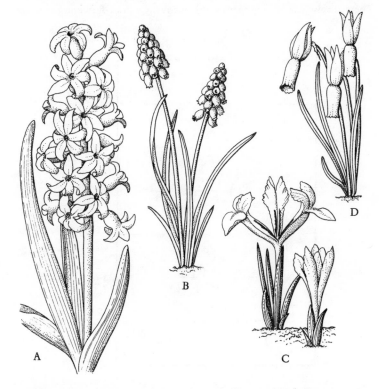

Bulbs to plant in September for spring: (A) hyacinth; (B) grape hyacinth; (C) *Iris danfordiae;* (D) *Narcissus cyclamineus*

Early-flowering bulbs are always pleasing, with their promise of spring. *Anemone blanda* will flower through winter to mid-spring, with myriads of starry, deep blue flowers, and deeply cut leaves; pink, white and mauve varieties also occur. Plant the tubers 2 in. (5 cm) deep in rich, leafy soil.

Chionodoxa luciliae grows to about the same height of 6 in. (15 cm) and requires similar cultivation. Its flowers are blue with white centres, several to a stem, and there is a pink form called 'Pink Giant'.

Dwarf narcissi worth trying are the hoop-petticoat daffodil, *Narcissus bulbocodium* (now sometimes referred to as *Corbularia*), with a flared trumpet and mere strips of perianth segments behind. Others are *N. cyclamineus*, which has backward-pointing segments like donkey's ears, and narrow tube trumpets; and the baby, 3 in. (7.5 cm) *N. asturiensis*, a real miniature daffodil. There are also dwarf tulip species and, of course, winter-flowering crocuses.

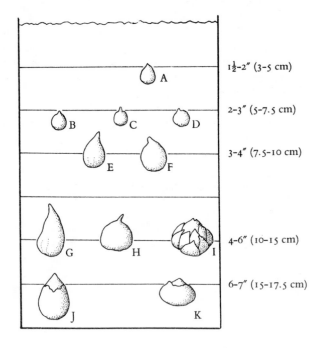

A depth chart for bulbs: (A) scillas; (B) grape hyacinths; (C) snowdrops; (D) crocuses; (E) chionodoxas; (F) early narcissi; (G) tulips; (H) gladioli; (I) lilies; (J) hyacinths; (K) narcissi

Grape hyacinths (muscari) are small enough at 6-10 in. (15-25 cm) for cultivation in pans of good potting compost; some of the easiest are *Muscari botryoides* var. *album*, a white-flowered fragrant type, and the blue *M. armeniacum*, which has double grape-shaped blossoms in showy spikes.

Snowdrops, both single and double, and winter aconites (*Eranthis hyemalis*) bloom in January or February and are followed by *Ipheion uniflorum*, a fragrant spring flower with soft, thin and narrow leaves and many single, pale violet flowers on 4-6-in. (10-15-cm) stems.

Most of these little bulbs need good drainage and are especially suitable for rock garden pockets, small beds or the edges of mixed borders. Set all bulbs at the right depth, slightly more on light soil, and use a dibber or bulb trowel for planting. The latter is marked across the blade with the various depths. As a rough guide, plant scillas at 1½-2 in. (3-5 cm) deep, muscari, snowdrops and crocuses 2-3 in. (5-7.5 cm), chionodoxas and early narcissi 3-4 in. (7.5-10 cm), tulips and gladioli 4-6 in. (10-15 cm), and hyacinths and narcissi 6-7 in. (15-17.5 cm).

The smaller bulbs should never be kept out of the ground longer than necessary; bluebells, snowdrops and winter aconites often fail to come up if the bulbs dry out. If they persistently fail, here is a tip I learned from that great gardener, the late E. A. Bowles; find somebody with plants in flower and leaf and transplant them. Aconites, crocuses and snowdrops never fail to establish themselves when transplanted in flower.

Bulbs for naturalizing, such as snowdrops, crocuses, narcissi and scillas, should be scattered at the site and planted where they come to rest. This gives a much more natural effect than trying to set them out at even spacing or in lines. They look equally at home in rough grass, or round island beds on lawns, in orchards, meadows, alpine lawns and in open shrubberies. Bulbs for naturalizing can often be bought in bulk, which represents a considerable saving. *Iris danfordiae* is best in rockeries.

Any good garden soil suits narcissi, but heavy ground should be improved for tulips and bulbous irises by working sand and peat into the upper layers. Because of the risk of tulip fire disease, it is advisable to plant tulips late in the season (well into November) when there is less risk of infection. As an added precaution dip the bulbs in a fungicide like benlate for fifteen minutes prior to planting.

SUMMER BULBS

Lilies are in a class of their own and are usually planted in late winter or spring. Most of the early-flowering Asiatic hybrids are stem rooting and should be planted 4-6 in. (10-15 cm) deep in well-drained soil, covered with 1 in. (2.5 cm) of soil and on top of that a layer of decomposed farmyard manure or garden compost. A layer of leaves on top of this will keep the bulbs moist. Most lilies thrive in full sun if their roots are kept moist and cool, or in partial shade, but do check each species or variety prior to planting.

Gladioli are planted in spring, but August to November is the right time to put in colchicums and the autumn-flowering crocuses like *Crocus sativus*, described in October, as well as the late blooming pink *Nerine bowdenii*.

AUTUMN BULBS

Other bulbs to establish in late summer include the golden, crocus-like sternbergias, which require sun and a sheltered well-drained site where they should be planted 6 in. (15 cm) deep. Madonna lilies (*Lilium candidum*) should go into the ground before growth restarts around September. Give this lily full sun, rich, cool but well-drained soil and barely cover the bulbs.

Colchicums, whose fat crocus-like flower goblets appear, without the leaves, in September and October, are useful in many situations, such as rough grassland or between shrubs in open glades. They are also most effective when planted underneath deciduous trees growing as lawn specimens. Not only do they then show to advantage, but they can be left undisturbed. The only attention mine receive, apart from weeding, is an occasional mulch of leaf-mould when the leafy stems and seed pods have died down in spring.

The double *Colchicum autumnale* hybrid called 'Water Lily' is particularly fine, especially when grown on the sunny side of a fairly small tree. The violet-pink flowers, cut into numerous segments, are very showy and, as they sit squatly near the ground, resemble cactus dahlias or water-lilies. Others to note are *C. speciosum illyricum*, soft rosy-carmine with white centres and yellow anthers; *C. autumnale* 'Album', a fine white with long stem-like perianth tubes; and 'Lilac Wonder', a tall 6-8-in. (15-20-cm) amethyst-violet sort with many blooms on each plant. This variety will even flower 'dry' on a saucer stood in a sunny window-sill; naturally it must be planted afterwards if you wish to keep it for another year.

Colchicums belong to the lily family and have long, irregular-shaped corms with curious foot-like appendages to one side. They have grooves next to the corms with a hollow at the base in which new growth develops. They should be planted about 4 in. (10 cm) deep.

All parts of the plants contain an alkaloid poison called colchicine; if seeds are soaked in a weak solution of this the resultant seedlings are dwarfed and malformed because colchicine causes chromosome changes. This property has been exploited by seedsmen in order to produce new plants. Theophrastus (368 BC – 288 BC) tells us that slaves, when provoked, used to eat parts of colchicum to make themselves ill (they apparently knew of an antidote when necessary). On the other hand, he also says that death from colchicine poisoning was slow and lingering – sometimes taking up to a year. However, the plant has modern uses as a painkiller, especially for gout, but because of its toxic nature should never be allowed within reach of small children.

Summer bulbs: *Acidanthera bicolor murielae* (left); *Lilium candidum*, Madonna lily (centre); *Galtonia candicans*, summer hyacinth (right)

Making Lawns

Foreigners rhapsodize about our lawns but, if the truth be told, it is our equable climate and our normally adequate rainfall that are largely responsible for their velvety green finish. There are periods, perhaps in spring and summer, in almost every year when it pays to water lawns.

Feeding is just as important. No intelligent gardener would expect to take a crop of vegetables off the same ground year after year without digging in manure or at least applying generous doses of fertilizer. Yet thousands of gardeners mow from their lawns the equivalent of two or three hay crops every year and never think of putting any food back for the turf.

For a really good lawn two feeds of a general lawn fertilizer in spring, one in mid-March and another in mid-April, will do a power of good. An autumn feed in September or October of a slow-acting fertilizer is often as valuable as *two* spring feeds, although ideally the autumn feed as well as two spring feeds should be applied.

LAWN WEEDS

Most gardeners find weeds their greatest lawn problem. Theoretically, lawn weeds should be no problem with selective weedkillers, and if these are used intelligently weeds are controlled fairly easily, even if some can be stubborn and may need several applications before they are entirely destroyed.

Selective weedkillers can be applied as a liquid from a watering can fitted with a sprinkler bar or applicator, consisting of a plastic tube, up to 18 in. (45 cm) long, with fine holes through which the liquid trickles evenly on to the lawn.

Alternatively, apply weedkillers on the 'weed and feed' principle by means of a powder or granular fertilizer which is combined with a selective weedkiller. This method saves time, of course, because one only has to go over the lawn once, but it is a less efficient way of applying weedkiller. Ideally, apply fertilizer first, followed about a fortnight later by weedkiller. The idea behind this technique is that weeds are encouraged to grow lustily and produce a large leaf area to absorb the weedkiller into the sap stream where it can be translocated throughout the plants.

Broad-leaved weeds, such as dandelions, daisies, and plantains, are readily controlled with weedkillers based on 2,4-D, MCPA, mecoprop, fenoprop or ioxynil, but others like clover are more persistent. In some parts of our lawns the soil is alkaline which encourages both clover and earthworms. We tried watering on a weedkiller containing both ioxynil and mecoprop. The first application had virtually no effect, but as we have hard water we were advised to add two teaspoonfuls of household detergent to each gallon of the solution. This worked perfectly and the clover disappeared. Now we will be working sedulously to bring the lawns into an acid condition by applying sulphate of ammonia (an acid nitrogenous fertilizer) in spring. The recommended rate of application is a $\frac{1}{4}$ oz. to the square yard (6 g to the square metre) every ten days or so until 2 oz. (50 g) have been applied. However, sulphate of ammonia must be well watered in as it can scorch the grass. Failing an opportune shower of rain, put a sprinkler on the lawn for half an hour to wash it off the grass, and down to the roots.

With creeping weeds like clover, yarrow and yellow trefoil it is best to rake the stems up clear of the grass if possible so that they can be thoroughly wetted by the weedkiller. It is sometimes necessary to give a second treatment to these stubborn weeds.

MOSS

Moss is usually, but not always, found in lawns that are rather sunless and badly drained. There are many different mosses in Britain, and some are quite happy on light, quick-draining soils. The presence of moss is normally an indication of run-down turf, caused by shortage of fertilizer, poor drainage, too little topsoil, impaction, too close mowing or heavy rolling. Try to ascertain which of these are the likely causes. Proper lawn management – scarifying or raking the turf and spiking or aerating it – helps to prevent moss from becoming a serious nuisance. Once it appears, it must be dealt with firmly as it can grow and spread even during low light conditions in winter when grass is dormant.

Books have often recommended that moss should be raked out, but this is not a good idea because it only spreads the plants about and the smallest piece is capable of growing. The right course is to kill the moss. Various mosskillers are available, some based on mercury compounds; they work well and it is usually not necessary to rake the dead moss out – it will disintegrate and disappear in due course.

EARTHWORMS

Worms do not like acid soils and grass usually grows best on soils that are slightly acid. As already mentioned under clover, dressings of sulphate of ammonia will bring the ground into an acid state and discourage worms, though a few are nothing to worry about. They feed near the surface in spring and autumn, and if their casts are not too numerous they are easily brushed off (as they should be) before the lawn is mowed. Unless swept away they are likely to be trodden into the turf where a flattened wormcast may cause a bare patch and encourage weed seeds.

Particularly numerous worms become a nuisance and it may be necessary to destroy them. Various wormkillers are available. Some, like derris, act as an irritant bringing the worms to the surface, and then there is the nasty job of sweeping them up and destroying them. Derris is poisonous to fish and should not be used near ponds or streams.

Wormkillers based on chlordane kill the worms below ground so there is not the necessity for sweeping them up. Chlordane gives control of worms and other soil pests for a year or more, but keep pets and children off lawns for two weeks after treatment with this wormkiller.

LAWN MAINTENANCE

The most time-consuming lawn chore is mowing. It was in 1831 that Edward Budding invented the mowing machine, and its design and cutting principles changed little until the first rotary mowers appeared just after the Second World War.

Before the advent of the motor mower, lawns were cut by hand machines, and most gardeners used a roller on the turf several times in the spring. The weight of a motor mower, of the cylinder-roller type, proved heavy enough to keep the lawn smooth, and extra rollings became unnecessary. Indeed on some soils, the weight and frequency of cutting led to compaction and hence the need for spiking or aerating the turf.

Then came rotary mowers which worked without rear rollers, but these did not leave the lawn with its banded cuts of light and dark stripes, so rotary mowers with roller attachments came on the scene.

Lastly came the hover mowers that float on a cushion of air. The early models did not collect the mowings, and many modern types still do not do so, which means that either the mowings must be left on the lawn or they must be swept up with a besom broom or a leaf-sweeper.

There are two schools of thought about the effect of allowing mowings to lie on lawns. Some contend that they make the turf spongy (create a thatch is the professional term) and say that moss and weeds are encouraged thereby. It is also held that a thick mat or thatch prevents light rainfalls from reaching the grass roots before evaporating into the air.

Others claim that the decaying mowings feed the lawn and it grows better than if the cuttings are removed. Personally I am of the opinion that mowings are best removed and that the maintenance regimes developed and carried out for many years by professional groundsmen produce the best turf.

Traditional lawn maintenance takes up a great deal of time and costs money for fertilizers and weedkillers. But if you value the lawn, the annual work of maintenance is not really all that arduous once it has been well fertilized and freed from weeds.

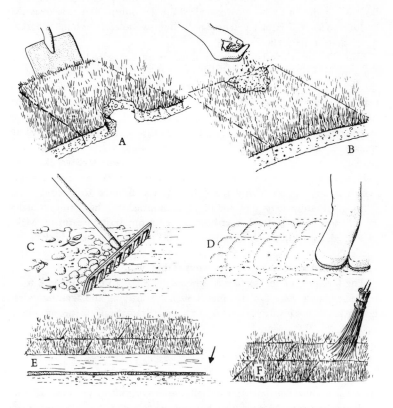

Care of the lawn: (A) to repair a worn turf edge, cut and lift a turf; (B) reverse it and sow seed in bare patch; (C) prepare for laying turf by raking level; (D) tread firmly; (E) lay turf; (F) brush soil in gaps between turves

NEGLECTED LAWNS

Often when one moves to a new house one finds the lawn has been sadly neglected. Several times I have been asked to look at a lawn that was so weed-infested that the owner was on the verge of digging it up and starting all over again.

In every case where the lawn was level and smooth, I have advised against such a drastic step and suggested instead a programme of weedkilling and feeding. After a couple of years or so this has paid off. Only where the lawn was very uneven, have I recommended digging it up.

The first task with a shoddy lawn is to level it. If there are humps and hollows in the turf, the mower will scalp the humps and ride over the hollows to leave bare pale patches on the humps and areas of longer, darker green grass in the hollows.

Minor hollows can be gradually filled in by sifting soil into them and brushing it well in so that only the tips of the grass shoots are revealed. If this treatment is repeated several times the hollows can be levelled up in a season. Deeper hollows need to be dealt with more drastically, the turf lifted, the hollow filled with soil and the turf relaid. When applying sifted soil do not worry that you may be putting weed seeds on the lawn. They will mainly be annual weeds and will disappear after a few mowings; any perennial weeds that germinate can be dealt with by a selective weedkiller.

Humps are not so easily treated. Hollow-tined forks or lawn aerators which remove plugs of soil from the turf can be used to remove cores from small humps over a period of a few months, and they can eventually be rolled or trodden flat. Larger humps need more drastic treatment. Make H-shaped slits in the turf, then lift and roll the two middle pieces back with a spade. Remove enough soil from the hump to allow the two pieces of turf to be replaced at the same level as the rest of the lawn.

The levelling of the surface is probably the most important task for a neglected lawn. All other treatments, such as scarifying and aerating, while beneficial, do not improve the look of a lawn as dramatically as the smoothing process.

AERATING THE LAWN

Aerating is always beneficial, especially on heavy soils or where these tend to lie wet at times. Make slits or holes in the turf with a spiking machine, or remove cores of soil as described above.

The cores can be brushed up and the holes filled with coarse sand. This helps to let water drain away from the surface and hopefully it will be less muddy to walk over in periods of prolonged wet weather.

On normal soils slitting or piercing with a small spiked roller is adequate. It lets air and water down to the grass roots and encourages growth.

SCARIFYING

Even when grass cuttings are allowed to lie on the lawn in summer, I still find it advantageous in autumn to remove decaying grass and to bring to the surface long trailing stoloniferous shoots which for the most part will be bare of leaves.

Raking out this debris with a wire rake is hard work and time-consuming, but there are small electric scarifiers which do a good job quickly and adequately. Hire shops usually stock scarifiers and spiking machines.

MAKING A NEW LAWN

There are two ways of making a new lawn: laying turves or sowing seed. If you are in a hurry and can afford it, you lay turf. If not, you sow seed.

In both cases, soil preparation is the same. Dig it over, remove large stones, roots and perennial weeds and rake the ground level, or at least smooth on a slope. Next firm the soil by treading it, slowly and deliberately, in both directions – across and lengthways, before applying and raking in a general fertilizer at the rate of 2 oz. per square yard (50 g per square metre).

Turves can then be laid on this well-prepared bed; standard sizes are 3 ft by 1 ft (90 cm by 30 cm). If you are buying turves insist on seeing a sample, and if possible try to be at home when the turves are delivered. Check them as they come off the lorry and if they are not as good as the sample – weed-free and compact – refuse to take delivery.

Turfing may be done at any time in open mild weather in autumn, winter or spring, but is risky in summer unless the turf can be watered copiously in dry weather. Stagger the joints as you lay the turves (as in bricklaying), and stand on a wooden plank as you work to avoid damaging both the prepared ground and the newly laid turves. Start at one side and work in straight lines. When the lawn is finished, brush a mixture of coarse sand and sifted soil into the cracks.

Where a lawn is to be seeded try to have the surface soil prepared, as already described, a few weeks beforehand. This allows annual weeds to germinate so that they can be hoed off and the site left clean prior to seed sowing.

Grass seed can be sown at almost any time from April to September as long as it is possible to water the site when necessary. I would never sow grass seed before the last week of April, by which time the soil will have begun to warm up. The warmer the soil the faster the seed germinates, and the less time the birds have to steal it.

The choice of seed mixtures lies, broadly, between a mixture of hard-wearing grasses like rye grass, or a mixture of fine grasses without rye grass. For hard-wearing lawns, with foot traffic and children playing games, a mixture containing rye grass is to be preferred.

Recently a new dwarf strain of rye grass called 'Hunter' has appeared and is becoming popular. It is hard-wearing and does not need cutting as often as ordinary rye grass; it withstands drought conditions well and is of a pleasing dark green colour.

Allow $1\frac{1}{2}$ oz. of seed per square yard (35-40 g per square metre) of lawn. Mark out the area with white tape or string into square yards and sow the requisite amount in each space. Lightly roll it into the surface. Choose a day when it is moist below but dry on the surface. Protect against birds if necessary although most grass seed is treated with a repellent. Make the first cut when the seedlings are 2 in. (5 cm) high, keeping the mower knives high at 1 in. (2.5 cm); water in dry weather.

 OCTOBER

The Month in the Garden

Autumn has finally arrived and preparations for another gardening year make October a very busy month. There are still flowers to brighten our gardens, and myriads of black, blue and scarlet berries glistening on various shrubs and trees. This is the time of year when the fat pods of the rather nondescript *Iris foetidissima* split to reveal rows of coral-red seeds, set like jewels against a cream and green background. Green, gold and scarlet leaves flutter from the trees, and berberis bushes are heavy with rows of rich red fruits, reminiscent of the beaded fringes worn by North American Indians.

Plants providing two displays in a year are real boons, and worth a dozen ephemeral beauties. In the planning of a garden one should always include a number with attractive fruits as well as flowers, like the wine-red fruited *Malus* 'Eleyi' which bears crimson flowers and purplish-green leaves. There are also shrubs which display fine autumnal tints in addition to good flowers, like the deciduous azaleas and the witch hazels (*Hamamelis* species).

Make the October garden interesting with a few highlights, like siting groups of colchicums or autumn crocuses (*Crocus speciosus* or *C. zonatus*) in open glades between shrubs and trees. The fat ruby and white goblets of the colchicums and the misty-blue crocus chalices are now at their best.

General Tasks In October the leaves come hurtling down, covering lawns, rock gardens, flower borders and paths. They must be constantly swept up in order to discourage worms – and their casts – from damaging lawns and to prevent small alpines from rotting underneath them in rock crevices, and they can be dangerous on paths when they become wet and slippery. Leaves must be dredged from pools because their putrefaction releases salts into the water, some of which can injure fish.

Apart from wire rakes and brooms, there are various tools which can make this tiresome task easier, even enjoyable. There are garden sweepers which are pushed along like vacuum cleaners and draw the leaves into large receptacles or bags, ideal for large gardens with broad paths, drives and lawns. To my mind, however, the most useful tool for smaller gardens – and equally useful in large ones – is the mains electric machine called the Green Machine. This blows the leaves together in neat heaps so that they can be lifted easily into a barrow and wheeled away. It is held in the hand, weighs only 5 lb. (2 kg), and when switched on the motor drives a fan inside to create a blast of air. The air escapes through a long hollow tube at the front, its volume controlled by a finger-operated trigger switch. The machine is ideal for getting leaves out of awkward corners, between the stems of herbaceous plants and in rock pockets, drains and gutters.

Two other important tasks are bulb planting (see September, *Bulbs for Forcing and Garden Decoration,* p. 196), and the propagation of hardy shrubs from seeds or cuttings. A greenhouse is unnecessary and although a cold frame or cloches can be useful they are not essential for either method.

Hardwood Cuttings By October the new young shoots of shrubs will have ripened and become firm and woody. They can then be used to make hardwood cuttings. Sturdy stems are cut from healthy plants, their unripe tips removed just above a joint and, at a point 6-12 in. (15-30 cm) lower down (depending on the size of the stem) cut immediately below a joint. Dip the cuttings in a hormone rooting compound and insert for two-thirds of their length in sand or sandy soil in a sheltered spot. They will probably have rooted by spring in the case of forsythia, many roses (especially climbers and vigorous varieties like 'Queen Elizabeth'), kerria, ivies, lavender, rosemary, privet and philadelphus. Evergreens, like cupressus and *Prunus laurocerasus* (Portugal laurel) which do not need their tips removed, may take a little longer.

The great advantage of cuttings is that all the young plants will be identical to the parent stock, while shrubs raised from seed will exhibit individual characteristics.

On the other hand, shrub seedlings usually grow away quicker than hardwood cuttings and are a good method where large quantities are required. The seed must be stratified in order to hasten germination: gather berries as they ripen and spread them on seed-trays half filled with sand; cover the boxes with wire netting to stop birds and mice from taking the fruits, then stand them outside in an open position. The weather does the rest – alternating bouts of freezing and thawing, drought and rain, as well as sun and wind, rapidly soften and rot the flesh, leaving the seeds exposed. After cleaning they can then be sown in pots or boxes and left to germinate.

Trees and Shrubs Make and insert hardwood cuttings as already described, including box, brooms, cistus, tamarisk and olearias, all of which can be left with a heel of old wood attached and the tips left intact. Others which can have the tips removed include spiraeas, weigelas, chaenomeles, cornus, cotoneasters, deutzias, escallonias, hardy fuchsias, hypericums and *Viburnum* *tinus.* The lower leaves of all hardwood cuttings should be removed.

Stack some of the fallen leaves for use in potting and leaf-mould; the rest can go on the compost heap.

Plant new shrubs and trees towards the end of the month. Complete the planting of evergreens or else wait until April.

Plant new deciduous hedges.

Climbers Tie in long shoots and remove dead or broken branches.

Roses Reduce the length of very tall shoots on bushes to reduce the danger of wind rocking.

Prepare the ground for new rose bushes, for planting next month; work in plenty of organic material and add a handful of bonemeal to each 1-ft (30-cm) run of trench.

Lawns Continue scarifying, aerating and fertilizing existing lawns. Break up wormcasts and keep leaves swept from the grass. Turf new lawns and use turves to repair worn patches.

Hardy Plants Continue preparing herbaceous borders for winter.

Plant new perennials, excluding *Aster amellus* varieties, poppies, pyrethrums, *Scabiosa caucasica* and delphiniums if the soil is very heavy. These are best left until spring.

Divide and replant old clumps of early-flowering perennials like doronicums and campanulas. Leave pyrethrums and achilleas until spring.

Dig and manure new beds for next season before the weather turns cold.

This is a good time to move paeonies.

Bulbs Continue planting bulbs for forcing in pots or bowls; store outside under 6 in. (15 cm) of sand or light soil.

WEATHER

Although patience is a virtue in the garden in spring, the reverse is true in autumn when procrastination can be the thief of more than time. Inevitably conditions are getting worse week by week, and the wise gardener always tries to do the autumn digging and clearing-up operations as early as possible.

In addition to shortening daylight hours and falling temperatures, the soil becomes more and more difficult to handle as rain begins to replenish ground water supplies. 'Spring rain damps, autumn rain soaks' and 'In spring a tub of rain makes a spoonful of of mud; In autumn a spoonful of rain makes a tub of mud.'

Although they say in Kent that there are always nineteen fine days in October, this seems to err on the side of optimism and is not likely to be true over most of the country.

The one redeeming feature is St Luke's little summer, a short period of fine warm days which often occurs around 13 October. 23 October on the other hand, the day of St Simon and St Jude, is accounted certain to be rainy, and weather records show that the end of October and beginning of November are often stormy periods with the arrival of vigorous Atlantic depressions. 'On St Simon and St Jude, Winter approaches at a gentle trot.'

The French believe that all ploughing should be done by All Saints' Day, 1 November, and the British gardener should try to complete most of his autumn cultivations by the end of October. If subsequent weather is bad, the early work will be fully justified; and if the autumn remains fine well into November, nothing has been lost.

Complete the planting of small and

rockery bulbs early in the month.

Plant narcissi and hyacinths, but leave tulips until next month, as this lessens the risk of fire blight disease.

Plant lilies.

Lift half-hardy bulbs such as acidantheras, ixias and sparaxis; dry and store in a cool, dry but frost-free place.

Lift gladioli about the middle of the month, trim off the top growth and dry the corms. Store them in shallow trays in a cool, frost-free place.

Rock Garden Plants Remove fallen leaves; hand weed and lightly prick the soil between plants. Check all labels and put down slug bait in damp weather.

Top dress cushion-type plants like androsaces and mossy saxifrages with limestone or granite chippings to protect them from slugs and winter wet.

Cut back straggling stems and protect choice specimens with alpine cloches or panes of glass raised and supported on bricks.

Plant out seedlings or rooted cuttings raised earlier in the year.

Water Plants Dredge out fallen leaves and any decaying vegetation.

Feed fish well this month to prepare them for winter, giving them a high protein diet.

Keep all pools full of water.

Annuals, Biennials and Bedding Plants Complete all summer bedding changes: planting bulbs, polyanthus, forget-me-nots, double daisies, wallflowers, etc.

Dismantle and store unwanted containers, hanging and wall baskets.

Plant window boxes with spring material.

Sweet peas can be sown outside early in the month.

Plant out hardy biennials in their flowering positions.

Cut down dahlias as soon as frost blackens the foliage, lift the tubers and stand them upside down in a dry frost-free place for a week to dry out. Dust the crowns with flowers of sulphur and store them in damp peat in a cool, frost-free place.

Most chrysanthemums can be left outside, or they can be lifted, boxed in potting soil and stored in a cold frame or greenhouse. Water sparingly.

Complete the lifting of tender bedding plants such as cannas, heliotrope and fuchsia standards; store them under heated glass for the winter.

Patio Plants Continue any constructional work.

Replant containers for winter and spring displays. For winter interest, plant with dwarf conifers, ivies and winter-flowering heathers.

Vegetables Lift and store beetroot and marrows.

Gather in the last of summer crops. Clear the ground, dig and manure it.

Plant winter lettuce under cloches, and, in the south of England, spring cabbage during the first week of the month.

Herbs Gather and dry branches of bay for winter use.

Fennel and mint can be lifted and boxed in peat to be kept in a warm kitchen or greenhouse for use in winter.

Small parsley seedlings can be planted in parsley pots or small containers.

Fruit Order new fruit trees and bushes; prepare the soil for their reception and plant immediately on arrival.

Continue to pick tree fruits as they become ready, mainly pears and apples.

Unless already completed, cut out old fruiting canes from raspberries, loganberries and blackberries; tie in new shoots on supporting wires or frames.

Clean and cultivate any spare ground, removing weeds – especially those near existing trees or bushes.

Complete greasebanding and spray the ground around dormant bushes with paraquat. This will kill all existing weeds.

Plants under Glass Admit as much air as possible, according to the weather. Alternatively, install a small fan and keep this permanently switched on. It keeps the air moving and prevents mildew and other diseases. It also distributes heat more effectively. See also January, *Greenhouse Gardening*, p. 18. Do not spray or water more than absolutely necessary, especially over plant foliage.

Dry off begonias, gloxinias, achimenes and other summer-flowering greenhouse bulbs this month. Begonias can then be lifted, cleaned and stored in dry peat in a temperature of around 10°C (50°F). Gloxinias, achimenes and hippeastrums are better left in their pots; lay them on their sides and keep them in a frost-free place.

Thin out shoots of climbing greenhouse plants, particularly plumbago, passiflora, *Jasminum polyanthum* and tibouchinas.

Check that frame lights are closed when frost threatens; make regular checks on heating appliances and thermostats in the greenhouse.

House Plants Keep plants away from frosty windows at night, but give them all possible light during the day.

Water carefully and only when required.

Cease feeding from the middle of the month.

Pick off dead leaves regularly.

PLANTS IN THEIR PRIME

Trees and Shrubs Abelias; *Arbutus unedo;* berberis (some species); callunas; *Ceanothus* 'Burkwoodii'; *Ceratostigma plumbaginoides; Cotoneaster horizontalis; Elaeagnus pungens;* ericas; *Escallonia macrantha* and other species and hybrids; *Euonymus europaeus* (spindle); *Hamamelis virginiana;* hebes; *Perovskia atriplicifolia; Ulex europaeus* 'Plenus' (gorse).

Climbers Callicarpa (berries); celastrus (berries); *Clematis flammula, C. rehderana, C. vitalba; Jasminum officinale;* late roses.

October berries: *Euonymus europaeus,* spindle (left); *Cotoneaster horizontalis* (centre); berberis (right)

Hardy Plants *Anemone japonica* varieties; *Aster ericoides, A. novae-angliae, A. novi-belgii* varieties;

Boltonia asteroides; helianthus species and varieties (perennial sunflowers); *Kniphofia uvaria* and various garden hybrids; *Liriope spicata;* physalis (fruits); *Sedum spectabile* and varieties.

Bulbs Colchicums; autumn-flowering kinds of crocus; *Cyclamen neapolitanum; Galanthus nivalis* 'olgae' (snowdrop); *Leucojum autumnale; Nerine bowdenii; Schizostylis coccinea* and varieties; *Sternbergia lutea.*

Rock Garden Plants *Achillea tomentosa; Gentiana farreri, G. sino-ornata; Polygonum vacciniifolium;* violas; *Zauschneria californica.*

CROPS TO ENJOY

Vegetables Broccoli; cabbage; carrots; cauliflower; celery; leeks; lettuce; parsnips; spinach; turnips.

Also beetroot, carrots, onions, potatoes and shallots in store.

Fruits Apples and pears in variety; grapes; medlars; late plums; quinces; late raspberries and strawberries.

PLANT ASSOCIATIONS

A group of *Gentiana sino-ornata* with flowering heathers.

A bed of mixed Michaelmas daisies.

Pink and white autumn anemones with *Sedum spectabile* in front.

GARDEN PROBLEMS

Mildew on greenhouse plants: aim at a more buoyant atmosphere.

Frosted half-hardy perennials; bring under frost-free cover in plenty of time.

Fallen leaves smothering small plants.

Rotting leaves in garden pools; trap these with a net spread over the top or dredge out regularly.

Plants of the Month

SAFFRON CROCUSES

In September and October *Crocus sativus,* the saffron crocus, comes into flower, spangling short grass, rock garden pockets and open patches between shrubs and hardy plants with its narrow goblets of orange-centred, misty blue flowers. If left undisturbed it seeds itself with happy abandon.

Saffron was perhaps the most valuable and important spice of the Old World and was widely grown in Asia Minor long before nutmegs, cloves and other riches of the East reached Europe. Its uses included dyeing cloth, bleaching hair, and providing spicy flavouring and colouring for food. Medicinally, saffron was used as an opiate against hysteria, was made into pills to stop nose-bleeds or to promote eruptions in measles, and was distilled into a nerve tonic. It was also thought to prevent sea sickness if worn in a bag over the stomach, and to induce immoderate laughter when taken internally.

Saffron is obtained from the orange stigmas in the centre of the flowers, about four thousand three hundred blooms being necessary to produce a single ounce of crude saffron. Small wonder that the cost, plus the uncertainty of the harvest, has now largely removed it from the market.

Crocus sativus, saffron crocus

It must have been popular in Tudor times since a law passed during the reign of Henry VIII prohibited the dyeing of Irish linen sheets with saffron. Apparently such sheets were not washed frequently enough, in the belief that they had antiseptic qualities, a practice which was thought by doctors to contribute to the spread of plagues.

There are several stories concerning the introduction of saffron to England. Some say it was brought by the Romans, but the tale I like best concerns an Essex pilgrim who, after visiting the Holy Land, and 'proposing to do good to his countrey', stole 'a head of saffron and hid the same in his Palmer's staffe, which he had made hollow . . . and so he brought the root into this realme with venture of his life, for if he had been taken, by the law of the countrey from whence it came, he had died for the fact' (Hakluyt in *Rembrances for Masters S.,* 1582). Other stories credit the introduction to a Sir Thomas Smith of Saffron Walden in about 1330.

However it occurred, there was certainly a flourishing saffron industry in that part of Essex for hundreds of years, giving the town its name. Stray blooms can still be found in the hedgerows, and the arms of Saffron Walden, granted a charter during the reign of Edward vi, bear three crocus flowers.

Metasequoia glyptostroboides

METASEQUOIA

Metasequoia glyptostroboides is one of the world's most interesting trees for although long known in Pliocene fossils, living specimens were unrecorded until 1941.

In that year three trees were discovered by a Chinese forester, but they were not identified until 1946 after a Chinese botanist called Dr H. Hu compared a specimen with fossil representations. Through the agencies of Harvard University and the Chinese it is now known that the plant is more plentiful than was at first realized, growing over an area of some two hundred and fifty square miles in Western Hupeh, where in one valley alone there is a stand of more than a thousand trees. In its native territory it is known as water fir and the foliage is used – and actually harvested – for feeding cattle. Plants reached Europe around 1948, and now many specimens grow in Britain where it has been given the more manageable name of dawn redwood.

Metasequoia, which is related to sequoiadendron (formerly sequoia), the world's largest tree, is a deciduous conifer growing to 100 ft (30 m) in its native environment. Already some British specimens are 40–50 ft (12–15 m) high and producing cones, although these have not yet produced seed, possibly because the male cones do not ripen sufficiently in these islands or are killed in winter. The plants' lacy, light green leaves are most attractive in spring and summer and turn russet-red prior to falling in autumn.

Growing in the Shade

Gardeners frequently request me to recommend plants for growing in deep shade, under trees or in the shadow of a north wall. Such plants may be limited in number and their colours less brilliant than those of sun lovers, but there are enough to make shady spots colourful and interesting for many months of the year.

The most important preliminary is to get the ground in good condition. Few plants will tolerate dry shade, but many grow well in damp shade. Prepare the soil by deep digging and work in plenty of organic material, such as decayed farmyard manure, old mushroom compost, leaf-mould or rotted garden compost. This will hold moisture as well as provide food for the plants, and dry shady soils can be kept moist by watering. In later years the humus content can be kept up by regular mulches of similar material. Get rid of weeds before planting; some, like ground elder, thrive only too well in shade and unless eradicated before plants are inserted will be a constant source of aggravation.

CLIMBERS

Hydrangea petiolaris is perhaps the showiest for a north wall. A strong growing, self-clinging species, it may need a little support at first while getting established, but thereafter romps its way up walls, fences and even tree trunks, producing flat 3-4-in. (7.5-10-cm) clusters of greenish-white flower-heads bordered by conspicuous white sterile florets. They appear in June, each sterile blossom consisting of four uniform petals. The simple leaves are deciduous.

Another self-clinger, the vigorous *Schizophragma hydrangeoides*, also produces flattish flower clusters, but they are 6-8 in. (15-20 cm) across, their chief feature being one large, heart-shaped, creamy-yellow bract up to 1½ in. (4 cm) wide and 3 in. (7.5 cm) long on each sterile flower.

Ivies thrive on north walls. Besides the many small-leaved varieties of *Hedera helix*, there are large cream-variegated types like *H. colchica* 'Dentata Variegata'. Although honeysuckles are often recommended for shade they will not flower well without plenty of sun and light, a point which matters little with the gold- and green-variegated *Lonicera japonica* 'Aureo-reticulata' since – in spite of Bean declaring that it flowers freely – I have rarely seen this variety in bloom.

Some vines grow well in deep shade, particularly *Parthenocissus (Vitis) henryana*; its hand-shaped leaves, with three or five leaflets, are dark green with the main veins picked out in pink and silvery-white.

SHRUBS

Glossy-leaved evergreen camellias are without parallel for a shady border. They are beautiful at all seasons, never more so than in late winter and early spring when festooned with myriads of symmetrical, single or double rosettes of flowers, in shades of pink, red, white and striations of these shades. These shrubs can also be grown in tubs of lime-free but humus-rich soil and moved about in key positions as required.

Several viburnums do well in shade, particularly the winter-flowering, evergreen laurustinus, *Viburnum tinus*. The flat heads of white, pink-budded flowers appear continuously from late autumn until early spring – although more profusely in sun than in shade. *V. rhytidophyllum*, another evergreen, has large oblong leaves covered with rusty-brown hairs beneath, and flat heads of white flowers, or pink in the variety 'Roseum'. We have a hedge of *V. farreri* against a north fence; it is now 12 ft (3.6 m) high, its naked branches studded each winter with clusters of fragrant, white, pink-budded flowers.

Aucubas of all kinds can go in shade and will grow quite large; they can be useful for masking ugly features. All are evergreen, the most attractive being the gold- or cream-spotted kinds like 'Crotonifolia' and 'Variegata', female plants, and 'Maculata', male. It is necessary to grow both sexes in order to obtain the showy round, scarlet berries which persist all winter. There are also varieties with yellow berries.

Hollies will grow in shade, and again trees of both sexes are necessary in order to ensure berries. If there is a male plant in the neighbourhood you may be able to concentrate on female hollies, leaving bees to do the pollinating. Skimmias also carry the sexes separately, except for *S. reevesiana* which is hermaphrodite. They are small, glossy-leaved evergreens, only 3-4 ft (90-120 cm) high, and very suitable for front row positions in borders. The small white flower heads are fragrant, exceptionally so on male plants, and the bright scarlet fruits are as vivid as holly berries and persist until the plants bloom again the following spring.

Hypericum calycinum, the rosé of Sharon, is a most adaptable plant, for not only will it grow in shade, but also in comparatively dry places such as on banks. It grows about 12 in. (30 cm) high, with showy 3-in. (7.5-cm), five-petalled, golden flowers which have central bosses of yellow stamens. This gives them a pin-cushion appearance and though they bloom most freely in June, flowers appear intermittently until September. This evergreen ground-cover plant benefits from being cut back fairly hard each spring.

Bamboos and box, periwinkles (*Vinca minor* and *V. major*) with single and double flowers, and the scarlet-berried butcher's broom (*Ruscus* species) are others to grow in shade, as well as *Fatsia japonica*, which produces its ivy-like flowers in December; *Mahonia aquifolium*; *Symphoricarpos albus*, the snowberries; and *Rhododendron ponticum*. Mention should also be made of the Japanese *Pachysandra terminalis*, especially the cream- and green-variegated 'Variegata'. Growing about 9 in. (23 cm) high, with small, diamond-shaped and toothed evergreen leaves and sprays of small white flowers in February and March, it thrives in damp shade but will also grow under dryish conditions. It makes an ideal ground cover, and is to my mind more attractive than the American species *P. procumbens*.

PERENNIALS AND BULBS

There are a considerable number of herbaceous plants suitable for shady situations, including the early-flowering hellebores. The lenten roses (*Helleborus orientalis*), given damp shade, will seed themselves about without help from the gardener. Their round, single rose-like flowers of white, cream, pink, red, deep crimson and, more rarely, yellow, appear in January, sometimes earlier, and persist for weeks. It is usually necessary to remove some of the older, discoloured leaves when the buds appear, otherwise they hide the blossoms. Then there is the taller, 2-4 ft (60-120-cm) prickly-edged, tripartite-leaved and green-flowered *H. corsicus* which stands out well in a dim corner. This also seeds itself, as do the lesser green-flowered *H. foetidus* and *H. lividus*.

Plants for shade: (A) *Vinca minor*, periwinkle; (B) *Phyllitis scolopendrium*, hart's tongue; (C) *Endymion* (*hyacinthus*) *non-scriptus*, bluebell

One plant I would not wish to lose is the white-flowered toothwort, *Dentaria pinnata*, so-called because of the shape of its white tuberous roots. This thrives in the deepest shade in our garden, producing masses of pretty white flowers on 1½-ft (45-cm) spikes, with light green, deeply cut leaves long before most other flowers have awakened from their winter slumber.

Kirengeshoma palmata, the yellow waxbell, growing in the same shady spot is as late as the toothwort is early, for the blooms do not appear until late September and October. The smooth, 3-ft (90-cm), slightly purplish stems carry thin, maple-shaped leaves and terminal clusters of long, drooping, bright yellow, waxy-textured flowers. It is a plant which resents dryness round the roots.

Other plants for shady borders and corners include lilies of the valley, *Convallaria majalis*, with single or double white or pink flowers; Solomon's seal, *Polygonatum multiflorum*; *Meconopsis cambrica*, the Welsh poppy, with yellow or orange flowers; and the blue representatives of this exotic family like *M. betonicifolia*.

In addition, there are *Gentiana asclepiadea*, the willow gentian, with arching sprays of deep blue or white blossoms on 18-in. (45-cm) stems in late summer; the autumn-blooming Japanese anemones, *Anemone hupehensis* (*A. japonica*) hybrids; trilliums which flower early in spring; *Euphorbia robbiae*, low-growing with green flowers; and uvularias with drooping yellow flowers.

Many of the primulas and, of course, any of the hostas are plants for shady, moist spots.

Among bulbous plants are bluebells; *Anemone blanda*, richly blue but with pink and white cultivars; *Cyclamen neapolitanum*, autumn-flowering and useful under trees; and several alliums like the white *A. triquetrum*. Few annuals tolerate much shade, but where there are patches of sunshine for part of the day try impatiens, nasturtiums and the biennial foxgloves.

Finally, there are ferns like *Phyllitis scolopendrium*, hart's tongue, which are natural dwellers in shade and variable in shape, texture and habit.

The Unscrupulous Conmen

Many freelance or jobbing gardeners do a good job at a reasonable rate, cash down for obvious reasons. Leaving aside the morality of this, there is the much more serious problem of unskilled operators who go round offering to prune or lop trees, shrubs and hedges.

I have seen some appalling examples of such work, including the damage sustained by two elderly ladies who had their treasured wall-trained peaches reduced to mere stumps. They had paid several hundred pounds for the privilege and tearfully asked me when they might expect to have fruit again. The answer had to be 'never'.

How to find an honest and capable tree surgeon? Efficient local authorities should be able to supply a list of contractors they have found reliable. Alternatively, write to the Arboricultural Association, Ampfield House, Ampfield, near Romsey, Hants. This has a list of about fifty consultants and contractors whose work has been inspected and whose standards may be relied upon. The contractors must also have insurance cover of £250,000, and their work embraces planting, pruning, cable bracing and felling of trees as well as tree nutrition and disease control. Before allowing *any* firm to start work on tree surgery or tree felling, insist on seeing a current receipt of the insurance premium covering third party liability.

There are also patently dishonest characters who con people into having their drives or paths resurfaced. While infuriating, these smooth operators cause less lasting damage than the unskilled wreckers who mutilate trees so badly that they never become a thing of beauty again. At least the shoddy work of the drive cowboys can be put right, albeit at considerable expense.

The pattern of approach by such a character is a ring at the door, a lugubrious look, and a declaration that the drive has some holes and is in urgent need of repair which, if not soon attended to, will result in complete disaster and a huge repair bill if there is a severe frost next winter. By a strange coincidence he has a load of bituminous macadam left over from another job in the neighbourhood, so he is able to do your drive at once for a very reasonable price. Usually he puts what is virtually a useless skim of bituminous macadam over the surface and demands four or five times the charge of a reputable firm. A favoured technique is to turn up early in the day when the husband is at work, and the wife is so taken in by his patter that she thinks it is too good a bargain to miss.

If you need to have a drive laid, or an old one repaired and resurfaced, ask around in the neighbourhood for the names of reliable firms. Local building contractors of good standing are often able to recommend a firm they have found reasonable and efficient over a number of years.

It is also worth asking your local council for recommendations on drive construction firms. For a major job always obtain two, preferably three estimates and make sure the firms are estimating on the same specifications. Insist on having estimates in writing.

Many factors must be considered when a new drive becomes necessary. Is it to be used only by light car traffic, or will the local refuse man, coal lorry or oil tanker be trundling frequently up and down? A well-constructed drive consists of a solid base, topped by a layer of bituminous macadam. The upper layer is made up of stone chippings impregnated with bitumen. For a good drive the soil should be excavated 6 in. (15 cm) deep, and the base firmly rammed or rolled if it has loosened during the excavation process. A foundation, consisting of concrete or brick rubble, should be put in and firmed; on top of this is laid – for a normal private drive – a 2-in. (5-cm) 'wearing course' of small stone chippings and bitumen. A drive for heavy traffic should have a $1\frac{1}{2}$-in. (4-cm) layer of heavier stone material and above this the 'wearing course' of finer chippings.

Stipulate that no clay is included in the base material because it may swell when wet and shrink when dry, causing much trouble.

I would also advise the insertion of concrete slab kerbs, 2 by 6 in. (5 by 15 cm) deep at the sides of the drive. They will prevent the sides of the drive from crumbling and protect adjoining grass or borders. It is of paramount importance that a drive on a slope must be so constructed that rainwater runs off and does not lie in puddles on the surface. This needs a skilled artisan and is another reason for using a reliable firm.

Finally, beware of one who offers to guarantee the work on your drive for five, eight or ten years. Ten to one his caravan and lorry will have moved on to another district inside a month or so. Bona-fide contractors do not give such guarantees because they cannot be responsible for the quality of the macadam, but they will always come and relay any surface that may for one reason or another disintegrate.

There are also unscrupulous characters in the plant business. A common trick is to offer tender annuals and tomato plants long before it is safe to plant them outside. Since frosts are possible until the end of May such plants are doubtful buys unless they can be kept in a frost-free greenhouse, watering and tending them in the meantime until the end of May. They probably came orginally from a grower who raised the plants too early and was then faced with the necessity of warning prospective customers that they must give them protection for a few weeks or have the plants (particularly tomato) spoiled by growing them too long and leggy. The alternative was to pass them on to someone else for disposal.

This practice of offering tender plants liable to be killed by April or May frosts is not confined to barrow boys. There are plenty of garden centres and high-street shops where tomato or marrow plants, petunias, salvias, geraniums, begonias, fuchsias, marigolds and other frost-tender plants are offered for sale as early as the first week of April.

Some garden centres display coloured posters showing plants that are frost hardy, others, like alyssum, which will shrug off a few degrees of frost, and those which will certainly be killed or severely damaged by frost.

There are glowing advertisements for unusual shrubs or fruits. Sub-tropical fruits like Chinese gooseberries (*Actinidia chinensis*), tree tomatoes (*Cyphomandra betacea*), and loquats (*Eriobotrya japonica*) may bear the odd fruit in a warm southern garden, but it is doubtful whether they will even survive in the colder north.

The more honest traders do recommend growing such plants in a greenhouse where at least they will not die, although the promised 'baskets of fruit' rarely materialize.

All sorts of claims are made for plant novelties. There is a slight element of truth, but some advertisers shamefully overdramatize the traits in order to sell the plants. There are offers of plants to 'rid your house of flies', meaning insectivorous plants like the Venus flytrap (*Dionaea muscipula*) which may catch the odd insect but loathes the dry atmosphere of the normal household. Another will 'drive moles from your garden'. This usually refers to the caper spurge (*Euphorbia lathyris*) and is a much quoted remedy. In a pharmocognosy garden near our home where they grow quantities of medicinal plants, I saw a bed of caper spurges honeycombed by moles. These little pests have to be got rid of by more conventional methods.

Inexperienced gardeners often buy the 'blue geraniums' believing them to be blue versions of the scarlet bedding geraniums (pelargoniums). Yet the name is correct. The plants are hardy herbaceous *Geranium* species, commonly known as crane's-bill, of which there are good blue varieties.

The 'hardy citrus' is not any of the kinds you buy at the greengrocers, but the Chinese *Citrus trifoliata,* which more correctly should be called *Poncirus trifoliatus* as botanists have removed it from the genus *Citrus*. This does flower and bear small fruits in a sheltered situation, but they are hard and inedible except for the grated skin which can be used in drinks. However, a cross between this species and the sweet orange (*Citrus sinensis*) has produced the citrange which, with some winter protection, is practically hardy in warm, sheltered situations and bears acid but juicy orange-coloured fruits.

NOVEMBER

The Month in the Garden

When I was a child November seemed to be the most dismal month of the whole year. Fogs were common – real 'pea soupers' in the south of England – which stripped the leaves from privet and various other evergreens, caused bonfire smoke to move sideways and add to the yellow murk, made travelling difficult and caused bronchial sufferers real distress. Perhaps the only benefit was the fact that lichens and black spot on roses were unable to tolerate the acid sulphurous fumes and therefore never occurred in gardens subject to fogs.

General Tasks The Clean Air Act has put paid to fogs. Today, November is often a mild and at times sunny month, and we can get on with the work of tidying the garden, creating new herbaceous borders and renovating old ones, planting fruit trees and bushes, and pruning the apple and pear trees.

It is also an ideal time to plant new rose bushes, in well-prepared and manured ground. Always take out a planting hole that seems larger than will be needed, and fork over the subsoil before spreading a layer of well-rotted farmyard manure or compost. Cover this in turn with garden soil, then place the rose bush in the hole, with its roots spread out and

any damaged parts removed. Pack the bush with moist peat and bonemeal and then the excavated soil. Firm as planting progresses, and stake standards to prevent wind-rocking later.

With grafted trees and bushes, it is most important to bury the union between rootstock and scion, to prevent injury by frost and also to give the roses a chance to make roots on their own account instead of being entirely dependent on the briar on which they were grafted.

In general, rose bushes should be planted about 2 ft (60 cm) apart, or 2½ ft (75 cm) when exhibition blooms are required. Standards should be set 3-4 ft (90-120 cm) apart if grouped, but undoubtedly look most effective when planted among bush trees.

Existing rose bushes need some attention at this time, to keep them tidy and weed-free and to ensure that they are in good condition for the following season. Start by cutting out briar growths as close as possible to the stocks, and remove perennial weeds. Fork between the plants; if the soil is very heavy or sour, a dressing of lime can be applied before forking takes place. Manuring is best delayed until springtime.

Although many growers follow the time-hallowed habit of pruning in spring, those roses which have made strong shoots, 4-5 ft (1.2-1.5 m) in length can, for the sake of appearances and to prevent them being blown about in the wind, be cut back by 2 ft (60 cm).

Many ornamental grasses can be planted in early November, such as pampas grass and eulalias – and bamboos in sheltered positions. Although peat or leaf mould can be added to the soil it is best not to introduce manure at this stage of their lives.

Larger bulbs like hyacinths and narcissi can still be planted, but they will probably perform less satisfactorily if planting is delayed much longer. However, November and even early December are suitable times for planting tulip varieties as they are less likely to contract tulip fire disease so late in the year. We never plant ours until mid-November.

Another important task is to collect suitable material for winter-protecting tender subjects. We cannot foretell the possible severity of winter weather, and suddenly we may need straw or bracken, leaves, hessian frames or sheets of glass as well as string to protect special treasures.

WEATHER

'Set trees at All Hallowtide (2 November), and command them to grow; set them after Candlemas (2 February) and entreat them to grow'. Late autumn is always the most suitable time for transplanting trees and shrubs. Soil temperatures are still comparatively high, and autumn and winter rains are helpful. In winter or early spring, soil temperatures may still be low, and there is always a danger of dry spells which are harmful to plants whose roots are not well established.

Although November is normally the last month of autumn, it can often be the beginning of an early winter. The turning point seems to come at Martinmas, for although St Martin's Summer is said to last for three days and a bit, by this date 'winter is on its way'.

A saying from Huntingdon reminds us that 'Wind north-west at Martinmas, Severe winter to come', but if St Martin's Day, 11 November, is fair, dry and cold, it is thought that winter will not last long. This belief, that an early cold spell is something of a false alarm, has prompted many country sayings: 'If there is ice in November to bear a duck, There'll be nothing after but sludge and muck', which may owe more to hope than certainty. A more reliable adage is: 'When in November the water rises, It will show itself the whole winter', which is another reason why autumn work in the garden should be carried out sooner rather than later.

Trees and Shrubs Deciduous trees and shrubs can be planted this month, in clean, well-prepared soil. Tread the ground around the roots from time to time as the work proceeds.

If new trees arrive in frosty weather,

keep them under cover until conditions improve.

Tall trees should be staked; protect the stems with hessian or cloth tied and carefully secured with soft string; a piece of inner tube from a car or bicycle can also be used as protection. Never let string or wire cut into the tender bark. Purpose-made plastic ties can be looped round the trunk and stake and loosened as the tree expands.

Plant a *Cotoneaster horizontalis* or *C. dammeri* beside a drain cover. It will grow over and hide the cover, but can be lifted gently if this has to be opened.

Continue to take hardwood cuttings (see October, *Hardwood Cuttings*, p. 212), especially of ribes and willows.

Climbers Plant *Clematis* x *jackmanii* and a pink climbing rose together near a stout pole. Run wires from the top of the pole down to the ground, about 12 in. (30 cm) away. Wrap wire or plastic netting around this wigwam and allow the climbers to clamber up and mingle.

For quick ground cover in a large shady garden plant ivies, *Hydrangea petiolaris* or *Parthenocissus quinquefolia* (Virginia creeper); encourage these to sprawl instead of climbing.

Roses Plant new bushes and standards; climbers and ramblers should be set 12-15 in. (30-35 cm) back from walls and fences. Stake and tie as necessary.

Make hardwood cuttings of strong growing roses like 'Queen Elizabeth', 'Iceberg' and 'Peace'.

Replace worn out roses with new ones, but not in the same soil. See March, *Roses*, p. 60.

Lawns Complete turfing new lawns and patching old ones.

Spike and aerate established lawns if this was not done in October.

In new gardens, outline the lawn area, dig and manure the ground and remove perennial weeds. Leave the soil rough – although as level as possible – until spring for the weather to break it up. It will then be easier to prepare for sowing.

Drainage improvements on very wet or low-lying land should be carried out now.

Hardy Plants Finish digging and tidying herbaceous beds and borders.

Cut stems of herbaceous perennials back nearly to the ground, except in very cold or exposed areas when they should be left until spring.

Protecting plants in the winter: (A) when the pool freezes, pour boiling water on a floating ball, and remove, (B) bale out some water and (c) cover hole with hessian; (D) and (E) use glass lights to protect plants; (F) cover alpines; (G) tie evergreen leaves of red-hot pokers together

Bunch the evergreen leaves of kniphofias (red-hot pokers) and tie them together. This protects the crowns of the plants and prevents water from entering and freezing.

Collect leaves of oak and beech, which take a long time to rot, and heap these over and around tender plants like agapanthus, nerines and *Amaryllis belladonna*. If they are still green or showing flowers, wait until these die down before covering the crowns. Other leaves can be composted for mulching round rhododendrons and lilies.

Bulbs Plant tulips and complete the planting of hyacinths and narcissi. Bring in bowls of bulbs from the plunge bed; acclimatize them in a cool room before subjecting them to higher temperatures. See also September, *Bulbs for Forcing and Garden Decoration*, p. 196.

If lilies arrive this month, plant at once if weather permits. Otherwise store them in boxes of barely moist peat in a cool, frost-free place until spring. Alternatively, pot the bulbs, still keeping them cool.

Clean, dry and store gladioli and *Acidanthera bicolor* 'Murielae' corms.

Annuals, Biennials and Bedding Plants Examine dahlias and other bulbous plants in store. Shrivelled tubers can be revived by plunging them for several hours in tepid water, then drying them off and covering them with peat.

Rock Garden Plants Remove fallen leaves from small plants.

Stand a pane of glass on short stakes or bricks over plants like androsace which dislike winter wet. Secure the glass with large stones.

Top dress small compact plants with granite or stone chippings, crushed crocks or clean shingle. This will smother weed seedlings and keep the crowns of the plants dry.

Water Plants Dredge out fallen leaves from pools.

Feed fish with high protein food until the middle of the month, then stop.

Overhaul pool pumps and other equipment.

Patio Plants Trees, shrubs and heathers from pots can be planted in containers this month; keep them in a sheltered place during the first winter. In very severe weather it may be necessary to move them under frost-free cover; alternatively heap straw or leaves round the containers as a temporary measure.

Keep stonework clean by scrubbing. Treat paths with an algicide to make them non-slip.

Vegetables Lift parsnips for storing, especially in cold exposed areas.

In the south, try an outdoor sowing of broad beans during the first half of the month. Choose varieties likely to over-winter like 'The Sutton', 'Aquadulce', 'Claudia' or 'Bonny Lad'.

Shorten the top growth of Jerusalem artichokes; lift the tubers as required for use.

Chicory, rhubarb and seakale can be taken into a greenhouse at the end of the month for forcing.

Herbs Put protective glass covering – cloches or framelights – over parsley so as to have it available all winter.

Lift a few roots of mint, pot in good soil and take into the kitchen or a warm greenhouse to sprout (see September, *Herbs*, p. 190).

Fruit Root-prune fruit trees, especially plums, which have failed to fruit. Take out a trench about 4 ft (1.2 m) away from the trunk, exposing the roots. Leave the fibrous feeding roots alone but cut through and sever stout and strong anchoring roots. Work round the root area in this way stopping at 2 ft (60 cm) from the trunk. Return the soil afterwards over the fibrous roots. Some gardeners root-prune one half of the tree one year and complete pruning the next.

Winter-prune apples and pears (see *Pruning Calendar*, p. 239).

Plant new fruit trees and bushes; lightly prune young fruit trees, newly planted, to establish the framework.

Complete pruning of raspberries, removing old canes and suckers at base and tying in new canes to the wire supports.

Plants under Glass Start forcing azaleas.

Tidy all plants, removing dead flowers and leaves.

Avoid splashing water about; do necessary watering in the mornings.

Ventilate plants in frames whenever possible; close lights in fog or severe cold. Keep the soil moist but not wet.

House Plants Keep plants tidy, giving them plenty of light during the day. Protect from excessive temperature fluctuations, and maintain damp but not wet conditions.

PLANTS IN THEIR PRIME

Shrubs and Trees *Arbutus unedo* (strawberry tree); *Elaeagnus pungens*; *Erica carnea* varieties; *Fatsia japonica*; hebes (some); *Prunus subhirtella* 'Autumnalis'; *Viburnum farreri*. Berries on hollies, skimmias, cotoneasters and others.

Hardy Plants *Helleborus niger* (certain forms in sheltered places); *Liriope spicata*; winter pansies.

Bulbs Colchicums; *Cyclamen neapolitanum*; *Schizostylis coccinea* and varieties; *Sternbergia lutea*.

GARDEN PROBLEMS

Frost lifting newly planted subjects.
Wind tearing at loosely tied climbers.
Mice eating fruit, vegetables and tubers in store.
Mildew in greenhouses; ventilate whenever possible and keep water off floors. If mildew persists, spray with a suitable fungicide.
Check pools, gutters and drains for fallen leaves.

CROPS TO ENJOY

Vegetables Jerusalem artichokes; broccoli; Brussels sprouts; cabbage; celeriac; celery; leeks; parsnips; savoys; spinach; turnips. Beet, carrots, onions, potatoes, shallots and turnips in store.

Fruit Grapes, apples, pears, and nuts in store.

PLANT ASSOCIATIONS

Erica carnea with euonymus. Red and white heathers (*Erica carnea*), and varieties with golden foliage in front of dwarf silver or gold conifers.

Red *Cotoneaster dammeri* berries undercarpeting a variegated-leaved holly.

Pernettya mucronata berries associated with the red stems of *Cornus alba* 'Sibirica'.

Plants of the Month

WEEPING WILLOWS

Weeping willows are popular in Britain, and also in Australia; curiously, Napoleon I was the link that established them in both places.

Salix babylonica, weeping willow

The species *Salix babylonica* has never been found wild and is known only in cultivation. Its weeping form was introduced to Britain about 1730, and the most famous tree seems to have been that cultivated by Alexander Pope in his garden at Twickenham. This was raised from a live twig tied round a parcel of figs received from abroad by Lady Suffolk at a time when Pope was visiting her.

Subsequently these weeping trees became immensely popular, many being taken abroad by colonists going overseas. Among the many willows which thus found new homes, one went to St Helena and was flourishing there at the time of Napoleon's exile. He sat so often in its shade that a seat was built beneath it.

The former French Emperor, however, was far from being a model prisoner and frequently complained about conditions, including the lack of shade, on the island. In 1819 he wrote to a friend in Paris, 'No doubt the English have in mind my death, and when it comes to pass I ask that I may be buried beneath the willow neath whose shade I so often sit.' In 1821 he did die; strangely, at the time of his death a violent storm destroyed the tree. Nevertheless he was buried in the spot of his choice, and Madame Bertrand planted a few twigs from the fallen tree around his grave, one of which grew lustily. Here Napoleon's body remained until 1840 when it was taken to its present resting place in Les Invalides in Paris. In the years between, however, many people visited the grave, especially ship passengers making the long journey to Australia from Britain or vice versa. It became customary to gather a few twigs from the willow as a memento and to keep them in water for the rest of the voyage, by which time they had usually rooted, and so Napoleon willows became treasured souvenirs in many new homes.

MONKEY PUZZLE TREES

The monkey puzzle tree or Chile pine, botanically known as *Araucaria araucana,* is the only conifer of tree-like proportions from the Southern Hemisphere which is hardy in the British Isles.

Its curious branches do indeed resemble a tangle of monkey's tails, being long and narrow, curved at the tips and tightly clothed with hard, dark green, prickly leaves. They are not only tightly clustered – about twenty-five leaves to 1 in. (2.5 cm), according to W. J. Bean – but stay fresh on the tree for ten to fifteen years and are then retained for several more. In time, monkey puzzle trees grow to 80 ft (24 m) and bear catkins and cones, the latter taking two years to develop their seeds.

The monkey puzzle was brought to England in 1795 by Archibald Menzies, the surgeon-botanist who accompanied Captain George Vancouver on the *Discovery,* the ship sent to the Americas to discover 'the existence of any navigable communications between the North Pacific and Atlantic Oceans'. During the course of this long survey voyage they put in for stores at Valparaiso in Chile. There Menzies met the Viceroy, who turned out to be an Irishman who had adopted Spanish nationality. Invited to dinner, Menzies was intrigued by some unusual nuts served at the meal. In the interests of science he pocketed a few and managed to sprout several on the long journey back to England. They were later handed over to Sir Joseph Banks and given the name *Araucaria* because the trees were native to an area of Chile populated by the Araucana Indians.

Araucaria araucana, monkey puzzle tree

Pruning

Pruning is a necessary evil. Necessary, because it removes superfluities which affect the health and shape, fruit and flower production of the plant. Evil, because the sharp instruments used to carry it out create wounds, and wounds can open the way to infection and other troubles.

The reasons for pruning are as varied as the plants to be cut; to create stocky plants, especially in bedding plants and annuals; to remove dead, damaged, diseased or badly placed branches; to obtain better quality flowers or fruits; to balance root and top growth; to improve the shape; to let in more light; to discourage irregular cropping (too much fruit one year and none the next); to produce plenty of young shoots on plants which bear their flowers on the annual wood, like *Jasminum nudiflorum* and blackcurrants, or which colour up well for winter effects, as in the case of some *Cornus* species; and to replace worn-out branches with new and vigorous growths.

PRUNING DO'S

Do use sharp tools.

Do remove dead and diseased wood regardless of season, or the trouble may spread.

Do take out rubbing and crossing branches which can damage bark and cut out light.

Do protect wounds more than 1 in. (2.5 cm) across with a sealing agent to prevent the entry of fungus spores, wood-boring insects and rain which can ultimately cause decay. Grafting wax or proprietary bituminous paints are both effective.

Do cut immediately above a bud, in the case of woody shoots especially.

Do remove old flowers (unless you intend saving the seed) from perennials and such shrubs as lilacs and rhododendrons, to prevent sapping the plants' energies by unnecessary seed production.

Do thin over-heavy crops of tree fruits for the same reason.

PRUNING DON'TS

Don't leave large cuts untreated.

Don't strain secateurs by cutting over-large, heavy branches; it spoils the secateurs and bruises plant bark. Use pruning saws instead.

Don't leave snags, but trim pruning cuts smooth with a sharp knife. When sawing off branches make a cut underneath the limb first, then cut down from the top. This prevents tear and damage to the tree.

Don't make large wounds on trees and shrubs prone to silver leaf disease (see August, *Plant Disorders,* p. 176) during the infectious season. This includes all stone fruits and ornamental cherries and plums; these must be pruned during the relatively safe period between April and mid-July.

Don't leave suckers on grafted trees and shrubs, but take them out as low down on the stock as possible. Roses, lilacs and many ornamental shrubs are prone to this trouble.

Don't leave dead flowers on ornamental plants unless seed is required.

Don't cut back frost-damaged branches in spring until all likelihood of severe frost is past.

Don't prune for the sake of pruning – have a reason.

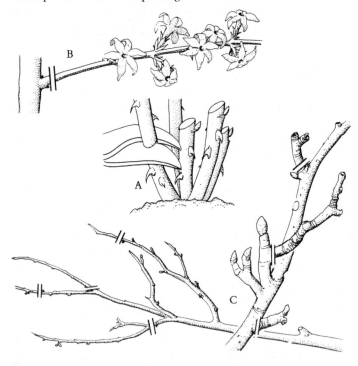

Different types of pruning: (A) hard pruning of new rose bushes; (B) cutting back flowering shoots of *Jasminum nudiflorum* hard after blooming; (C) in fruit trees, remove useless wood, shorten leaders and hard prune laterals

PRUNING SOFT FRUIT

During many years spent as a horticultural adviser I have visited very many gardens with soft fruit problems. Almost invariably the main causes of poor fruit or indifferent cropping were one or more of the following:

1 Overplanting, with too many bushes crowded together.
2 Poor varieties.
3 Lack of regular attention, particularly pruning.
4 Worn-out bushes which had become prey to pests and diseases.

Light, food, water and air are all necessary for the cultivation of good fruit, and annual pruning ensures the retention of the best branches to carry the crop. The removal of broken, dead, rubbing and very old shoots controls the spread of diseases and concentrates the plants' energies on a smaller number of branches, which accordingly bear larger and better fruits.

Age is important. When does a bush become old? The market grower, who is a keen judge when it comes to yields, considers that eight to ten years is enough for blackcurrants, fifteen years for white and red currants, ten to fifteen years for gooseberries, and about ten years for raspberries. By this reasoning many back garden bushes should have been consigned to the bonfire long ago. Nevertheless, this is largely a matter for personal consideration; some well-tended bushes may last much longer, but for poor croppers replacement may be the wisest policy.

Blackcurrants Blackcurrants fruit on wood made the previous season, so pruning is relatively simple. The old fruited wood is removed soon after cropping has finished, which in practice means taking away approximately a quarter of each bush. Old wood is easy to spot, being much darker in colour than the younger wood. Take the branches back either to ground level or to a strong new shoot lower down on the branch. This treatment encourages a constant renewal of young branches from the base for future cropping.

Red and white currants These fruit on wood which is at least two years old, similar to an apple tree. It is therefore necessary to build up a framework of well-spaced branches round an open centre. These will be retained for a number of years and replaced as necessary. The general shape will resemble the ribs of an upside-down, open umbrella.

Side shoots (laterals) from these branches carry the fruit in clusters near their bases. Annual pruning involves cutting the laterals back to within two or three buds of the main stem and cutting the leading stem of each branch back by about half its length.

Many growers prune red currants in summer, particularly those trained as cordons or espaliers. The laterals are pinched back to about 4 in. (10 cm) in July and pruned again to $\frac{1}{2}$ in. (12 mm) when the leaves have fallen.

However, since birds, particularly bullfinches, often strip the buds from white and red currants in winter, it may be wiser to defer pruning until March.

Gooseberries These fruit on both the old and the young wood. Start by removing any diseased, crossing, badly placed, dead or damaged branches, then shorten or take out any which trail on the ground or congest the centre of the bush. Finally, shorten the remaining shoots to such a pattern that you will be able to pass your hand easily between the branches when gathering the fruit.

Gooseberries grown on a leg or short trunk will not produce replacement branches from ground level. They are commonly pruned in the same fashion as red currants, with the leaders tipped and the laterals shortened to 5-6 in. (12.5-15 cm). Where birds are troublesome, pruning may have to be deferred until spring.

Raspberries Summer-fruiting raspberries present no pruning problems. They bear their crop on wood made the previous season, so in autumn the current season's fruiting canes are taken back to soil level. They are easily recognized, being darker in colour and rather flaccid-looking. Prune out also any weak new canes and reduce the rest to five or six of the strongest; tie them to the wires about 8 in. (20 cm) apart. The only other pruning – apart from removing canes coming up in the wrong places, such as paths – takes place in February, when the unripe tips of the canes are taken out, in order to encourage lateral shoots to carry the fruit. Newly planted canes should be cut back to 6-12 in. (15-30 cm) following planting.

Autumn-fruiting raspberries bear their crop on wood made in the *same season*. They are therefore left unpruned after the crop has been gathered, until the end of February when they are cut back to ground level. Since the whole process of cane-making and fruiting has to be carried out within the space of a few months, the plants should be helped along with good feeding. Mulches applied at pruning time are highly beneficial in this respect.

Blackberries, boysenberries and loganberries The pruning technique for all these fruits is very simple. Cut out all old canes as soon as possible after fruiting, then tie in the new young canes in a fan shape, allowing plenty of space between the branches.

Pruning Calendar

Although the months indicated in this calendar give a general guide to the time of year when specific pruning operations can be carried out, it is not mandatory. Abnormal weather, particularly in the north of Britain, may make it advisable to delay spring pruning; and sometimes, through illness, absence from home and other reasons, pruning will be impossible.

The following pruning recommendations apply mainly to established plants; the training, including pruning, of young fruit trees especially is quite distinct, and reference should be made to an authoritative book on this subject.

Many trees and shrubs, such as evergreens, viburnums and escallonias, will not require regular pruning, although some thinning and shortening back may be necessary to keep them in bounds. This can be carried out after flowering or during the winter months.

Since the gardener's year tends to follow seasons rather than calendar months, the pruning calendar begins in autumn.

OCTOBER

Biennials Remove old stems and seed heads of *Eryngium giganteum* and honesty; shake them over spare ground to encourage self-set seedlings.
Blackcurrants Take out the old fruited wood at ground level or to a strong young secondary shoot.
Hedges Clip over. See also December, *Hedges and Screens*, p. 263.
Herbaceous Perennials Except in very exposed districts, cut back dead stems of herbaceous plants to ground level. These include asters, anaphalis, echinops, eryngiums, achilleas, lupins, delphiniums, heleniums, helianthus, heliopsis, and solidagos.

NOVEMBER

Apples Carry out winter-pruning. Shorten summer-pruned stems of trained trees to 1 in. (2.5 cm) on bush and standard trees, remove crossing, badly placed, diseased or damaged branches, tip leaders and treat laterals according to growth of fruit spurs and wood buds. See July, *Fruit*, p. 148.

Deciduous Hedges Clip hawthorn, myrobalan plum, briar, blackthorn and hornbeam, also beech unless this was trimmed in July. Hedges can be laid during the next few weeks: remove old or dead branches and bend down some of the new ones to fill in the gaps, partly cutting them underneath so that they will go down readily.

Pears Cut back laterals to within a few inches of their bases. Shorten leaders by about one-third. Thin out old unfruitful spurs.

Wisterias Reduce summer-pruned growths to two-thirds or so of the older wood. See also August, *Climbers*, p. 166.

DECEMBER

Hollies *Ilex* sp. Shape the trees by careful cutting when removing branches for Christmas decoration. Take out any green-leaved shoots on variegated varieties as soon as they are visible.

Ornamental Trees Except for prunus, flowering almond and cherries, this is a good time to remove or lop branches and generally thin bushes and trees in shrubberies.

JANUARY

Apples and Pears Complete winter pruning.

Peaches and Nectarines These fruit on one-year-old wood, so the shoots need annual replacement. Encourage two or three basal shoots from the point where they are cut back and rub out any others as soon as they appear.

FEBRUARY

Actinidia Thin out and trim trailing branches before new growths appear next month.

Apricots These bear fruit on the old wood but give better quality fruit on one-year-old growths. Most wall specimens should be pruned as for peaches. See January above.

Chimonanthus praecox (winter sweet). Shorten side shoots on main branches to about five or six buds.

Clematis x jackmanii and varieties. Cut back all growths to within 12 in. (30 cm) of the ground; prune *C. viticella* forms similarly. Exceptions occur when any of these are growing up a tree and allowed to ramble. They will then require little or no pruning.

Climbing Roses Remove some of the old wood, but leave as much of the young wood as possible. Cut back frosted tips.

Cobnuts and Filberts To keep the bushes low so that they can be easily tended, and the nuts gathered with ease, build up an open centred tree on a short trunk. Remove entirely any branches which are likely to defeat this aim. Shorten side shoots to 3 in. (7.5 cm) and remove basal shoots.

Currants: Red and White These fruit on the old wood. Prune as suggested on p. 237. Leave pruning until March if birds are troublesome. See under June, p. 245.

Hydrangea Hortensia varieties. Thin out older shoots and weak twigs, and cut back old flowered shoots to within a few inches of the old wood. In very mild districts this can also be done soon after flowering is finished.

Jasminum nudiflorum After flowering, reduce the strongest shoots to a convenient length for tying in; cut back the remainder to within 1-2 in. (2.5-5 cm) of the old wood. Where there is plenty of space, simply tie in the main shoots with no shortening and thin out any crowded growths as soon as flowering is finished.

Newly Planted Shrubs Cut back fairly drastically to encourage strong new growths from low down on the bushes. The only exceptions are plants grown as standards.

Polygonum baldschuanicum Regular pruning is unnecessary, but where space is limited, cut back hard this month.

Raspberries Tip summer-fruiting canes. Cut autumn-fruiting kinds hard back. See also under August.

Tamarix pentandra (tamarisk). For dwarf bushes, cut back previous year's wood to within 6-8 in. (15-20 cm) of base. Otherwise no pruning. See also under May.

Willows and autumn-flowering Spiraeas like 'Anthony Waterer', *S. bullata, S. douglasii*. Thin out weak growths and cut back last year's wood to within a few inches of the older wood. For larger bushes, leave a few strong branches at three-quarter length.

MARCH

Buddleia davidii The species and its forms flower on wood made the same year and should be pruned hard back, almost to the old wood in spring. They will then produce plenty of strong flowering shoots.

Callicarpa Flowers and fruits produced on current year's growth; shorten the longest shoots in March.

Caryopteris (blue spiraea). Cut back previous year's shoots fairly hard.

Clematis montana Tidy up if necessary immediately after flowering; remove weak growths.

Cornus alba and C. stolonifera These and their forms are grown for the bright colour of their stems in winter. Cut back the previous year's growth to within a few inches of the old wood.

Corylus maxima 'Purpurea'. Prune this ornamental red-leaved filbert now, cutting back last year's shoots to within a few inches of the old wood. The new growths will have particularly bright foliage.

Cotoneaster The deciduous kinds can be hard pruned to keep them shapely.

Currants See under February.

Cytisus nigricans This flowers on wood made during the current year; prune hard back before new shoots appear. See also under June.

Erica Shear off the old flower stems on autumn-flowering heathers.

Escallonia floribunda and other autumn-blooming species. Remove some of the old wood and shorten back laterals.

Figs Cut back frosted growths.

Forsythia Prune wall and hedging plants hard after flowering has finished to encourage plenty of new shoots to carry next year's bloom. Prune plants in the open to shape and to keep them within bounds. See also under April.

Fuchsia Remove tips of frosted branches. In a bad year these may have to be taken back to ground level.

Gooseberries See *Pruning Soft Fruit*, p. 237.

Herbaceous Perennials Where stems were left for winter protection cut these hard to ground level now.

Passiflora (passion flower). Remove weak branches, leaving only enough to cover thinly the allotted space. Side shoots should be cut back to just a few inches.

Peaches (under glass especially). Disbud and thin young fruits. These should ultimately be reduced to one for every 9 in. (23 cm) of wall space.

Philadelphus (mock orange). Hard prune occasionally at this season if plants have become overgrown. They will not flower this year but should make good plants for next.

Roses Always cut to an outward pointing bud.

Hybrid teas and perpetuals: Remove overcrowded, crossing, diseased and weak shoots. With strong bushes or those intended for garden decoration, prune fairly lightly, weaker kinds a little harder, and new bushes or any designed to grow exhibition blooms fairly severely. See also March, *Roses,* p. 60.

Cluster-flowered (floribundas): Prune at the end of the month. Cut lightly, reducing weak growths and shortening the rest. Any new bushes should be hard pruned back to a few inches from the ground in their first season. Roses can also be pruned during the winter months in sheltered places, but rather lightly in case of subsequent frost damage.

Spartium junceum Cut back straggly shoots.

APRIL

Arundinaria (hardy bamboos). Thin out crowded shoots, cutting them to ground level. When dried, some of these will make useful bamboo canes.

Aucuba japonica (laurel). This is the best time of year to undertake hard pruning when needed. Use secateurs for ordinary trimming, not shears which cut and mutilate the foliage.

Berberis, evergreen kinds. Thin out crowded shoots and generally tidy up.

Buxus (box). Hedges can be trimmed.

Calluna vulgaris (heather, ling). Shear off dead flowers and cut back long trailing shoots with secateurs.

Ceanothus coeruleus (C. azureus), C. dentatus Build up a framework of branches, then prune back previous year's growth to within two or three buds of this foundation.

Chaenomeles (Japanese quince). Carry out necessary thinning or shortening back of side shoots; spur-back side growths on wall-trained specimens.

Cherries Prune as little as possible, but if it becomes necessary do it this month and paint the wounds.

Cotoneaster, evergreen kinds. Hard prune overgrown plants, otherwise lightly thin, and trim the bushes annually.

Deutzia Thin out the oldest wood annually, leaving the young shoots.

Elaeagnus (oleaster). Prune to shape and thin out as necessary.

Erica (heather). Shear flowers from winter-blooming varieties.

Forsythia This usually flowers on wood that is two or more years old. Reduce growth occasionally to younger, more upright shoots. Wall specimens: keep side growths constantly pinched out to within 1 in. (2.5 cm) of the older wood. See also under March.

Hamamelis (witch hazel). Any necessary thinning out.

Hebe Prune back old stems every few years to keep bushes shapely. Young growths arise from the old stems.

Helianthemum (rock rose). Shorten back stems after flowering to keep plants compact, and to prevent them smothering nearby small plants.

Herbaceous perennials Reduce the number of shoots, especially the weaker ones, of delphiniums, phlox, Michaelmas daisies, helianthus, heliopsis, heleniums, and the like, to encourage finer blooms in due course.

Holly Prune hedges.

Hydrangea paniculata 'Grandiflora'. Cut back almost to ground level for large flower heads later.

Hypericum (rose of Sharon). Thin and tidy straggling shoots as necessary.

Ivy on walls Clip hard back, also trim shoots on plants growing in more open situations.

Laurus nobilis (bay). Thin and trim to shape.

Lilacs On shrubs which bear few or no flowers, thin the branches, cut away inner and weak shoots, and remove all suckers. See also under June.

Pyracantha (firethorn). Prune only if necessary and then right back into old wood.

Rhododendrons Prune back really hard shrubs which have grown too tall and spindly; new growths will appear freely from the old, cut branches. Bushes so treated completely recover and make handsome specimens in about two years.

Rosemary and Lavender Trim back straggly bushes to encourage new shoots.

Roses Complete all pruning.

Santolina (lavender cotton). Hard prune if necessary, otherwise simply cut back straggling shoots in autumn.

Senecio laxifolius Prune straggly shoots to make the bushes more compact.

Stachyurus Thin as necessary.

MAY

Aubrieta Cut back straggly shoots to make compact clumps.

Buddleia globosa Thin out or reduce lanky branches from time to time when necessary.

Caryopteris Shorten lanky branches, remove weak shoots annually.

Choisya, Camellias, Carpenteria, Abelia Treat as buddleia (see above).

Clematis florida and C. patens group. These flower on short growths from the previous season's wood; as soon as they finish flowering, cut off the blooms just above the strong buds lying behind them. Space the main branches to prevent tangling and take out weak or worn-out stems.

Clematis macropetala, C. armandii Cut back after flowering to fit allotted space; thin out overcrowded growth.

Cherries, ornamental As plums (see p. 245).

Garrya elliptica Trim back if necessary and spur-prune wall specimens by reducing length of side shoots.

Gooseberries Thin fruits.

Hedges Trim evergreen hedges and topiary specimens.

Herbaceous Plants As for April.

Kerria After flowering, take out the old flower shoots to a strong shoot lower down on the branch.

Lilacs, Rhododendrons, Azaleas Remove old flower heads to prevent seeding.

Pittosporum Carry out any necessary pruning at this time.

Plums Any necessary pruning can now take place, such as the removal of diseased, rubbing or crossing branches. Some shortening of branches can take place but cut as little as possible and paint the wounds.

Prunus laurocerasus (cherry laurel). Prune with secateurs, not shears, to keep hedges and specimen plants shapely.

Raspberries Remove suckers.

Ribes Occasionally thin out and shorten back the branches of flowering currants.

Tamarix tetandra (tamarisk). Shorten back straggling bushes. See also February.

Viburnums, evergreen kinds. Prune if necessary this month.

JUNE

Border Flowers Remove faded blossoms of annuals, lupins and other perennials.

Buddleia alternifolia Once flowering has finished, shorten back the drooping stems or even cut out some of the lower branches. To form a standard tree, retain a strong upright shoot and remove all the others; tie the shoot to a stake and remove further shoots as they appear except any coming out near the top of the standard. When the plant reaches the required height and has enough side branches, stop it at the top. As the trunk strengthens the stake can be removed.

Currants: Red and White cordons and espaliers. Summer-prune – spur back new laterals to within 5 in. (12. 5 cm) of the base. Remove suckers.

Cytisus (brooms). When flowers have faded, cut back almost to the old wood. Leave plenty of young shoots to keep the bushes compact and shapely. Do not reduce too drastically into the old wood or the plants may die. See also March.

Gooseberries cordon type. Summer-prune as for currants and remove suckers.

Lilacs Remove suckers and reduce a few of the weaker shoots. With old straggly bushes cut back branches to strong shoots lower down. This may lose a season's flowering next year, but ultimately results in a better shaped plant. See also April.

Philadelphus (mock orange). Treat straggling bushes as for lilac (see p. 245).

(see p. 245)

JULY

Apples and Pears Summer-prune trained trees like espaliers, cordons and dwarf pyramids. There are several systems; the simplest is to shorten all side shoots (laterals) to within five leaves of spur clusters. See also November.

Beech Hedges Clip over to encourage new young shoots. These will retain their leaves in winter.

Border Plants Remove spent flowers from roses, perennials, annuals and bedding plants.

Plums Thin fruits if necessary.

Strawberries Restrict number of runners to four per plant if these are to be propagated; otherwise remove all of them.

Water Plants Pull out dead flowers and yellow leaves from water-lilies; shorten growths of aquatics which have flowered, like *Iris laevigata* and calthas. Reduce or thin underwater vegetation if necessary.

Weigela florida and forms. Remove flowering stems as soon as blossoms have faded, leaving one or two strong young shoots lower down on the branches.

AUGUST

Apples and Pears Finish summer-pruning (see July).

Aubrieta and Phlox subulata Treat as for violas (see p. 247).

(see p. 247)

Hedges Clip privet, hawthorn, *Lonicera nitida,* chamaecyparis species and varieties, box, yew, *Viburnum tinus* (laurustinus), hornbeams, escallonia species, cotoneasters, hazel and hollies. Trim again in October.

Hydrangeas Remove faded flowers back to the first plump bud. Remove weak stems entirely.

Lavender Remove old flower stems. Do not cut back much into old wood or the plants may die.

Loganberries Take out old fruited canes to ground level, as well as new weak ones. Tie in the rest.

Lonicera (honeysuckle). After flowering, remove some of the older branches and shorten long straggling stems.

Raspberries Remove old fruited canes to ground level, and weak new growths and suckers between rows. The latter can be used to make new rows if required.

Roses and Dahlias Disbud for larger flowers; remove faded blooms.

Violas and Pansies Cut back hard to induce basal shoots suitable for cuttings.

Wisteria Prune long straggling young shoots made during current year back to within five or six buds of base. See also November.

SEPTEMBER

Blackcurrants Take out old fruited wood to ground level or, if there is a shortage of young basal shoots, back to a strong young side shoot on the old branch. The fruits are carried on one-year-old wood so this drastic pruning is necessary annually.

Hydrangea anomala petiolaris (H. scandens) Cut back if necessary to restrict growth after flowering.

Hybrid Berries and Blackberries Remove as many old fruited stems as possible without denuding the bushes; tie in the new canes, well spaced.

Roses ramblers. Remove old flowered stems to ground level or, if there is a shortage of replacement shoots, to good side shoots on the old stems. Space the new stems well out and tie in place.

# DECEMBER

The Month in the Garden

There is no need to avoid a brisk walk round the garden on a bright December day, since there are still plants to be enjoyed in a well-stocked garden.

Winter heathers are among the most rewarding, the splendid carpets of colour derived from various *Erica carnea* varieties bringing a note of cheer on the most dismal day. Then there are such trees as the evergreen *Arbutus unedo*, the so-called strawberry tree which bears bunches of pendent, lily-of-the-valley-like flowers of pinkish-white, with round, edible fruits resembling strawberries (from earlier blossoms) at the same time. With its small, dark green serrated leaves, this is a tree with many attributes, growing in time up to 30 ft (9 m).

The rosebud cherry, *Prunus subhirtella* 'Autumnalis', chooses to flower in mild winters and, although subdued by frosts, usually recovers to provide another burst of bloom. The semi-double, shell-pink flowers hang several together, in short clusters from the naked wood.

There are also plenty of berries, and at this season one can admire the bark of such trees as the green-and-white-striped, snake-barked maple, *Acer davidii*, or the patina of *Prunus serrula*, which gleams like mahogany in the wintry sunshine, the bark peeling off in circular strips to give the trunk a banded appearance. There is colour, too, in the young shoots of *Cornus alba* 'Sibirica' which are red just now, or yellow in *C. stolonifera* 'Flaviramea'. Most people enjoy the corkscrew branches and twigs of the twisted hazel, *Corylus avellana* 'Contorta'.

General Tasks Since snow and prolonged frosts may come at any time, every effort should be made to catch up with the unfinished tasks of autumn.

WEATHER

'December takes away everything and returns nothing'. Perhaps it is the short days and the cloudy skies of December which make it seem a dismal month, and the relative absence of colour in the garden cannot help. Fine, mild weather is, however, seldom welcomed at this time of the year. 'A fair day in winter is the mother of a storm' is often true, and out-of-season conditions always seem to prompt a feeling that retribution is to follow. Such unusually fine days in winter are often known as a 'borrowed day' which has to be paid back later. Other names are 'weather-breaker' and, in Scotland, a 'pet' day. The fate of pets, they say, awaits it, and spoilt weather is expected to follow soon.

Sometimes the repayment for the borrowing is on a long-term basis, hence 'Christmas on the balcony; Easter by the fire'. If the sun shines through the apple trees on Christmas Day, it is said that there will be an abundant crop the next year. If warmth at the end of the year is really followed by a cold late spring, with late apple blossoms escaping the frosts, this may well be true.

With the rebirth of the sun at Christmas, the New Year opens up the promise of a new gardening year. At the same time it is wise to try and learn from the weather lessons of the past twelve months, and remember the Spanish proverb 'Do not abuse a year till it has passed' and the opinion of André Maurois: 'An Englishman's soul is like the English skies; the weather is nearly always bad, but the climate is good.'

With shorter daylight hours, completion of digging, pruning, tidying and planting becomes increasingly difficult, so press on whenever the opportunity occurs.

Make new gravel paths and renovate old ones. Lay crazy paving. Clean out rubbish heaps and burn uncompostable material.

Trees and Shrubs Check trees and shrubs for dead, diseased and damaged branches. Remove these entirely and paint all wounds with a sealing compound like Arbrex.

Fork the soil lightly between shrubs and sprinkle coarse bonemeal at 4 oz. per square yard (100 g per square metre) on top.

New shrubs and trees arriving this month should be planted at once if the weather is suitable. If not, heel them in until conditions change. If the roots are dry, soak them for an hour before planting.

Shake newly fallen snow from evergreens.

Climbers Check wall shrubs and climbers for loose ties and shoots; secure against strong winds and possible bad weather.

Hardy Plants Take root cuttings of anchusas, herbaceous phlox, *Papaver orientale* and *Primula denticulata*. See July, *New Plants from Old*, p. 154. Protect doubtfully hardy perennials with dry leaves, bracken or plastic sheeting.

Cover *Iris unguicularis* with glass to induce clean, long-stemmed flowers; place cloches over *Helleborus niger,* the Christmas rose, for early flowers. Set slug traps if necessary.

Treat newly arrived perennials as for shrubs. Alternatively, pot them up and keep under shelter until spring.

Bulbs Finish planting tulips and other

bulbs. Bring bulbs from plunge beds into the home or greenhouse to maintain continuity of bloom.

Rock Garden Plants Remove wet leaves around the collars of alpines or they may cause damage as they rot. This particularly applies to primulas, meconopsis, androsaces and any plant with furry leaves.

Water Plants Keep pools full of water, and a heater going in one area during prolonged frost.

Remove ice and protect fish and plants as described in May, *Water Gardens*, p. 112.

Vegetables Protect broccoli heads by bending the leaves over the curds.

Finish the digging of vacant plots, weather permitting.

Tie up bamboo canes and tidy away netting and stakes.

Fruit Finish top-fruit pruning if possible (see November, *Pruning Calendar*, p. 239).

Plant out new trees and bushes when weather is open; tread back newly planted trees and bushes after a hard frost.

On still, frost-free days winterwash top fruit with a tar-oil formulation. See also August, *Plant Disorders*, p. 176.

Plants under Glass Water sparingly, but admit air when conditions allow.

Remove dead flowers and leaves regularly.

House Plants After Christmas rest plants in overheated rooms by giving them a spell in a cooler room or in the greenhouse.

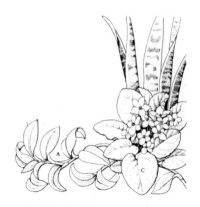

House plants for the winter: (A) *Zebrina pendula;* (B) *Sansevieria,* mother-in-law's tongue; (C) *Saintpaulia ionantha,* African violet

PLANTS IN THEIR PRIME

Trees and Shrubs *Arbutus unedo; Aucuba japonica* and forms (berries and leaves); barks of various acers and *Cornus alba* and *C. stolonifera; Prunus serrula* and *Rubus biflorus.* the whitewashed bramble; cotoneasters (various kinds with berried fruits); *Erica carnea* varieties, *E. x darleyensis* 'Silberschmelze'; *Fatsia japonica; Hamamelis mollis; Ilex aquifolium* (hollies); *Lonicera fragrantissima, L. standishii;* mahonias; *Prunus subhirtella* 'Autumnalis'; pyracanthas (berries); *Rhododendron mucronulatum* (in sheltered places); *Viburnum farreri. V. x bodnantense, V. grandiflorum. V. tinus* and varieties.

Climbing Plants *Jasminum nudiflorum* (winter jasmine).

Hardy Plants *Helleborus niger* (Christmas rose); *Iris unguicularis; Liriope spicata; Petasites fragrans;* winter pansies.

Bulbs Some species and forms of galanthus (snowdrops); *Cyclamen coum; Sternbergia lutea.*

CROPS TO ENJOY

Vegetables Jerusalem artichokes; Brussels sprouts; cabbage; carrots; leeks; onions; parsnips; potatoes, scorzonera; seakale beet; swedes; turnips.

Fruit Apples and pears in store; grapes.

PLANT ASSOCIATIONS

Jasminum nudiflorum over a wall above mahonias with heather in front.

Viburnum fragrans combined with winter heathers.

GARDEN PROBLEMS

Snow on evergreens.
  Plants lifted by frost.
  Mice attacking seeds, bulbs and fruit in store.
  Storage rot among fruits in store.
  Loose shoots torn from their supports by wind.
  Outdoor pipes and taps freezing.
Turn off the water, drain or lag exposed pipes.
  Leaves falling from indoor azaleas and *Solanum capsicastrum,* **due to lack of humidity.**

Plants of the Month

HOLLY

Decorating homes with evergreens at Christmas time is a practice dating back to pagan times. In Ancient Rome the custom was associated with the great festival of Saturnalia, which began on 19 December and continued for seven days. During this period gifts were exchanged as well as sprigs of holly as symbols of friendship and goodwill. The evergreens were then hung up to provide a sanctuary for any spirits which came to watch the revels.

This custom was continued by early Christians, although they changed its meaning so that the evergreens became a symbol of immortality and rejoicing at the birth of Christ. The Druids regarded holly as a force for good and used it as a charm to banish evil spirits from the dwellings of Ancient Britons. Likewise, it was once a Persian practice to sprinkle water, in which holly bark had been steeped, over the face of a new-born baby as a protection against evil. Fifteenth-century maidens in England placed holly sprigs in their beds to prevent unwelcome visits from goblins and witches – a prank which many a twentieth-century child has played on unsuspecting guests.

Medicinal properties have been attributed to the leaves, bark and berries of holly, for treating such varied ailments as colic, gout, skin diseases, gallstones and even broken bones. At the 'Verderers' Court' in the Forest of Dean, witnesses at one time took the oath on a spray of holly, instead of the Bible.

The wood, being hard, evenly grained and light in colour, has been used for inlay work, musical and drawing instruments as well as for fine furniture and farm tools.

Ilex aquifolium, our native holly, has produced a number of varieties, some with smooth leaves, others prickly, and yet others with gold or silver variegations or bearing near-white, yellow or orange berries instead of red.

The leaves of *I. vomitoria,* a South American species, are widely used on that continent for the making of a refreshing and stimulating tea called *Yerba Maté* or simply *Maté.* It is made by pouring boiling water over the powdered leaves, and imbibed through a hollow tube which has a bulbous tea strainer-like base.

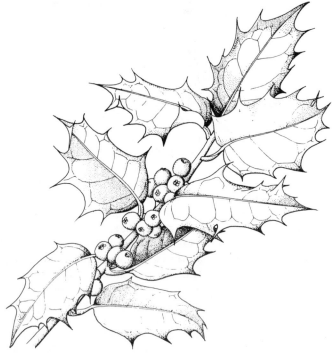

Ilex aquifolium, holly

MISTLETOE

A Norse legend relates how the much loved Baldur, son of Freya, the earth goddess (whom we commemorate each Friday) dreamt that he would shortly die. His mother took counsel with Thor (for whom we name our Thursday), and as a result Freya visited and extracted promises from earth, fire, air, water and all the animals and plants not to harm him. Only mistletoe was omitted, being thought too insignificant to matter. Loki, an evil spirit who hated Baldur, learnt of this and fashioned a dart from mistletoe, then guided the arm of blind Hödur as he took aim at Baldur, who fell lifeless.

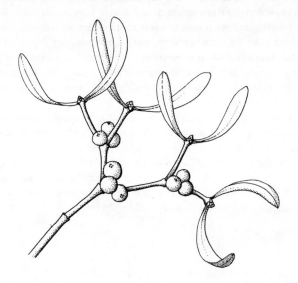

Viscum album, mistletoe

Long before the Romans invaded Britain, mistletoe held a prominent place in the rites and sacrifices of the Druids. Great medicinal virtues were attached to its leaves and berries, especially for treating epilepsy, sores and toothache and as an antidote to poisons. The plant was considered especially potent when growing on an oak, since that tree was sacred to the Druid god Tutanec. Only a Druid priest could gather such a sacred plant, which he did with a golden knife, another priest catching the falling branches, for if these touched the ground much of their potency would be lost.

Among various virtues with which mistletoe has been credited was the old Swedish belief of its power to protect against fire if hung from the ceiling, and that a knife-handle fashioned of oak-mistletoe would ward off attacks of epilepsy.

In Scotland, mistletoe found growing on the famous oak of Errol was at one time important to the fortunes of my husband's – the Hay – family. On All-Hallows Eve each year, a sprig was cut by one of the clan, using a new dirk, and this talisman ensured a year's charm against sorcery and a guarantee of preservation and success in battle.

The practice of kissing under the mistletoe bough is peculiarly English, but may be derived from an old Scandinavian custom. Because of its sacred nature warring armies, meeting where mistletoe grew, would lay down their arms for a day; from this grew the practice of hanging a sprig of mistletoe over doorways as a token of welcome to visitors who were greeted with a kiss of welcome. But back in the present day, what every Englishman does not realize is that for every kiss, a berry should be removed if blessings are to be received by both kisser and kissed.

To plant mistletoe, which is semi-parasitic on apple, hawthorn, poplar, mountain ash, whitebeam, willow and sundry other hosts, the seed should be planted when ripe between March and May. Some people simply squash the berries on the undersides of a young branch, which is fine if birds leave them alone, while others make a V-shaped cut, raise the bark and slip the seed inside. Growth is slow at first, but once a leaf shows the plant grows quickly and tends to break out in different places on the tree.

Paths

Paths are an important feature of any garden and should be given serious consideration from the very beginning of design and planning – or as more often happens, of replanning. Too often, paths are laid on virgin plots without much thought, merely to facilitate such work as soil levelling and transporting manure, peat and other materials. Once they are laid, they stay because re-routing them is a huge task.

Consider first whether the paths will be used for heavy barrow or truck traffic or mainly for light pedestrian use. Paths for the former purpose need a really solid foundation.

For light traffic there are various choices, including gravel, and grass paths, which are quite suitable although mowing the grass some twenty-five times a year is a chore that many people would be happy to do without.

Paths to take heavy traffic must have a good foundation, well rammed down, of 2-3 in. (5-7.5 cm) of old brick rubble or similar material; on top of this, a 1-in. (2.5-cm) layer of crushed boiler ash or bituminous macadam. Alternatively, lay a concrete or a paved path, the latter on a concrete base.

Simulated paving blocks in various sizes which provide a fair imitation of the expensive York stone are widely available. They are also less dangerous – for they do not attract slimy, slippery-green algae growth as much as does York stone.

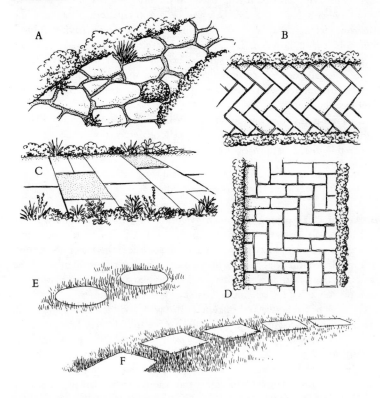

Different types of paths: (A) broken or 'crazy' paving; (B) 'herring bone' brick pattern; (C) formal paving slabs; (D) random brick paving; (E) tree trunk sections set in turf; (F) paving slabs in turf

BRICK PATHS

Occasionally one comes across paths made of old bricks, either set flat or on edge, or paths made of old tiles laid edgeways in concrete. The tiled kinds are fine, though sometimes not very smooth and rather uncomfortable to walk on, but brick paths can be slippery in frosty weather or when covered with slimy algae. Soft bricks also tend to crumble or flake after frosts; for a brick path it is therefore worthwhile seeking out a supply of well-fired, wire-cut bricks. They have smooth sides, tops and bottoms and can be laid flat.

Another idea is to have an edging of bricks either side of a path made of broken or formal paving. Such paths look very attractive and can be laid in various patterns. The main path between the brick edges can also be filled with large cobbles, and again these can be laid in a pattern of perhaps one square or rectangle of cobbles to every three or four squares of paving. A long, solid cobble path, however, is very uncomfortable to walk on.

Most stone, concrete or brick surfaces become slippery with a covering of algae, especially on steps or slopes. Such surfaces should be sanded in frosty weather or watered with a solution of tar-oil wash, as is used for spraying fruit trees in winter.

Concrete paths of various colours can be laid with coloured cement blocks, although to my mind a sandstone finish looks especially attractive and I prefer this to the pattern of green, red or white squares so often seen in modern gardens.

CRAZY PAVING

Broken or crazy paving has much to commend it, but should always be laid on a 1-in. (2.5-cm) layer of concrete. I also prefer to fill the cracks between the pieces of paving with concrete because if this is not done, moss and weeds eventually appear. While it is easy enough to get rid of weeds by watering them with a weedkiller, such as glyphosate or a paraquat/diquat formulation, this is just one more job to tackle in early summer.

Gaps can be left between the paving, filled with good soil and planted with low growers. Especially suitable for this purpose are aubrietas, London pride, thymes, dwarf campanulas, *Alyssum saxatile*, aethionemas, arabis, armerias (thrift), small bulbs like crocuses, chionodoxas and snowdrops, dwarf dianthus, dwarf genistas, *Hypericum polyphyllum* or *H. olympicum,* dwarf phloxes, sedums and violas. Obviously they should not be planted where they are likely to be trodden on or run over by a barrow or truck, but reserved for wider areas at the sides.

In small gardens, where space for plants is limited, it might be worth replacing paths and small lawns with broken paving. Many alpine plants are happy in paving, some in fact are happier than in a rock garden or border where they may lie wet and rot at the crown in winter.

Path width is important. Main paths must be wide enough to permit the passage of a barrow or truck, and ideally broad enough to allow two people to walk abreast. This means a width of at least 4 ft (1.2 m).

The siting of paths needs careful consideration. The fewer paths and the less obtrusive they are, the better. It is possible to make a cunning use of paths to improve the perspective of a garden – by making a path wider at the end nearest the house and narrowing as it stretches away, one can often make a short garden appear longer. Conversely, a long narrow garden can appear wider with paths that become wider as they stretch away from the house down the garden.

PATH COMPANIONS

A well laid-out garden should be full of surprises, each turn of the path revealing new vistas. A bed of shrubs or a low dividing trellis, covered with roses perhaps, may hide another feature, reached by a winding path.

In general in rectangular gardens, it is best to site the path, or paths, to one side rather than right down the middle; they should always lead somewhere, perhaps to a pool or a greenhouse, not finish abruptly for no reason. Curves and straight lines can be blended; in a long narrow garden avoid long narrow flower borders and formal paths, but let the border finish in broad curves or scallops, the path following suit.

Borders of herbaceous plants are often planted against a wall, fence or hedge, with the path in front, but sometimes it would be better to have the path next to the boundary and running behind the border. There are two reasons for this; first, it is easier to trim the hedge, or attend to climbers and shrubs growing against a wall or fence. Second and more important, is the fact that with a border well away from the hedge, the plants can be attended from both sides. In addition, plants growing against a wall or hedge are usually short of water and nutrients, and become drawn. They reach for the light so that many of them will need staking, while in free-standing beds they would probably not need support.

STEPS

With sloping gardens various areas can be levelled to make terraces con-nected with steps; if the difference in levels is not too great, they can be linked with sloping paths. If steps are built, they should be wide enough for two people to walk up or down them side by side, and they should be neither too shallow nor too steep. They should also be of the same width as the path leading to them.

Steps consist of two parts: the flat tread part, and the riser or upright wall that supports the tread. For comfortable ascent or descent the tread should be at least 10-12 in. (25-30 cm), preferably 15 in. (38 cm) wide, and the height between steps (the riser) not more than 8 in. (20 cm) and not less than 5 in. (12.5 cm). Very shallow steps are fiddling and irritating, and if they are high they are difficult for elderly people to negotiate. All steps should be of such a height and width that there is no uneasiness in negotiating them.

Gardening for the Disabled and Elderly

To many people the word 'disabled' brings to mind someone in a wheelchair. The symbol denoting that a garden or other place open to the public is suitable for people in wheelchairs is, indeed, a wheelchair; where the going would be too difficult for non-ambulant visitors, the symbol is a chair with a diagonal stroke across it.

But wheelchair cases account for a mere three or four per cent of all disabled people. There are probably about forty kinds of physical diability, and if we include old age, probably about one person in seven suffers from some disability or handicap.

Disabled gardeners can be divided into two categories: the non-ambulant or wheelchair people; and the ambulant, those who can get around even if they can move only slowly or with the aid of sticks and crutches.

Obviously there are many jobs chairbound gardeners cannot do: dig, for example, in the orthodox manner with a spade or fork; only a few will be able to mow a lawn, although some enthusiasts manage it. Pruning, staking and tying are only possible at certain levels, and only then if wheelchairs can go right up to the plants.

Although unable to use a conventional spade or digging fork, a wheelchair gardener can often cultivate the ground to a depth of several inches (deep enough for sowing seeds, planting vegetables or bedding plants) with the aid of a hand fork or a pronged cultivator, attached to a very long handle, which can be pulled through the soil towards the person in the chair.

Chairbound people often develop powerful shoulder and arm muscles so they usually master pulling tools better than pushing kinds. For hoeing the Swoe, which is a two-sided hoe, or the Wolf Push-pull weeder, which is shaped like a stirrup and has wavy edges on both sides, are as easy to use with a pulling as with a pushing motion; there is also more control over the tool when it is pulled rather than pushed.

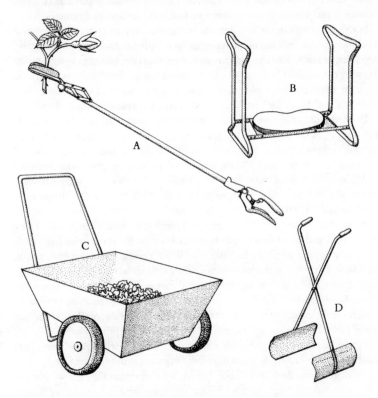

Gardening aids for the elderly and disabled: (A) 'cut and hold' flower gatherer; (B) easy kneeling stool; (C) two-wheeled truck; may be tipped forward and leaves or rubbish swept into it; (D) pick-up tool for lifting leaves or rubbish

For gathering flowers for the house or removing dead blooms from plants or rose bushes, there are 'cut and hold' flower gatherers. This type of tool is about 18 in. (45 cm) long and consists of a pair of blades operated by a trigger-grip handle which first cuts and then holds the flower. With this tool, the gardener can reach 2-3 ft (60-90 cm) into a bed or border. These flower gatherers are also a boon for people who suffer from rheumatism or other disabilities and find it difficult to make their way into borders or among beds of roses.

For both ambulant and non-ambulant gardeners, it is obvious that beds or borders should not be too wide; certainly no more than about 4 ft (1.2 m). Provided the beds are free-standing one can easily tend them from all sides.

For those who cannot manage the tools necessary to cultivate at ground level, raised beds will enable them to grow a wide range of plants, including vegetables such as lettuce, radishes and spinach, raise seedlings and cultivate strawberries. Raised beds may be built up to a convenient height with bricks, concrete blocks or even old car tyres stacked one on top of the other, then filled with rubble at the base, topped with about 2 ft (60 cm) of good soil.

Painted white, old tyre beds are not unattractive and they can be made into a feature if, as they are built up, trailing plants such as *Campanula portenschlagiana,* creeping Jenny (*Lysimachia nummularia*), or aubrieta are inserted between each tyre. Such 'towers of tyres' make excellent raised beds for children – even those who have to sit on the ground can enjoy growing plants in a bed one, two or three tyres high. You can usually obtain tyres free from a garage if you say you want them for a disabled person.

A number of firms manufacture tools with the disabled in mind. There are trowels and hand forks with bulbous handles for those who have difficulty in gripping ordinary handles; the Wolf Terrex spade and fork can be used for cultivation operations without the gardener having to bend his or her back. Some tools, such as secateurs and shears, and even wheelbarrows, can be used one-handed, and there are various gadgets – lawn tools and pruners – which can be operated from a sitting position. Watering can be carried out quite easily with a 'ring' system as described in April, *Watering*, p. 95. If a greenhouse is equipped with a door able to take a wheelchair, even very disabled people can enjoy growing plants in its warmth and comfort.

Gardeners who find their hobby becoming a burden as they grow older, or succumb to disabilities, or who know someone who is completely housebound, should not despair. Some of my happiest memories are of working with groups of disabled people at Norwood Hall Institute of Horticulture, where as Principal I was able to inaugurate classes for chairbound and disabled, including blind, people, in gardening and flower arrangement. For many, these classes brought a new interest to their lives, although able-bodied people must be at hand to help them in the first instance.

For a chairbound gardener some reorganization or redesigning of the garden may be necessary. It is desirable, for example, to have firm paths of gravel or paving on all sides of beds and borders, for easy access. The paths should be at least 3 ft (90 cm) wide with a space 4 ft (1.2 m) wide for turning. Steps are always a problem; where there is room it is a good idea to construct a gently sloping ramp alongside the steps, provided that it is not too steep for a wheelchair user.

Anyone interested in gardening but who finds difficulty in undertaking the numerous tasks involved should send a stamped addressed envelope to the Disabled Living Foundation, 346 Kensington High Street, London W14 8NS for their leaflet on Horticultural Therapy. This registered charity also issues lists of tools, with addresses of suppliers, as well as manufacturers of raised beds and planters, composts and fertilizers, publications, and gardening books in braille.

PREPARING FOR RETIREMENT

On reaching middle age, the wise gardener thinks ahead to the time when he will no longer be able to do as much work in the garden as he did in the past. Even when knowledgeable help is available in the neighbourhood, it will probably cost more than anyone can afford on a retirement pension. Assuming you will stay on in the same house rather than move to smaller premises, what can be done to reduce recurrent garden chores from the physical effort of view?

In retirement, we will probably have plenty of time, but less strength. There are many aids to gardening, especially tools and machines, some designed especially with the elderly and handicapped in mind, but here I wish to dwell on the various constructional changes we can make while we still have the strength and, hopefully, the money to make life easier later on.

Sloping gardens with steps and grass banks, for example, can be improved. It may be possible to eliminate the bank by building a brick or flat-stone retaining wall, on more than one level if the bank is very steep. Construct the wall in such a manner that the stones or bricks slope slightly backwards, with gaps left at intervals between the stones so that various trailing plants (aubrieta, alyssum, small campanulas and arabis) can be inserted in the spaces and packed around with good soil. Such small plants will look most effective when in flower and require little attention beyond cutting them back from time to time. Occasionally, a stone should be inserted into the bank lengthways to give the wall strength. Alternatively, the whole retaining wall can be concreted between the stones or bricks, although this will debar you from using it for plants, except as a background to low-growing shrubs.

If the bank is so steep that two walls must be constructed, one above the other, allow for a narrow border between them. The arduous job of mowing grass on a bank is eliminated and a pleasant feature is created. Maintenance of the plants growing in the walls is attended to in an upright position.

Wild Gardens Mowing grass is a time-consuming business and hard work with declining agility. In a small garden, the grass area can be replaced with paving. Larger areas that have always been mown can be allowed to become a 'naturalized' or wild garden area, where bulbs and some trees or shrubs can be planted, and the grass cut only once or twice a year. The first cut, if there are bulbs in the grass, would not be necessary much before the middle of June in the south, two or three weeks later in the north. Six to eight weeks must be allowed for the foliage, daffodils especially, to die down after the flowers have faded.

Semi-wild areas like this can look charming; if a winding path can be cut through the grass once a fortnight, a small close-mown lawn near the house will show up in splendid contrast to the meadow area.

Greenhouses and Sun Lounges A valuable investment for retirement is a small greenhouse or a sun lounge built on to the house, and heated so that one can potter about happily in winter or bad weather and grow plants in comfort with little physical effort. Much of the work of potting, sowing and the like can be undertaken while sitting down. The cost of heating a greenhouse may eventually be prohibitive, but much pleasure can still be had from a cold greenhouse, especially if it houses small winter bulbs and alpine plants. It may be too chilly in winter to work in the cold greenhouse, except in the middle of a sunny day, but, well-wrapped up, one can still spend many hours there in autumn, winter and early spring.

Screens and Paths Hedges that need clipping once or twice a year become increasingly burdensome over the years. A screen of shrubs that need very little in the way of pruning would be easier to manage. Compact, spreading varieties of yews and spruces are suitable, as well as mahonias, skimmias, escallonias and viburnums.

If there is room to plant a screening border, 8-10 ft (2.4-3 m) wide, inside the existing hedge, it might be worth while doing so well before retirement; after a few years, when the shrubs have filled in, the hedge can then be removed. A pleasant fence or a wall is even less effort – cedar wood does not need constant painting – and though both are initially expensive, subsequent maintenance is low-cost.

Paths should be paved, concreted or made of material which does not necessitate constant weeding or repair.

As to plant material, to avoid bending choose shrubs and trees rather than a lot of fussy small plants. Grow alpines and other small plants in raised beds or sink gardens. Patios are usually easy to maintain and are worth considering for areas near the house.

Finally buy good tools while you can afford them, especially some of the labour-saving types recommended for disabled gardeners.

Hedges and Screens

Well tended hedges are almost as much admired as our lawns by overseas visitors to Britain. Sadly, many farm hedges once cared for by craftsmen, sometimes for hundreds of years, are fast disappearing and too often those that remain are poor travesties, now that skilled men are no longer around to look after them.

In private gardens, too, the large formal hedges, the majestic battlements of yew, the masterpieces in box and holly, are now so costly to maintain that most people hesitate to plant anything which will need skilled trimming once or twice a year. Even with modern electric or petrol-driven hedge trimmers, hedge maintenance is still time- and energy-consuming.

So there are several options: erect fences or walls to ensure privacy and boundary enclosure; plant formal hedges that will need regular hard trimming; or install informal hedges which do not need such hard trimming. Another idea is to plant a screen in depth of shrubs, using a discreet mixture of evergreen and deciduous shrubs, many of which will need little maintenance and will give flowers or ornamental fruits or maybe both. The only snag to this is that such a screen in depth needs a border about eight feet wide.

Taking the formal hedges first, for a quick growing screen *Cupressocyparis* x *leylandii,* the Leyland Cypress in either its green or gold forms, is probably the fastest growing hedge plant I know. If planted in well-manured ground, watered assiduously in dry spells for a couple of years until its roots get well down, and meanwhile fed regularly with soluble fertilizer, this cypress can attain 10 ft (3 m) in three or four years. It can then be kept to any desired height by annually topping the young growth.

Other good evergreen shrubs for screening include Portugal laurel,

Prunus lusitanicus, which bears fragrant white flowers in June; *Viburnum tinus* which will take shade; various hollies and yews. There are, of course, many other conifers, golden, green or silver, which can be used to create an evergreen screen.

Turning now to flowering deciduous shrubs that can be welded into a screen in depth, there is *Viburnum farreri* which is very vigorous and bears its white, pink-tinged flowers generously in winter. The lilacs, single or double, give colour in June, as do the various mock oranges, varieties of philadelphus; my favourites being the double white 'Virginale', and 'Beauclerk' which has large single flowers.

Rose hedges are other possibilities and most growers recommend varieties for this purpose.

Of course, if one has an acid soil all the rhododendrons and camellias are there to choose from and give fine foliage and lovely flowers. Privet, hornbeam and beech hedges are popular in some areas for formal hedges and look fine when kept regularly clipped.

Low hedges to divide various parts of the garden – for example, to separate the flowers from the vegetables, or to screen certain features – are another possibility. In large gardens years ago when labour was cheap and plentiful, even beds in the vegetable garden were cased round with low box hedges. These were planted for the very good reason that they sheltered the plots from cold winds, thus making for earlier crops. For low separating hedges, lavender and rosemary are excellent but so are box and *Lonicera nitida,* which can be kept trimmed to two or three feet or lower.

In old gardens one sometimes comes across low box hedges that have become bare at the base. These may be dug up, their site dug over and enriched with some organic manure or bonemeal, and the bushes replanted a foot or two deeper than they were, so that only their green branches show above the ground. They will then produce roots from their stems and start a new lease of life.

Hedges can be planted in the dormant season, preferably in a trench at the recommended distances apart. Improve existing soil with rotted manure or compost to provide nourishment in the early years, also sand if the ground is naturally wet or heavy. Keep the plants moist until they get established and cut them fairly hard at first in order to provide a firm hedge base. This is the secret of a good dense hedge.

Plants for Specific Purposes

SOME CHOICE VARIEGATED PLANTS

Arum italicum 'Pictum'
Berberis thunbergii 'Rose Glow', barberry
Cornus alba 'Elegantissima', dogwood
C. a. 'Spaethii'
Elaeagnus pungens 'Maculata'
Fuchsia magellanica 'Variegata'
Hosta – several, plantain lily
Iris pallida 'Variegata'
Phlox paniculata 'Harlequin'
Phormium tenax 'Variegata', New Zealand flax
Tovara virginiana 'Variegata' painter's palette
Weigela florida 'Variegata'

PLANTS FOR DRY POSITIONS

Berberis sp., barberry
Betula – all, birch
Calluna vulgaris, heather or ling
Centranthus, red valerian
Cercis, Judas tree
Cistus, rock rose
Erica, heath or heather
Helianthemum, sun rose
Ilex aquifolium, holly
Kerria japonica, Jew's mallow
Populus sp., poplar
Tamarix sp., tamarisk
Ulex, gorse
Verbascum, mullein
Vinca, periwinkle

BAMBOOS, REEDS AND ORNAMENTAL GRASSES

Acorus calamus, sweet flag
Arundo donax, giant reed
Carex buchananii, sedge
Cortaderia selloana, pampas grass
Cyperus longus, galingale
Festuca amethystina, fescue
F. cinerea, blue fescue
Holcus mollis 'Albovariegata'
Milium effusum 'Aureum', Bowles' golden grass
Miscanthus sinensis
Molinia caerulea, purple moor grass
Phalaris arundinacea 'Picta', ribbon grass, gardener's garters
Sinarundinaria murielae, bamboo
Stipa calamagrostis, feather grass

NO NEED TO STAKE THESE PERENNIALS

Alchemilla, lady's mantle
Anaphalis, pearl everlasting
Anemone, windflower
Bergenia
Centranthus, valerian
Delphinium – belladonna group
Echinops, globe thistle
Eryngium, sea holly
Euphorbia sp., spurge
Geranium sp., crane's-bill
Hemerocallis, day-lily
Kniphofia, red-hot poker
Monarda, bergamot
Phlomis, Jerusalem sage
Scabiosa, scabious
Sedum, stonecrop
Solidago, golden rod
Tradescantia, spiderwort
Yucca, Adam's needle

RABBIT-RESISTANT PLANTS

Aconitum, monkshood
Anemone, windflower
Astilbe
Bergenia
Campanula lactiflora, bellflower
C. latifolia
Convallaria, lily of the valley
Corydalis
Digitalis, foxglove
Epimedium, barrenwort
Helleborus corsicus, hellebore
H. orientalis, Lenten hellebore
Kniphofia, red-hot poker
Polygonatum, Solomon's seal
Trollius, globe flower
Ulex, gorse

WINTER-FLOWERING PLANTS

Camellia
Chimonanthus praecox, winter sweet
Cornus mas, cornelian cherry
Crocus – various
Erica carnea forms, heather
E. x darleyensis
Galanthus, snowdrop
Garrya elliptica, silk tassel bush
Hamamelis, witch hazel
Helleborus, hellebore
Hepatica, liverwort
Iris danfordiae
I. histrioides
I. unguicularis, Algerian iris
Jasminum nudiflorum, winter jasmine
Lonicera fragrantissima, winter honeysuckle
L. standishii
Mahonia
Pachysandra terminalis
Petasites japonicus, butterbur
Prunus subhirtella 'Autumnalis'
Sarcococca – all, sweet box
Viburnum x *bodnantense*

V. farreri
V. tinus, laurustinus

WATERSIDE AND BOG
PLANTS

Acorus calamus 'Variegatus',
  sweetflag
Astilbe species
Butomus umbellatus, flowering
  rush
Caltha palustris, kingcup
Hemerocallis flava vars., day-
  lily
Iris kaempferi
Juncus effusus 'Spiralis',
  corkscrew rush
Lobelia cardinalis, cardinal
  flower
L. siphilitica, blue lobelia
Menyanthes trifoliata, bogbean
Mimulus luteus, monkey musk
Miscanthus sacchariflorus var.,
  variegata, hardy sugar cane
Myosotis palustris, water
  forget-me-not
Orontium aquaticum, golden
  club
Pontederia cordata, pickerel
  weed
Primula japonica, Japanese
  primrose
P. pulverulenta
Ranunculus lingua
Rodgersia sp., bronze leaf
Salix daphnoides, violet willow
Scirpus tabernaemontani.
  'Zebrinus', zebra rush
Typha minima, dwarf
  reedmace
Zantedeschia aethiopica, calla
  lily

CHOICE WATER-LILIES
Large pools
(*water depth to 3 ft: 1 m*)

Nymphaea
'Attraction'
'Colossea'

'Escarboucle'
'Gladstoniana'

Medium pools
(*water depth 1½-2 ft: 45-60 cm*)

'Chromatella'
'Conqueror'
'Gloire de Temple sur Lot'
'Gloriosa'
'Gonnère'
'James Brydon'
'MmeWilfron Gonnère'
'René Gérard'
'Rose Arey'
'Sunrise'
'Virginalis'

Small pools and tubs
(*water depth 10-18 in: 24-40 cm*)

'Aurora'
'Fire Crest'
'Graziella'
Laydekeri forms
Nymphaea odorata 'Sulphurea'
'Paul Hariot'
'Pink Opal'

PLANTS FOR SHADE

Anemone nemorosa forms,
  wood anemone
Aquilegia, columbine
Brunnera
Campanula latifolia, giant
  bellflower
Convallaria, lily of the
  valley
Dentaria, toothwort
Endymion, bluebell
Epimedium, barrenwort
Euphorbia robbiae, spurge
Gentiana asclepiadea, willow
  gentian
Helleborus, hellebore
Hosta, plantain-lily
Kirengeshoma, yellow wax
  bells
Lilium martagon, Turk's-cap-
  lily

Meconopsis, Welsh and blue
  poppy
Polygonatum, Solomon's seal
Uvularia, bellwort

EASY PLANTS FOR A
ROCK GARDEN

Arenaria montana 'Grandiflora',
  sandwort
Arnebia echioides
Aster alpinus, rock aster
Aubrieta
Berberis thunbergii
  'Atropurpurea Nana',
  barberry
Campanula carpatica,
  Carpathian bellflower
Cheiranthus 'Harpur Crewe',
  wallflower
Cistus – all, sun rose
Crocus species
Dianthus alpinus vars.,
  alpine pink
Edraianthus pumilio
Erica – most, heather
Galanthus, snowdrop
Gentiana septemfida, gentiana
G. sino-ornata
Geranium dalmaticum,
  crane's-bill
Helianthemum nummularium
  vars., rock rose
Iris pumila
Juniperus communis
  'Compressa', juniper
Leontopodium alpinum,
  edelweiss
Lychnis alpina, arctic campion
Onosma tauricum
Papaver alpinum, alpine poppy
Phlox douglasii
P. subulata, moss phlox
Potentilla fruticosa vars.,
  shrubby cinquefoil
Pulsatilla vulgaris, pasque
  flower
Ranunculus alpestris, alpine
  buttercup

Saponaria 'Bressingham
  Hybrid', soapwort
Saxifraga – most, saxifrage
Thymus cilicicus, thyme
Viola species, viola

RED-LEAVED PLANTS

Acer platanoides 'Crimson
  King', red sycamore
Berberis thunbergii – forms,
  barberry
Corylus maxima 'Purpurea',
  purple hazelnut
Cotinus coggygria
  'Rubrifolius', smoke tree
Malus 'Profusion', crab apple
M. x purpurea
Phormium tenax 'Purpureum',
  New Zealand flax
Prunus cerasifera 'Pissardii',
  purple-leaved plum
Sedum maximum atropurpureum

Vitis vinifera 'Purpurea',
  grape vine
Wetgela florida 'Foliis
  Purpureis'

GOOD POOL OXYGENATORS

Callitriche hermaphroditica
  (C. autumnalis)
C. palustris (C. verna), water
  starwort
Crassula recurva
Elodea canadensis, Canadian
  pondweed
Fontinalis antipyretica, water
  moss
Hottonia palustris, water violet
Lagarosiphon major (Elodea
  crispa)
Myriophyllum all ssp., milfoil
Potamogeton crispus, curled
  pondweed
P. densus, frog's lettuce

Proserpinaca palustris,
  mermaid weed
Ranunculus aquatilis, water
  crowfoot

CAREFREE FERNS

Asplenium viride, spleenwort
Athyrium filix-femina, lady fern
Blechnum penna-marina
B. spicant, deer fern
Dryopteris filix-mas, male fern
Matteuccia struthiopteris,
  ostrich plume fern
Onoclea sensibilis, sensitive
  fern
Osmunda regalis, royal fern
Phyllitis scolopendrium, hart's
  tongue fern
Polypodium vulgare, polypody
Polystichum munitum,
  Christmas fern
Woodwardia species

Index